LOCAL VEGETARIAN COOKING
INSPIRED RECIPES CELEBRATING NORTHWEST FARMS

Debra Daniels-Zeller
LOC Press

This book is dedicated to Tom and Jennifer who light up my life and to all the hard working farmers who grow our food.

Copyright © 2004 Debra Daniels-Zeller
Cover photograph by Anna Mia Davidson
Pen and ink illustrations © Karen Towey
Willie Green's Organic Farm logo used with permission from Jeff Miller

Daniels-Zeller, Debra 1952-
Local Vegetarian Cooking:
Inspired Recipes Celebrating Northwest Farms

ISBN: 0-9728334-0-4
1. Vegetarian Cookery
2. Washington -- Northwest Cookery

LOC Press
PO Box 412
Lynnwood, WA 98026
ddanzel@aol.com

Printed in the United States of America

Contents

Acknowledgments

The creation of this book has depended on the inspiration, dedication and participation of many people. A warm heartfelt appreciation goes to my friend Candy Jackson who inspired me to start this book. Thanks to my husband, Tom, who believed in this project from its inception and my daughter Jennifer who encouraged me to continue and helped me with organizational skills.

Without farmers this book would not have been possible. I offer my gratitude to the farmers who generously gave their time to make the profiles possible: Bill Weiss, John Huschle, Patricia Meyer, Steve Phillips, Nash Huber, Michaele Blakely, Jeff Miller, Roger and Suzanne Wechsler, Katsumi Taki, Heather Robinson and Ron Lawrence. Thanks also to Ronny Bell owner of Pioneer Organics and Anne Marie Phillips from The Essential Baking Company. Thanks (and kudos) to Howard Lev because without Mama Lil's Peppers, the world would be a dull place.

I am grateful to Hoby Jergens, Pam and Ron Nachbor for sampling and critiquing my breads and baked recipes. Thanks also to the students and assistants in my cooking classes who sample my many creations and make it a joy to teach.

Alicia Lundquist Guy provided support and encouragement, offering her editorial skills. My appreciation also goes out to Maryellen Young, Pam Nachbor and Paula Holden for their recipe proofreading skills and valuable perspectives. A warm thanks to Anna Mia Davidson for the beautiful cover photograph of farmer John Huschle. I'm grateful to Karen Towey for contributing all the pen and ink artwork. Thanks also to Jeff Miller for the use of Willie Green's logo.

A very special thank you to Goldie Caughlan, whose tireless dedication to the integrity of organic foods continues to inspire me.

About the Author

Debra Daniels-Zeller learned how to roll a pie crust and to enjoy the simple pleasures of food in her grandmother's kitchen. She has taught healthy vegetarian cooking classes in Seattle since 1990, and has written vegetarian recipe articles since 1992.

Introduction

I can't remember a time when I didn't think about my food, where it came from and who grew it. When I was young, we had convenience foods galore – TV dinners, frozen pot pies, boxed macaroni and cheese, instant potatoes and rolls of refrigerated biscuits and cookies all ready to bake. I imagined people who made cookie dough and stuffed it in the refrigerated roll. I wondered how frozen pot pies were made and who Betty Crocker was. Mom prepared simple meals using convenience items combined with fresh foods. I preferred her simple steamed vegetables, baked squash and fruit desserts. At my grandmother's house, we enjoyed vegetables and berries from her garden. The sweet raspberries, eaten one at a time on sunny Colorado afternoons, were a delight that lingers in memories today.

Life experiences influence the way everyone thinks about food and the way they eat. In the mid-1960's, during the farmworker grape boycott in California, I thought about what living in such poverty must be like and refused to eat grapes. When I was older, vegetarian friends prepared culinary inventions with fresh vegetables and I savored every bite. *Diet for a Small Planet*, *Animal Factories* and *Animal Liberation* were all books that changed the way I thought about the food I ate. Fad diets and food trends have held little interest for me. Where food comes from, how it was grown and who grew it are bridges that connect us to the earth. Knowing that farmers make a decent living and that the money we spend on food ensures organic farming will continue is the best way to feel good about what we eat.

This book came about because I wanted to save recipes I've been inspired to create – all my favorite recipes in one volume. A good friend sparked my interest when she talked about writing her own book and encouraged me to write one as well. As I shopped local co-ops and farmers markets putting recipes together, I thought about adding farmer profiles. Farmers' lives and how they began farming are intriguing stories, and the farming issues that concern them are important for everyone to consider.

Farmers are a diverse group of people. Where they came from, what events or ideas influenced them to farm and how they acquired land to farm are as varied as American life across the country. The myth of the country farmer — an older man in overalls who grew up on the farm without much knowledge beyond farming – has been perpetuated for decades. The reality is some grew up on farms, some had farming in their family background and others simply dreamed of being a farmer while working a nine-to-five job. Bob Meyer of Stoney Plains, for example, wasn't a full-time farmer until he retired. While many retirees are thinking of relaxing and taking cruises, Bob wanted to be out in the fields on his new tractor. He wanted to learn all he could about farming and crops. He retired to do what he loved. Some farmers rent the land they farm, or they may trade harvest produce boxes for additional acreage from surrounding farms while improving neighbors' soil with organic techniques. Other farmers own the homestead their parents farmed. Some begin farming because they remember their grandparents' farm. While farmers come from many walks of life, the farmers I spoke with all have one thing in common – they are passionate about what they do.

The recipes in this book are a tribute to local agriculture. Many recipes were popular in classes I taught and some are personal favorites. I love to experiment, play with food and create new dishes. Inspiration comes from farmers markets, and I often get weekly delivered produce boxes in the off-season (February through May) to motivate me. If you can't get to markets during harvest season, weekly produce delivery is available year-round. Use my recipes as a springboard for your ideas or prepare the recipes exactly as they're written. Beyond locally grown foods, choose food for the way it was grown and buy processed foods from companies that encourage sustainable agriculture and support fair wages for farmworkers.

Here in the Northwest there is great deal of support for local farms. Natural food stores and produce delivery services often feature names and profiles of Washington organic farms. Madison Market, PCC Natural Markets, Larry's Markets, Whole Foods Markets, Pioneer Organics, Central Market, Manna Mills, Skagit Valley Co-op and others all purchase a portion of their produce from local farmers. As we reconnect to food we eat by choosing to support local organic agriculture, we ensure sustainable farming will continue for generations to come.

Tips From The Kitchen

Many people are looking for simple, instant recipes because they have little or no time to cook. I'm not a fan of fussy recipes, but taking an hour to cook beans or grains and preparing fresh produce is a necessary step in nourishing yourself. Over the years, I've found that a few basic concepts work in maintaining a health-oriented kitchen. Below are some basic tips for those who need organization, ideas and inspiration.

1. Start with the best quality ingredients. Inferior-quality, cheap food at chain or warehouse grocery stores was grown for appearance and durability for shipping. Many of the least expensive foods are grown in foreign countries where pesticides are more liberally applied than food grown in this country. Select food based on the way it was grown rather than price.

2. Choose whole foods first. Focus on whole grains, beans and fresh seasonal vegetables. When you buy convenience foods such as salsa, tomato sauce or canned beans, base purchases on quality.

3. Cook seasonally. Prepare lighter meals and raw food dishes in the heat of the summer using summer vegetables, melons, berries, salad greens and tomatoes. In the winter, simmer hearty soups, braise winter greens and bake root vegetable gratins.

4. Select produce by the season (see p.301 for seasonal picks). Don't buy tomatoes in January when they are tasteless and expensive. Instead, use marinated vegetables or pickles to garnish salads during winter months. If you want strawberries in February, think ahead and freeze some of the harvest at the peak of the season. Canning is a helpful skill to learn if you want to enjoy more local, organic produce during the off-season (see p.305 for books about canning).

5. Maintain a well-stocked organized pantry. You'll have options for plenty of dishes and be able to create a variety of meals if you have different spices, herbs and condiments to use. Purchase items such as raspberry vinegar, salsa, chutney, marinated vegetables, mixed fruit jam or various spice blends at farmers markets or specialty food stores.

6. Keep track of food that you have on hand. When thinking about preparing a meal, write down two or three things that need to be eaten. Build your meal or dish around these ingredients. Balance carbohydrates and protein and include vegetables — raw or cooked. Think about how various seasonings and ingredients will blend together.

7. Choose locally raised, organic dairy products and eggs. True free-range chickens from local farmers provide quality eggs with rich flavor. Small artisan cheese companies raise their own goats or cows and make their own products (see Port Madison Farm, p.93 and Samish Bay Cheese, p.232). I use soy and rice milk for cooking, but for most recipes you can substitute organic milk. Organic butter and ghee are the best choices since pesticide residues and environmental toxins can accumulate in fats. For those who don't eat dairy or eggs, most of the recipes can be made with egg replacements and there are vegan cheeses that you can substitute in recipes. Vegans can bake and cook with coconut oil instead of butter or ghee.

8. Use only high-quality organic oil for cooking and salads. With organic virgin or expeller-pressed oils, no chemicals or solvents are employed to extract the oil. Try extra-virgin olive oil for salads and low-heat cooking. Light sesame oil can be drizzled onto salads and used to bake or sauté with low heat. It adds a nutty flavor to many dishes. Rapunzel makes delectable hazelnut oil that is perfect on salads. Purchase mono and polyunsaturated oils in dark containers because light as well as heat deteriorates oil. Coconut oil and ghee are stable fats. They don't degrade or change when cooking at higher temperatures (above 325°). Tropical Traditions (www.tropicaltraditons.com) is one good place to get virgin coconut oil. Just a little of this oil infuses an intriguing hint of coconut taste to foods.

9. Be adventurous and use recipes as a pattern. Except for bread, cakes, biscuits and muffins, there is room for change in most recipes. For example, if you don't have fennel or kale, try celery and collards or Swiss chard. Keep in mind what the end dish will look like. We eat with our eyes first – presentation is important! A variety of colors can entice. Contrasting textures keeps food interesting, and the right blend of flavors creates a sensual experience.

10. Think about five flavors when you put recipes together — sweet, sour, pungent, spicy (hot) and salty. Balance those flavors in dishes you create. Often a recipe may need a twist of lemon, a pinch of salt or a hint of sugar to bring the flavors together. Focusing on how food tastes and the flavors we experience in prepared dishes enhances our awareness about food. Becoming experienced pairing food with ingredients takes practice and a willingness to experiment.

Uncommon Ingredients

Agar (or agar agar)
A vegetarian gelatin from a red seaweed, agar is available in bars, flakes or powder. It sets like gelatin as it cools. Substitute it for gelatin in recipes.

Agave nectar
A natural sweetener from the agave plant, a cactus-like plant native to Mexico. The sugar in agave nectar is more slowly absorbed than sugar, yet it tastes 25% sweeter than sugar. It has little taste compared to honey or maple syrup.

Aïoli spread
A mayonnaise-like spread traditional in the south of France.

Almond butter
Raw or toasted almonds ground into a butter. Raw almond butter is the more healthful choice. Use it the same as you would peanut butter.

Amaranth
(see p.293)

Amasake
A traditional Japanese fermented rice beverage, amasake is made by combining cooked sweet rice with rice koji enzymes (from fermented rice) and incubating it for 6 to 10 hours. Although it is quite sweet with natural sugars, it also contains enzymes that aid digestion and elimination. Use it in puddings and desserts.

Arrowroot
Arrowroot is a starchy powder from a tropical plant native to South America and the West Indies. Less processed than cornstarch and without the chalky aftertaste, arrowroot is high in calcium and can be used to thicken sauces and puddings like cornstarch. Do not overcook arrowroot-thickened sauces or they may break down.

Barley flour
Low-gluten, whole-grain flour that adds softness to quick breads and muffins. Use as a substitute for whole-wheat pastry flour when baking.

Bragg Liquid Aminos
Amino acids are extracted from soybeans to make this condiment. The taste is bolder and more complex than tamari or soy sauce. Unlike tamari, it is not a fermented product. It is quite salty, so use it sparingly. Bragg Liquid Aminos

can be used when a bold savory taste is required. Use it in stews, gravies or baked vegetable cobblers.

Brown rice vinegar
Distilled from rice, the traditionally brewed variety is the best quality with excellent taste and a smooth flavor with 4.5% acidity.

Buckwheat (toasted and raw groats, flour)
(see p.293)

Burdock root
Native to Siberia, burdock root has been a long-time favorite in Japanese cooking. With a sweet, earthy flavor, it can be used like carrots in soups, stews and bean or grain dishes. Burdock is known for its blood-purifying capabilities. It helps eliminate toxins from the body.

Channa dal
In India, dal is a general name for legumes. Channa dal are hulled and split black garbanzos. Cooked, they have a pureed texture - excellent for soups and spreads. The texture and flavor is perfect for hummus.

Chanterelle mushrooms
Delicate with a complex rich flavor, chanterelles are an annual autumn treat not to be missed. You can also find them dried for use at other times of the year. They contain selenium and help eliminate toxins in the body. Like other mushrooms, they are a rich source of glutamic acid, which naturally enhances savory foods.

Chipotle chile pods and powder
Widely used in Mexican cooking, chipotle chiles are smoked jalapeños. They add a deep, rich smoky flavor to soups, stews and salsas. Chipotle is also available in powder form.

Coconut oil and milk
People in tropical countries have used unrefined coconut oil for thousands of years. Unrefined, it is easily digested and metabolized, but most of the coconut oil on the market is refined. Use the unrefined variety in baking and higher heat cooking. Unlike expeller-pressed olive, hazelnut or sesame oil, it is not altered when used in baking and high-heat cooking. Coconut milk is available canned in most grocery stores. Look for organic, expeller-pressed varieties in natural food stores. Use it in desserts, soups and other dishes for a rich taste. For more information, see www.tropicaltraditions.com.

Date sugar
Containing about 65 percent fructose and sucrose, date sugar is made from dehydrated dates. Used in cooking, the granules do not dissolve when added to liquid. Dates contain significant amounts of niacin, iron and potassium.

Dulse
Growing in frigid temperate zones in the Atlantic or Pacific Ocean, dulse is a red sea vegetable with a tart, salty flavor. It makes a good addition to or garnish for casseroles, soups and stews. Like other sea vegetables, dulse is an excellent source of minerals, especially iron and iodine.

Ener-G Egg Replacer
Often referred to simply as egg replacer in vegan recipes, this ingredient is a dry mixture that can be found in the baking section of natural food stores. It contains potato starch with some tapioca flour and leavening. Ener-G Egg Replacer doesn't have the rising power of eggs, so baked goods are not as light as baked products that use eggs or flax seed egg replacer.

Flax oil, flax seeds
The richest source of Omega-3 essential fatty acids, flax seed oil and the seeds are an important addition to any healthy diet. The oil is fragile and is damaged by heat, so use it in dressings and marinades. It makes an excellent salad dressing. Flax seeds can be combined with water and made into a flax seed egg replacer that is better than any product on the market. Blend together one tablespoon ground flax seeds and three tablespoons water to replace each egg in a baking recipe. Boiled and refined flax seed oil is called linseed oil and is only good for shining shoes.

Fruit sweetener
Found in the refrigerated section of natural food stores, fruit sweetener is a thick fruit concentrate made from combinations such as pineapple, pear and peach. Substitute fruit sweetener for honey or maple syrup, but remember it has the taste of the fruit it came from, so be sure your recipe is compatible with it. Store it in the refrigerator or it will ferment and become unusable.

Garam masala
Every Indian home has a unique mixture of garam masala. Most of the recipes have been handed down for generations. The mixture often includes cumin seed, black peppercorns, cloves, coriander seed, cardamom and cinnamon. The spices are dry-roasted individually, ground and then combined. This blend can be made at home or purchased ready-made at an Indian market or natural foods store.

Ghee

Ghee is butter that has been clarified and is free of all milk solids. It can be stored without refrigeration. You can purchase ghee in jars in specialty stores or make your own by letting butter simmer over a low flame for about 45 minutes. Don't let the butter brown. The milk solids will turn brownish and cling to the sides of the pan or drop to the bottom. Remove the foam from the top and discard. Then strain the ghee (clarified butter) through a triple layer of cheesecloth.

Ginger

A rhizome, or an enlarged underground stem, ginger is a distant cousin to bananas. Ginger has a pungent, assertive flavor and is known for its digestive properties. Dried ginger is not interchangeable with the fresh variety. Dried ginger is most often used in baked goods. When ginger is young, there is no need to peel before using. An easy way to add ginger to a recipe is grate the ginger and squeeze the juice from the pulp. Then, discard the pulp. A tablespoon of grated ginger equals about one teaspoon of ginger juice.

Kamut

(see p.293)

Kudzu (kuzu)

A white powder from a pervasive, vigorous plant, kudzu or kuzu has been used for over a thousand years in Japan. Nutritionally, kudzu helps create alkaline blood and is good for maintaining or restoring health. It is also a good remedy for hangovers, colds and the flu. The powder can be used in place of cornstarch or arrowroot for thickening purposes. It should always be mixed with cold water and added near the end of cooking if possible. Kudzu is more expensive than arrowroot because preparing the powder is a labor-intensive endeavor that can take up to 4 months.

Mama Lil's Peppers

(see p.108)

Millet

(see p.294)

Mirin

A Japanese rice wine related to sake, mirin is made by combining rice koji, cooked sweet brown or white rice and water. Fermented and aged, sweet mirin is used for cooking where a mild sweetness is desired in marinades and salads. Look for the traditionally brewed version in natural food stores. Inexpensive mirin has been chemically brewed and sweetened with sugar or corn syrup.

Miso

Fermented soybeans or other beans and grains are made into a paste called miso, a traditional staple in Japan. With an intense wine-like taste, miso can be used for flavoring a wide variety of dishes from soup to salad dressings. A concentrated protein source, miso contains eight essential amino acids, B vitamins, calcium and iron. Miso is low in fat but contains a lot of salt, so use it sparingly. Sweet and light-colored miso is higher in enzymes and simple carbohydrates. Red and brown misos are higher in protein with a higher salt content and contain more essential fatty acids from the soybeans. Dark miso has been fermented for a longer period of time. It has a bold, assertive flavor.

Nutritional yeast

Adding a cheese-like flavor to foods, nutritional yeast is a living organism that is grown on mineral-rich molasses or wood pulp. The yellow powder is rich in B-vitamins that come from synthetic vitamins fed to the culture during the growth stage. The end product is also fortified. It can be found in natural food stores. Many add it to tofu mixtures to create a more "cheesy" taste.

Oats (groats, rolled and steel-cut)

(see p.294)

Porcini mushrooms

Fresh *Boletus edulis* or porcini and other mushrooms are available from people who gather and sell wild fresh and dried foods at local markets. Dried porcini are cut and dehydrated at the peak of ripeness. You can also buy them in natural foods stores. They can be rehydrated in 30 minutes and are perfect in sauces, stews and savory casseroles. All mushrooms are rich in zinc and help neutralize toxic residues in the body.

Portabello (portabella) mushrooms

Given the right conditions, small crimini mushrooms grow into the large 4 to 6-inch portabello mushrooms. High in B vitamins and trace minerals, these large mushrooms are more intense than their young crimini cousins. Portabellos are perfect for marinating and grilling or roasting. Instead of rinsing, use a soft vegetable brush because they tend to soak up water when washed. Store fresh portabellos in a basket or tray, cover with a towel and refrigerate for no more than a few days.

Quinoa

(see p.294)

Rapadura

A natural sweetener, Rapadura is organic, unrefined, dehydrated cane juice. It is high in minerals, vitamins and micronutrients. This sweet ingredient contains 82 percent sucrose, but it is also high in chromium, a mineral that helps stabilize blood sugar levels. Rapadura doesn't pass quickly into the bloodstream like refined sugar or fructose does. Use it cup for cup to replace refined sugar. You can also purchase unrefined sugar in Latino or Indian markets. A product simply labeled "organic sugar" is more refined than Rapadura.

Rose water
Rose water is used for traditionally flavoring sweets in the Middle East and India. The better varieties are made from real roses, not chemicals. Read the label to make sure you are getting real rose water.

Sea palm
A brown seaweed, sea palm can be found on the north pacific coast of North America. Like other seaweed, it contains algin, which removes radioactive particles and heavy metals from the body. It contains important minerals to help strengthen bones and teeth. Use dried and ground sea palm as a condiment to enhance foods.

Sesame seeds, sesame oil, unrefined and toasted
Containing more protein than any nut, sesame seeds have about 35 percent protein and are about 50 percent oil. They also contain vitamin E, making the seeds and oil more resistant to rancidity than other vegetable oils. Though they are high in calcium, it is bound with oxalic acid and not easily absorbed. Soaking the seeds before toasting them reduces the oxalic acid content. Whole sesame seeds are excellent toasted, ground and blended with a little sea salt, making a delicious condiment topping for salads and casseroles. Sesame oil has been used for centuries in the Middle East. Buy organic, unrefined sesame oil and use it for dressings, sauces and low heat sautéing or baking. Toasted sesame oil is made from toasted sesame seeds. Enhance a dish after cooking, or add it to a marinade.

Shiitake mushrooms
Possessing a wild woodsy, earthy flavor, shiitake mushrooms are rich in D and B vitamins and help strengthen the immune and cardiovascular systems. Fresh, local shiitake mushrooms have the best flavor. Rehydrate dried shiitake mushrooms for two or three hours before using in soups and sauces.

Spelt
(see p.294)

Tahini
A smooth, creamy paste made from hulled, ground sesame seeds. Commercial tahini is produced from seeds that have been soaked in caustic chemicals to remove the hulls. They are then neutralized and bleached. This

type of tahini tastes bitter and slightly soapy. The best quality tahini comes from mechanically, not chemically, hulled seeds.

Tamari and shoyu

Tamari and shoyu are varieties of soy sauce. Both are inoculated with koji, fermented and produced in a traditional way. With most common soy sauces sold today, soybeans are broken down chemically and then blended with caramel coloring, salt, corn syrup, water and a preservative. Higher quality, traditionally processed tamari is fermented with a koji starter that uses only soybeans. Shoyu uses koji made with equal parts of cracked wheat and soybeans. True tamari contains no wheat, has a higher amino acid content, a thick texture and rich taste compared to shoyu, which has a subtle sweetness with an aroma of wheat fermentation. Containing more glutemic acid than shoyu, tamari is a better choice for cooking because glutemic acid enhances flavors. Tamari also retains a deep rich taste, even in long-simmering liquids.

Tapioca flour

Tapioca is a traditional Brazilian food that comes from yuca or cassava (a fleshy rootstock native to the topics). The starch is an excellent thickener and when added to non-gluten flours, can make them hold together like the gluten in wheat flour.

Teff

(see p.295)

Tempeh

An ancient Indonesian food, tempeh is made by splitting, cooking and fermenting soybeans. A white thread-like mycelium mold binds the beans after they are pressed. This mycelium mold makes tempeh quite easy to digest. The protein and minerals are easily assimilated. Tempeh also contains very little fat, and at 19.5 percent protein, it contains 50 percent more protein than the equivalent amount of hamburger.

Turmeric

An essential ingredient in curries and Indian cuisine, turmeric is the highest known source of beta-carotene. It strengthens the immune system and is useful as an anti-inflammatory. Combined with coriander and cumin in curry spice blends, it aids digestion and helps with the assimilation of protein. Turmeric lends food a yellow color and a slightly musky, astringent flavor.

Umeboshi

Salted pickled plums, umeboshi are traditional in Japan, where they're commonly served as a condiment tucked inside rice balls or combined with rice and wrapped in nori. Umeboshi are made from unripe ume (commonly called "plum" in Japan). These plums are soaked in brine, sun-dried and then returned to the brine. The red color comes from shiso leaves that are pickled with the ume. Once assimilated, umeboshi has antibiotic properties and helps eliminate lactic acid that contributes to fatigue and illnesses.

Wasabi

Often called Japanese horseradish, the two plants are not related; but both are quite hot, pungent and can immediately clear your sinuses and make your ears burn. With its biting, stimulating flavor, wasabi contains protein-digesting enzymes, making it a good digestive aid. In Japan, wasabi is often grated fresh. Purchase it dried in Oriental markets and natural food stores, but be aware that much of the commercial wasabi sold is horseradish or daikon powder with artificial color added. When blended with water, true wasabi turns a greenish gray. Add lukewarm water to the powder to make a paste. Let it sit for about ten minutes to heighten the flavor before using it.

Wild rice

(see p.295)

Wine

When cooking with wine to add flavor, don't use a wine you wouldn't drink. A poor quality wine contributes only what it has to offer.

The conventional belief that the alcohol evaporates a few minutes into cooking doesn't hold up under scientific investigation. Research from the USDA shows 85 percent of the alcohol is still in a boiling liquid containing wine when the pan is removed from the stove. After 15 minutes of simmering, 40 percent of the alcohol remains in the food. In an hour, there is still 25 percent of the alcohol. In 2 1/2 hours, only 5 percent of the alcohol can be detected. For most people this is not a problem.

Red wine

Syrah or Zinfandel are dry red wines; use them with rosemary or tomato dishes, in risotto, soups and for braising vegetables such as red cabbage. Merlot or Cabernet Sauvignon are good additions to pasta sauces, soups or stews. Port, sherry and Marsala pack more intense flavor, and they also have a long shelf life because they contain more alcohol.

White wine

Riesling has fruity overtones with an exotic aroma. Use Riesling or Pinot Grigio, a drier white wine, for braising vegetables and greens such as broccoli rabe or kale. Chardonnay has more body, but both pair well with winter root vegetables in gratins. Both Chardonnay and Riesling go well with apples and pears in warming winter desserts.

The Well-Grounded Breakfast

Profile: Bill Weiss, Homestead Organic Produce

Simple Beginnings
    Seasonal Fruit Salad
    Apples and Pears with Banana-Almond Dressing
    Almond Milk
    Port Madison Goat Yogurt Smoothie
    Trail Mix
    Old-fashioned Soaked Oats
    Quick and Easy Breakfast Snack Ideas

Serious Cereals with Whole Grains
    Whole Grain Tips
    Cream of Rice
    Spelt Porridge
    Almond Amaranth, Teff and Steel-Cut Oats
    Toasted 3-Grain Cereal
    Overnight Whole Oats and Rice

Priceless Pancakes and Toppings
    Tips for Perfect Pancakes
    Light Lemony Oatcakes
    Zucchini Griddlecakes
    Buckwheat-Banana Pancakes
    Blueberry Hotcakes
    Blueberry Topping
    Strawberry-Plum Sauce
    Raspberry-Orange Sauce
    Apricot-Almond Topping
    Apple-Cranberry Topping

Bake it Ahead
    Quick Bread Baking Tips
    Corn Biscuits
    Sundried Tomato Biscuits
    Ginger-Peach Scones
    Lemon-Cherry Muffins
    Maple Pumpkin Bread

Northwest Blueberry Bars
Mocha-Hazelnut Date Bars
Lemon-Pecan Biscotti
Cherry-Apple Oatmeal Cookies

Hot and Hearty
Scrambled Tofu
Breakfast Burritos
Roasted Chile, Squash and Potato Tacos with Goat Cheese
Chipotle Cranberry Bean and German Butterball Potato Tostadas
Quinoa, Corn and Caramelized Walnuts (with variation)
Red Lentil Pottage with Kale and Lavender Vinegar
Rosemary Roasted Vegetables
Savory Baked Home Fries
Maple-Miso Baked Winter Squash
Refried Black Beans
Orange French Toast

The Essential Baking Company

Conventional Problems, Organic Solutions

THINK ABOUT IT

Farm fields provide habitat for wildlife and birds. According to Skagitonians to Preserve Farmland, half a million ducks, over 1,3000 trumpeter swans, 30,000 snow geese, bald eagles, peregrine falcons and migrating songbirds are supported on Skagit Valley farmland. Birds, bees and animals are critical for fruit and seed production and without them, many plants would lose the ability to regenerate.

Bill Weiss's farm, Homestead Organic Produce, in Quincy

The Well-Grounded Breakfast

The foundation of our lives begins with agriculture. Incorporating locally grown foods into our diet supports our health as well as our community.

American breakfasts are as varied as our landscape. My dad has had the same basic breakfast for over thirty years – a well-done sausage, fried eggs, and a slice of toast with juice and coffee. At my grandmother's house, when I was young, we woke up on summer mornings to enjoy fresh peaches or raspberries from her garden and scrambled eggs with a slice of French toast on the side. We ate together. Breakfast was mandatory.

Schedules, food beliefs and habits determine what we choose, whether it's toast and tea, a protein-enhanced smoothie, eggs and hash browns, a bowl of steaming oatmeal, or simply a cup of coffee with a meal-replacement bar in the car. Though many people realize the importance of eating breakfast for better performance and energy later in the day, the reality is all too often a morning meal can be a hurried affair. Getting up earlier and taking time to enjoy a nourishing breakfast can jumpstart your day in a positive direction.

When we sleep, our bodies rest and recharge. What we eat in the morning influences our energy and mood throughout the day. Think about how you feel a few hours after eating your usual breakfast, and then consider what you ate. Did your energy dip shortly afterwards, or was your breakfast energizing? Did it sustain you until lunch?

Not everyone needs the same thing in the morning, but take time to eat healthy, high-quality foods. What works for some people is definitely out for others. Some can't face the thought of cooked food early in the day. Others find it difficult to get through the morning with a smoothie or a skimpy fruit salad. The best option is to find out what kind of breakfast sustains your energy. For an experiment, try different types of food every day for a week. Early in the morning, when I wake up, I do well with something light like fruit and yogurt. After working out, I like a substantial savory breakfast of whole grains with some protein such as tofu, lentils or an egg. Sometimes a change of pace with pancakes, warm whole-grain cereal, or a smoothie made with Port Madison goat yogurt, fresh fruit and a little flax oil is the right meal.

Beginning your day with fresh, seasonal fruit, especially in the summer, is cleansing and energizing. With a high water and fiber content, fruit helps eliminate toxins from your system. The natural sugars provide glucose that your brain needs to function. Follow fruit with complex carbohydrates and protein for a warm, energizing meal. If you're short on time, rather than skip the most important meal of the day, keep healthy quick options on hand like apples, sliced and spread with raw almond butter.

Create a morning meal that will entice you out of that warm bed to begin your day. If something unconventional like tomato soup works for you, explore the soup chapter for more ideas. The recipes in this chapter offer diverse breakfast ideas, but sometimes it pays to think outside of the box. While dairy and eggs take prominent positions in other cookbooks, they are given a minimal role here and are considered optional. If you buy eggs, choose organic, local farm-fresh eggs. Once you sample fresh eggs, you won't accept anything less.

Bill Weiss
Homestead Organic Produce

Drive east over the Cascades, and just north of George, near Quincy, you'll find Homestead Organic Produce, owned and run by Bill Weiss. The landscape is flat with telephone poles standing in for trees. Winters are cold, and summers sizzle with plenty of sun — just right for fruits and vegetables, like corn and melons, to get a higher sugar content as the heat climbs on summer days. At Homestead Organic Produce, you'll find a varied selection of summer produce including juicy melons, corn, tomatoes and sweet onions.

Bill Weiss was born and raised on the farm where he lives. His parents and grandparents were dry-land wheat farmers before farms were irrigated. In dry-land farming, different techniques are used to retain natural precipitation. As Bill grew up, farming got into his blood. He says that he didn't want much as a young man, but he really wanted to hang on to the family farm. Today Bill and his crew work hard on his farm growing melons, various vegetables, and alfalfa, which he sells to organic and conventional farms.

Every Saturday from Memorial Day through the first weekend in November, Bill and Anselmo, Bill's right-hand man, drive to the University District Farmers Market to sell their harvest. "East of the Cascades, people aren't quite ready for the sticker shock of organic produce," Bill says. The season begins with asparagus, then come snap peas and English peas, black raspberries, green beans, corn, peppers, tomatoes, sweet and storage onions, garlic and a variety of delectable melons. There is a twinkle in Bill's eye as he passes out chunks of a juicy ripe, crenshaw melon. One luscious taste can sell a melon; and if you can't decide, Anselmo will pick out the perfect one, just for you. Occasionally he might slip an extra pepper into your bag. Such personal service is the bonus you get buying from farmer friends. I find myself going to the market just to purchase organic produce from farmers like Bill Weiss.

Bill says one of the biggest issues facing farmers today is simply staying viable. "Even conventional farmers have a hard time staying in business," he says. For one thing, weather can be a roll of the dice with hail storms, early freezes and droughts. Farmers deal with it on a day-by-day basis. Agricultural policies and government price supports have favored large farms since the 1930's. Subsidies go to farmers on land with a history of growing commodities such as wheat, corn, cotton, soybeans, rice and sugar, and generally to farmers who have substantial acreage. Most of the subsidies go to the largest farms. To stay with it, a farmer has to deal with market fluctuations, have a bit of luck, and be as dedicated to farming as Bill is.

For 34 years, Bill grew tasty organic apples – Fuji, Granny Smith, Golden Delicious and Braeburn. After years of dealing with the coddling moth, the persistent worm in the apple, Bill took all the orchards out and decided to grow melons. Though the apple orchards are no longer there, wonderful memories remain. Bill used to host an annual apple pressing on the last weekend in October at his old homestead in Quincy. One year, we drove from Seattle on the long drive that Bill and Anselmo take to sell farm fresh produce every Saturday during the summer and autumn. In the typical Eastern Washington sunny, chilly coat-and-glove weather, many of us cored, mixed and pressed the apples with an old hand-cranked apple press until our juice covered fingers felt quite frozen. Later, inside the 1906 farmhouse, we warmed up and enjoyed a potluck dinner as we got to know each other in the old-fashioned dining room. At the end of the day, goodbyes were exchanged, then we took a few jugs of apple juice and headed back over the mountains. There's nothing like a trip to an organic farm on a beautiful, crisp, sunny autumn day to make you smile.

His days of growing and pressing apples may be behind him, but the tradeoff is worth it. In 2003, Bill was the only farmer still selling sweet local melons into November. It's a rare treat to serve Washington grown melons for Thanksgiving dinner. Being a successful farmer also means being able to anticipate how your crop will do at the market – a skill Bill has mastered.

Simple Beginnings

While an ideal breakfast includes sitting down and leisurely enjoying it, the reality is some days our schedules are too hectic to allow that luxury. Instead of surrendering to a meal replacement bar, consider options such as a quick fruit salad, a Port Madison Goat Yogurt Smoothie (p.8) or check out Quick and Easy Snack Ideas (p.9).

Seasonal Fruit Salad

(Makes 2 servings)

Use strawberries or melon in the spring. Try apricots, nectarines, blueberries or any other fruit in the summer. Apples, figs or pears are good fall choices.

> 1 1/2 cups plain yogurt (low fat, goat or soy)
> 1 tablespoon honey or fruit sweetener
> 2 tablespoons fresh lime, lemon or orange juice
> 1 teaspoon lime, lemon or orange zest, finely chopped
> 1 tablespoon freshly grated ginger
> 2 cups chopped seasonal fruit
> 1 tablespoon chopped nuts or grated coconut (optional)

Blend yogurt, honey, citrus juice and zest together. Squeeze the grated ginger between your fingers into the yogurt mixture. Discard the ginger pulp. Mix in the ginger juice, then blend in fruit and garnish with chopped nuts or coconut, if desired.

Apples and Pears with Banana-Almond Dressing

(Makes 2 or 3 servings)

This recipe is best with freshly made Almond Milk (p.8). The packaged version isn't quite the same.

> 2 ripe bananas
> 1/4 cup almond milk, see recipe below
> 2 1/2 cups chopped apples and pears (Fuji apples and Anjou pears are good choices)
> 1/4 cup raisins, chopped dates or apricots
> Sprinkling of coconut

Blend bananas and almond milk until smooth and creamy. Mix in apples, pears and raisins. Spoon into dishes. Top each serving with a sprinkling of coconut.

Almond Milk
(Makes 2 1/2 cups)

Almonds are high in calcium, contain several B vitamins and are a good source of vitamin E. This recipe doesn't take much time, but you should soak the almonds overnight first. The milk will last a week in your refrigerator.

> 1/2 cup raw almonds
> 1 1/2 cups water
> 1 tablespoon maple syrup

Soak almonds in 1 cup water overnight. Add almonds and water to a blender and blend until the liquid is smooth and creamy. Add remaining 1/2 cup water and maple syrup. When the milk is smooth, strain through a cheesecloth or clean nylon strainer. Squeeze out the remaining milk from the pulp. Discard the pulp or use it in a cookie or cake recipe. Pour almond milk into a glass jar and store in the refrigerator.

Port Madison Goat Yogurt Smoothie
(Makes 2 cups)

Goat yogurt is much thinner than regular yogurt. Port Madison goat yogurt makes the best smoothies I've ever tasted. For an extra icy treat, freeze ripe bananas before preparing this recipe. This gives the smoothie very thick, ice-cream-like texture.

> 2 cups fresh or frozen blueberries (or other seasonal or frozen fruit)
> 1 ripe banana
> 6 ounces Port Madison goat yogurt
> 1 tablespoon peanut butter
> 1 tablespoon flax oil

Blend all ingredients in a blender until smooth and creamy. Pour into a glass and enjoy.

Trail Mix

(Makes 2 cups)

This the original fast food breakfast and hiking snack. Use any kind of dried fruit — apples, nectarines, apricots. Medjool dates are large fresh dates found in produce departments.

1 1/4 cup mixed dried fruit, cut into small pieces
1/4 cup pitted, cut-up Medjool dates (about 3 medium)
1/4 cup raw hazelnuts or almonds
1/4 cup raw cashews
2 tablespoons raw sunflower seeds

Mix fruit, nuts and seeds together.

Simple Soaked Oats

(Makes 1 serving)

For variation, add 1 tablespoon toasted, chopped nuts or ground seeds.

1/2 cup soy, rice or almond milk (use plain or vanilla)
1/3 cup old-fashioned rolled oats
1 tablespoon ground flax seeds
Fresh blueberries or raspberries or other seasonal fruit

Pour soy or rice milk over oats. Soak 1/2 hour or in the refrigerator over night. Stir in flax seeds and top with berries.

Quick and Easy Breakfast Snack Ideas

♦ Sliced apples or pears with almond butter or cheese wedges.

♦ Dried apricots, dates or figs stuffed with almonds, walnuts or pecans.

♦ Slices of sprouted whole-grain bread spread with pumpkin seed butter, raw almond butter or peanut butter.

♦ Nut butter balls made with 1 cup peanut or almond butter, 3 to 4 tablespoons ground flax seeds, honey or maple syrup to taste and as many currants or raisins as you want. Roll the ingredients into 1-inch balls and freeze overnight. Keep in freezer for easy storage.

Serious Cereals with Whole Grains

The cornerstone of civilizations around the world, whole grains are a rich source of vitamins, minerals, complex carbohydrates, protein, essential fatty acids and fiber. When whole grains are refined for consumption, the nutrient-rich germ and the bran, which contains fiber, are removed, leaving only starch and protein. Whole grains nourish life, and throughout history no other food has been as important for sustaining civilizations. Whole-grain cereals are a perfect way to start your day.

Whole grain tips

♦ Buy at your local natural foods store where the turnover is rapid. Because of the natural oils in whole grains, the shelf life is shorter. Most grains have a shelf life of six months. Buy in small quantities and store grains in well-labeled containers, away from the light. Alternatively, store them in the refrigerator or freezer for longer storage.

♦ Measure the amount of grains desired. Place in a fine-mesh strainer and look through grains for small rocks or sticks to remove before rinsing. Very small grains such as amaranth or teff don't have to be rinsed, but if you want to do so, place them in a small jar, cover with a clean nylon or cheese cloth, then rinse and pour the water off carefully.

♦ Presoaking most grains (except quinoa and teff) overnight enhances digestibility. Some sources recommend adding lemon juice to the soaking water to help break down the grains and neutralize phytic acid, which interferes with some mineral absorption.

♦ To get a more intense, nutty flavor, try dry-roasting grains. Heat a heavy skillet over medium heat. Add grains, stir and cook. They will give off a nutty aroma when they are fully toasted. It takes approximately 3 to 8 minutes, depending on how dry the grain is and how big the grain is. Since the oil in the grain has been heated, it is best to use toasted grains within a day or so of toasting. You can also toast cereal flakes such as oatmeal or barley.

♦ Use a spice grinder or blender to grind or crack grains into smaller pieces. Grains will cook faster – in about 5 minutes. Cracked grains from the blender cook in 15 to 20 minutes. Toast grains first, then grind them in the spice grinder for a nutty breakfast porridge. Since the grain is cracked, the oil is exposed to air, so it's best to use the grain shortly after grinding it.

♦ See pages 289-94 for additional information about whole grains.

Easy Cream of Rice

(Serves 2)

Using cooked, leftover sweet brown rice, this warming cereal takes 5 to 10 minutes to prepare. Top with seasonal fruit instead of using dried fruit, if desired.

1 1/2 cups cooked sweet brown rice
1/2 cup soymilk,
1/4 cup cut-up, dried fruit (apricots, dates, apples)
Pinch of salt
Maple syrup or date sugar
2 tablespoons toasted nuts or ground, raw flax seeds

Combine rice, milk, dried fruit and salt in a saucepan. Stir and cook on low for 5 to 10 minutes. Add more milk, if desired. Top with maple syrup and toasted nuts or flax seeds.

Variations:

Cream of Buckwheat

1 1/2 cups cooked, raw or toasted buckwheat
1/2 cup amazake (any flavor) or soymilk
1/2 teaspoon cinnamon
1/4 teaspoon nutmeg
Pinch of salt
1/4 cup chopped dates
1/4 cup chopped toasted hazelnuts

Follow the directions above.

Cream of Coconut Millet

1 1/2 cups cooked millet
1/2 cup light coconut milk
1/4 cup toasted coconut
Pinch of salt
1 to 3 tablespoons Rapadura

Follow the directions above.

Spelt Porridge

(Serves 2)

A spice grinder or clean coffee grinder can grind whole grains for a quick hot cereal.

1/2 cup water
1/2 cup amazake
Pinch of nutmeg and salt
1/2 cup ground spelt
1/8 cup chopped dates or other chopped dried fruit
Soy, almond, rice or dairy milk to taste

Combine water, amazake, nutmeg, salt, ground spelt and dates in a small saucepan. Bring to a boil, stir, reduce heat and simmer for 5 minutes or until done, adding more water as needed. Serve with milk.

Variations:

Kamut or Wheat Porridge

1/2 cup water
1/2 cup apple juice
Pinch of cinnamon, nutmeg and salt
1/2 cup ground kamut or wheat berries
1/8 cup chopped, dried apples or dried cranberries
Soy, almond or rice milk to taste

Follow the directions above.

Toasted Rice Porridge

Toast the presoaked rice in a heavy frying pan over medium heat for 7 minutes or until rice turns a darker shade and smells toasted.

1/2 cup water
1/2 cup vanilla soy, almond or rice milk
Dash of vanilla extract or butterscotch flavoring
1/2 cup toasted ground rice
1 tablespoon Rapadura
Soy or rice milk to taste
1 tablespoon chopped, toasted hazelnuts

Follow the directions above. Top with hazelnuts.

Almond Amaranth, Teff and Steel-Cut Oats
(Serves 2)

Amaranth is a hearty, nutritious grain that is loaded with calcium. Teff, the tiniest grain, originally came from Ethiopia and is reported to have more calcium than amaranth. Oats are rich in silicon, which helps bones absorb calcium. Indulge in this breakfast and feed your bones.

2 tablespoons almond butter
1 cup water
1 cup vanilla soymilk
1/3 cup each: amaranth, teff and steel-cut oats
1/2 teaspoon each: vanilla and almond extract
1 peeled and cored sweet-tart apple or pear, cut into tiny chunks
Pinch of salt
Maple syrup, to taste
2 tablespoons chopped almonds
Fresh seasonal berries

Combine almond butter and water in a saucepan. Blend with a hand blender until creamy. Add soymilk, amaranth, teff, oats, vanilla, almond extract, apple and salt. Bring to a boil. Reduce heat to a simmer. Cook for 30 minutes, adding more water if necessary. Top with maple syrup, chopped almonds and berries.

Goebel Hill Farm

Heather Robinson and Hal Buttery own and run Goebel Hill Farm, off highway 92, just beyond Granite Falls. They got started on their 4 1/2-acre certified organic farm with raspberries in 1998. Heather says her biggest farming challenge is the weather. Too hot, and blueberries shrivel while raspberries turn to mush. Too much rain, and mold quickly appears on the raspberries. They once offered you-pick raspberries, and then later sold products and produce at the University District Farmers Market, but being a small farmer is difficult. Market fees and the cost of transportation add up. You can purchase Heather's raspberry and blueberry products at the Machias fruit stand, which is east of Everett, close to Lake Stevens. Besides growing big, juicy, delicious berries and apples and making jam, Heather also makes great raspberry and blueberry vinegar. Her raspberry vinegar is an essential staple in my kitchen.

Toasted 3-Grain Cereal
(Serves 2)

This warming, nutty, 3-grain cereal is just the ticket for those cold, hard-to-start mornings.

> 1/3 cup each: raw buckwheat, millet, steel-cut oats
> 1 1/4 cups water
> 1 cup soymilk
> 1/2 teaspoon cinnamon
> 1/2 teaspoon nutmeg
> Pinch of salt
> 1/3 cup dried fruit (raisins, currants, chopped apricots, dried cherries, plums or nectarines)
> 2 to 4 tablespoons toasted chopped walnuts or pecans

Toast buckwheat in a hot skillet over medium heat. Stir for a few minutes, then add the millet and oats and continue to dry-roast the grains until they are lightly browned and fragrant. This takes about 5 minutes. Remove from heat.

In a small saucepan, combine water and milk, add the grains, cinnamon, nutmeg, salt and fruit. Bring to a boil, then reduce heat and simmer for 15 to 20 minutes or until liquid is absorbed. Garnish with toasted walnuts and serve with additional milk, if desired.

Overnight Whole Oats and Rice
(Serves 2)

You can substitute barley, buckwheat or millet in this recipe, or add a few tablespoons of amaranth or teff to the oats and rice for interesting variations. Soak grains before cooking for better digestibility, if desired.

> 1/2 cup each: oat groats and brown rice (long or short grain rice)
> 2 1/2 cups water
> 1 cup soymilk
> 1 vanilla bean, slit down the middle
> Pinch of salt
> 1/4 cup chopped, dried fruit (optional)

Place rinsed or soaked grains, water, milk, vanilla bean, salt and dried fruit in a crockpot. Set on low and cook overnight. Stir, remove vanilla bean and serve with additional soymilk.

Priceless Pancakes and Toppings

One of the original fast foods, pancakes or flatbreads have been around since someone first discovered that a bit of grain paste blended with water and laid on a hot stone near a fire developed a nice crust and was worth eating.

Most pancake recipes and mixes use wheat flour. However, wheat is an overused food in our country and it's no surprise wheat is one of our most allergenic foods. Whether you are allergic to wheat or not, using other grains, gives you an opportunity to see how various grains react with other ingredients and affect the taste and texture in pancakes. Kamut, spelt and barley contain gluten and are similar to wheat in performance. Recipes using low or non-gluten flours have additional binding ingredients added to give a wheat-like texture. The following pancake recipes were featured in Vegetarian Journal in August 1999.

Tips for perfect pancakes

◆ Sift or mix together dry ingredients, making sure there are no small lumps.

◆ Beat liquid ingredients separately. Egg replacer and liquids should be well blended.

◆ Combine dry and liquid ingredients. Use the batter immediately since the leavening process begins once the dry ingredients are combined with liquid. Double-acting baking powder means the leavening begins when combined with a liquid and acts again when heated.

◆ Use less salt with alternative grain flours because wheat-free pancakes need additional leavening to rise, and both baking powder and baking soda contain sodium. According to *Laurel's Kitchen Bread Book,* one teaspoon of baking soda contains 1,360 mg. of sodium.

◆ Cook pancakes on a preheated nonstick or lightly oiled griddle. The griddle is ready when water dripped onto it sputters.

◆ Measure 1/4 cup of batter for a 3-inch pancake. Pour batter at intervals over the hot surface.

◆ When bubbles appear all over the surface and then break, flip the pancake and cook the reverse side. The first side will take a few minutes longer than the second to cook.

◆ Serve pancakes as soon as they come off the griddle. You can keep them warm in a 250° oven for a short period of time.

Light Lemony Oatcakes
(Makes ten 3-inch pancakes)

These crepe-like pancakes are perfect for rolling up your favorite fillings or simply dusting with powdered sugar. In this recipe, tahini is used as a substitute for the binding quality of an egg.

1 cup vanilla soy or rice milk
1 tablespoon lemon juice
1 heaping cup old-fashioned oats (oatmeal)
1/2 tablespoon baking powder
1 teaspoon baking soda
1 teaspoon lemon zest
1/8 teaspoon salt
1 1/2 tablespoons tahini
1 tablespoon maple syrup or honey

Combine soymilk and lemon juice. Set aside. In a spice grinder or blender, grind oats into flour. Combine oat flour, baking powder, baking soda, lemon zest and salt. Mix well.

In a blender or with a hand blender, combine soymilk-lemon mixture, tahini and maple syrup or honey and blend until smooth and creamy. Mix wet and dry ingredients together. *(Hint: Use a deep-sided bowl when mixing with a hand blender.)*

Heat griddle on medium heat. Spoon about 1/4 cup per cake onto the heated griddle. Mixture will be quite thin. When bubbles form and break, turn carefully and cook until lightly browned.

Lemon tips

♦ Zest before juicing the lemon. To zest, wash the lemon, then use a peeler or microplane zester to remove only the outer part of the peel. Avoid grating the white inner peel since that only adds bitterness.
♦ Get more juice from a lemon by warming it slightly before squeezing it. If it is not room temperature, either roll it in your hands for a few minutes or place it in hot water for a minute. Then, roll the lemon on the counter and juice it. Don't roll too hard or the juice may become bitter.

Zucchini Griddlecakes

(Makes about fourteen 3-inch griddlecakes)

Kamut is a distant relative of wheat. It contains gluten, but some people who are sensitive to wheat can eat kamut without any allergy problems. If you don't have Ener-G-egg replacer, use 1 tablespoon ground flax seeds blended with 3 tablespoons water as a substitute, then add only 1/4 cup soymilk.

1/4 cup old-fashioned rolled oats (oatmeal)
2/3 cup kamut flour
1/3 cup cornmeal
2 teaspoons baking powder
1/2 teaspoon baking soda
1/2 teaspoon nutmeg
1/8 teaspoon salt
1/2 cup grated zucchini
1/2 tablespoon Ener-G egg replacer
2 tablespoons water
2/3 cup pineapple juice
1/3 cup soy or rice milk
1 tablespoon fruit sweetener, or frozen apple juice concentrate

Grind oats into flour in a spice grinder. Combine oat and kamut flour, cornmeal, baking powder, baking soda, nutmeg and salt in a bowl, mixing well. Stir in zucchini, coating all grated zucchini with flour. In another bowl, beat Ener-G egg replacer and water with a fork until foamy. Mix in pineapple juice, soy or rice milk and fruit sweetener until well blended.

Mix wet and dry ingredients together until a batter forms. Spoon onto preheated griddle. Cook until bubbles form and break. Flip the pancakes and cook for a few minutes on the reverse side. If mixture thickens as it sits add more soymilk to maintain consistency.

Buckwheat-Banana Pancakes

(Makes about ten 3-inch pancakes)

My favorite pancakes, the assertive taste of buckwheat is balanced with banana, which also helps to bind this gluten-free flour. For a substantial breakfast, serve these with smoky tempeh strips (Fakin' Bacon) or an egg and fresh seasonal fruit.

> 1 heaping cup buckwheat flour
> 2 1/2 teaspoons baking powder
> 1 tablespoon date sugar or Rapadura
> 1/8 teaspoon salt
> 1 cup carob soymilk
> 1 teaspoon vanilla
> 1 medium-sized ripe banana, mashed (about 1/2 cup)
> 2 tablespoons finely chopped walnuts (optional)

Sift together or combine dry ingredients, mixing well. In a blender or with a hand blender, mix soymilk, vanilla and banana. Stir wet and dry ingredients together. Spoon onto a preheated lightly oiled or nonstick griddle. Sprinkle with walnuts, if desired. When bubbles form, turn pancakes and cook until lightly browned.

Blueberry Hotcakes

(Makes about ten 3-inch cakes)

Here, tapioca flour serves as the binding ingredient for rice and millet flour. Alternatively, you can use arrowroot instead of tapioca flour.

1/2 cup each: rice and millet flour (or use 1 cup of either flour)
1 1/2 tablespoons tapioca flour
1/2 tablespoon baking powder
1/2 teaspoon baking soda
1/4 teaspoon salt
1 medium-sized ripe mashed banana
1 cup pineapple or pineapple-coconut juice
1 cup fresh blueberries

Sift or stir together dry ingredients, mixing well. In a blender or with a hand blender, combine mashed banana, and pineapple juice. Mix wet and dry ingredients. Gently stir in blueberries. Spoon onto preheated lightly oiled or nonstick griddle. When bubbles form and break, turn pancakes. Cook reverse side for a few minutes.

Blueberry Topping

(Makes about 1 cup)

Have a double dose of blueberries with this topping on blueberry hotcakes. For variation blend ripe, peeled peaches, apricots or nectarines. Use a little lemon juice with these fruits to retain the color.

2 cups fresh blueberries

Puree in a blender until smooth. Serve fresh.

Strawberry-Plum Sauce
(Makes 1 cup)

Though this is sweetened with strawberry jam, you can also use other jams, such as blueberry or raspberry, to vary the flavor. I like to use Italian plums for this recipe, but you can also use a sweet-tart variety such as Santa Rosa.

8 small ripe plums, pitted and halved (about 1 cup)
Zest and juice of 1/2 lemon (2 tablespoons lemon juice)
2 tablespoons fruit-sweetened strawberry jam

Place ingredients in a blender and blend until smooth and creamy. Serve immediately or refrigerate and serve later. Keeps about 1 week in the refrigerator.

Raspberry-Orange Sauce
(Makes 1 cup)

Agar is a sea vegetable and thickening agent. It can be found in natural or Asian food stores. This sauce is best eaten warm because it thickens when it cools. Reheated, it turns into wonderful syrup again.

1 cup fresh or frozen raspberries
Juice and zest of 1 orange
2 tablespoons fruit sweetener
1 tablespoon agar (or agar agar) flakes

Combine all ingredients in a saucepan. Slowly bring to a boil, stirring frequently. Reduce heat, simmer for about 5 minutes. Sauce will begin to thicken. Remove from heat. Serve warm. Store refrigerated for about one week.

Apricot-Almond Topping

(Makes about 1 cup)

Apricots and almond butter give this topping a compelling creamy consistency. This also makes a good sauce for fruit salads.

    10 dried apricots
    Apricot nectar or apple juice to make 1 cup
    1 tablespoon almond butter

Soak apricots in apricot nectar overnight. Blend with almond butter in a blender until smooth and creamy. Store refrigerated for up to one week.

Apple-Cranberry Topping

(Makes 1 3/4 cup)

Chunky, warm apples simmered with cranberries — sweet and tart flavors blended together into one mouth-watering sauce!

    1 1/2 cups peeled, chopped cooking apple (Granny Smith, Fuji,
    Winesap or McIntosh)
    1/4 cup dried cranberries
    1 cup apple cider or apple juice
    2 tablespoons apple cider vinegar
    2 tablespoons fruit sweetener or honey
    1 teaspoon cinnamon
    1/2 tablespoon arrowroot

Combine all ingredients in a saucepan. Stir until arrowroot is dissolved. Bring mixture to a boil, reduce heat, cover and simmer for about 12 minutes or until apples are very tender. Serve over hot pancakes.

Bake it Ahead

Living in a society that pushes sweet muffins, breads, cakes and cookies in large portions at us at every opportunity, it's no wonder so many of us have a sweet tooth or a weight problem. Bake with whole-grain flours, use alternative sweeteners and try using less oil in recipes. The results can be delicious as well as healthy. Using whole-grain flour makes quick breads and muffins more dense than commercial versions, but they are infinitely more satisfying.

Quick bread baking tips

♦ Preheat oven before baking. Have all ingredients at room temperature. Cold dough and batter bake unevenly and take longer to cook.

♦ Lightly oil a baking dish or line it with parchment paper before baking. Cold pressed vegetable oils don't work as well as solid oils because high heat degrades and changes oils such as olive or hazelnut oil. Refined oils are already damaged and altered and are not healthy options. Use solid oils like coconut oil or ghee when heating above 325°. These oils take heat without changing their chemical structure.

♦ Combine dry and wet ingredients separately, then blend the two together.

♦ Blend wet and dry ingredients gently. Do not overmix, as this will develop the gluten and produce tough bread or rubbery cake. Stir only about 15 strokes.

♦ Make sure the batter is fairly thick — from a thick oatmeal-like consistency to an almost cookie dough consistency. If a batter is too thin in a quick bread recipe, it will not bake correctly and will never get completely done.

♦ As soon as the batter is mixed, place it in a prepared baking pan and put it in a preheated oven. Baking soda and baking powder begin acting as soon as they contact moisture. Double-acting baking powder reacts again when heat is applied.

♦ Refrain from opening the oven door until the bread is within 5 to 10 minutes of being done. The heat in the oven decreases every time the door is opened, causing the bread to cook unevenly.

♦ To determine when a quick bread is done, insert a toothpick or wire cake tester into the center of the bread. It is done if the tester comes out clean. Let the bread or cake sit for 15 minutes in the pan on a baking rack before removing it from the pan.

♦ To remove bread from the pan, slide a knife around the edges, then invert the pan over the cooling rack, tap the bottom lightly and shake gently.

Corn Biscuits

(Makes 9 large or 12 small biscuits)

These easy drop biscuits are a reinvented version of my grandmother's biscuits. My grandmother used all white flour and her biscuits were very light. To make a lighter biscuit, use half unbleached flour.

1 cup plain soymilk
1/2 tablespoon lemon juice
1 3/4 cup whole-wheat pastry flour
3/4 cup cornmeal
4 teaspoons baking powder
1/2 teaspoon baking soda
1/2 teaspoon salt
3/4 cup corn (fresh off the cob or frozen, thawed)
1/4 cup melted butter or coconut oil
1 tablespoon maple syrup

Preheat oven to 450°. Oil a baking sheet or line it with parchment paper.

Combine soymilk with lemon juice. Set aside. In a medium-size mixing bowl, combine dry ingredients. Mix well. Stir in corn. Add butter and maple syrup to soymilk-lemon mixture. Make a well in the center of the dry ingredients and add the liquid ingredients. Stir until a soft dough forms. If necessary, add enough flour to make a stiff dough — like a cookie dough consistency. Drop dough from a spoon onto prepared baking sheet. Bake 15 minutes or until biscuits are lightly browned on top.

Tip

Deciding whether to drop biscuits from a spoon or roll them out depends on the amount of liquid in a recipe. For rolled biscuits, the dough should be sticky enough to hold together but firm enough to lay out on a board for cutting. Drop biscuits have a thick, cookie dough texture that can easily be pushed off a spoon. When pressed for time, drop biscuits are easier to make.

Sundried Tomato Biscuits
(Makes 12 biscuits)
These biscuits are excellent with scrambled eggs or tofu, or try Port Madison goat cheese spread on top.

2 tablespoons chopped sundried tomatoes
1/2 cup boiling water
2 cups barley or whole-wheat pastry flour
1 teaspoon baking powder
1/2 teaspoon baking soda
1/2 teaspoon salt
1/4 cup cold butter or coconut oil
2 medium eggs, beaten (or flax seed egg replacer, p.17)

Preheat oven to 400°. Pour boiling water over sundried tomatoes and set aside. Let soak for 20 minutes. Combine dry ingredients. Mix well. Cut in butter with fork or pastry blender until mixture resembles coarse crumbs. Blend eggs with the tomatoes. Add egg-tomato mixture and stir until a soft dough is formed. Drop from a spoonful onto an ungreased baking sheet. Bake 15 minutes, or until golden brown.

FOOD FOR THOUGHT
Eastern Washington is wheat farming country. The third largest commodity crop in the United States, about 17 percent of the wheat growers produce two-thirds of our wheat. Wheat farms are typically massive farms, and commercial growers apply an average of over 300 pounds of pesticides per acre. Although Montana, North Dakota and Colorado are the leading states with certified organic wheat production, in 2004 Washington totaled 2,115 acres that qualified for organic wheat certification. Organic wheat farms tend to be much smaller than conventional farms, and farmers alternate crops with legumes to improve soil quality. No chemical pesticides or sprays are allowed. They also underseed wheat with clover, a cover crop that improves soil quality and helps block out weeds. Organic farmers pay up to $5.00 an acre for transition to organic, plus the cost of certification, including new applicant and site fees. Organic fertilizer costs are also more expensive. It isn't easy being an organic wheat farmer and with more work involved, it can be tempting to return to conventional farming.

Ginger-Peach Scones

(Makes 12 scones)

Bake these scones ahead for a leisurely, summer breakfast. To toast walnuts, heat a skillet over medium heat, add walnuts. Stir and cook until toasted.

1/2 cup rolled oats
2 cups whole-wheat pastry or barley flour
1 tablespoon baking powder
1/3 cup Rapadura
1 teaspoon ground ginger
1/4 cup cold butter or coconut oil
1 medium-size, ripe banana, mashed
5 tablespoons vanilla soy or rice milk
1 medium-large peach, peeled and chopped (about 3/4 cup)
1/4 cup candied ginger, chopped to the size of a raisin
1/4 cup toasted, chopped walnuts (optional)
1/4 teaspoon cinnamon, mixed with 1 tablespoon Rapadura

Preheat oven to 375°. Line a baking sheet with parchment paper. Place oats in a blender or spice grinder and blend until you have oat flour. Combine oat flour, whole-wheat pastry flour, baking powder, Rapadura and ginger together. Mix well, making sure no small lumps remain. With a pastry blender, fork or your fingers mix in butter until mixture resembles a coarse meal.

In a blender or with a hand blender, combine mashed banana and soymilk. Blend until smooth and creamy. Combine wet and dry ingredients. Gently stir in peaches and candied ginger. Add toasted walnuts, if desired. Mixture will be sticky, not quite a formed dough. With your hands, form mixture into a soft dough by turning a few times, adding a small amount (a few tablespoons) more flour if necessary. Turn out onto a lightly floured board and knead lightly until dough sticks together — about 5 turns. Pat into a 9-inch round and cut in half. Cut each half into 6 triangles. Place wedges one inch apart on a baking sheet. Sprinkle with cinnamon sugar. Bake for 18 minutes or until lightly browned. Remove from oven. Cool slightly before removing to a cooling rack.

Lemon-Cherry Muffins

(Makes 10 to 12 muffins)

These light tasty muffins are perfect for a mid-morning or an afternoon break. Serve with organic tea or coffee.

1 cup whole-wheat pastry flour
1/2 cup each: barley flour and oat flour
2 teaspoons baking powder
1 teaspoon baking soda
1 tablespoon finely chopped lemon zest
1/2 teaspoon salt
1/4 to 1/2 cup Rapadura
1/2 cup chopped, dried sour cherries
1/4 cup toasted, chopped walnuts or pecans
Juice of 1 lemon
Soy or rice milk to make 1/2 cup (when added to lemon juice)
1 medium-size mashed banana
1 egg, beaten (or use egg replacer)
2 tablespoons melted coconut oil or butter

Preheat oven to 400º. Lightly oil muffin tins. In a large mixing bowl, combine flours, baking powder, baking soda, lemon zest, salt and sugar. Mix well, making sure there are no small lumps. Stir in sour cherries and walnuts. Set aside.

Combine lemon juice and enough soy or rice milk to make 1/2 cup. Blend in mashed banana and egg, beating well. (*Hint: A hand blender works well for this.*) Stir in melted oil.

Make a well in the center of the dry ingredients. Pour in the wet ingredients and mix, but do not overmix. Batter should be blended, but a little lumpy. Spoon into muffin tins. You can make 10 larger or 12 smaller muffins. Place in the oven and bake for 25 minutes. Remove from oven and place on a cooling rack for about 10 minutes before removing from the muffin tins. Loosen the muffins with a knife, cutting carefully around the edges. Gently pull them out.

Maple Pumpkin Bread

(Makes two 9 X 5-inch loaves)

Baked pumpkin and maple syrup combine to give this autumn favorite a moist, sweet taste. Use other varieties of squash such as acorn, butternut or sweet dumpling. You can also use yams or sweet potatoes instead of pumpkin.

2 1/2 cups whole-wheat pastry or barley flour
1 tablespoon baking powder
1 teaspoon cinnamon
1/2 teaspoon nutmeg
1/4 teaspoon cloves
1/3 cup coconut oil or butter
1 1/2 cup baked sugar or Cinderella pumpkin
1 cup maple syrup
1 cup currants or raisins
1/2 cup dried cranberries or cherries
3/4 cup lightly toasted, chopped pecans or walnuts

Preheat oven to 350º. Lightly oil two 9X5-inch loaf pans. Combine dry ingredients, mixing well. Cut in coconut oil with a fork or pastry blender until well blended.

In a separate bowl, mix pumpkin and maple syrup. (*Hint: A hand blender works well for this.*) Combine wet and dry ingredients. Mixture will be quite thick, like a very thick cookie dough — if it isn't, add a bit more flour. Fold in fruit and nuts, then spoon into loaf pans and bake for 45 minutes or until a tester or toothpick comes out clean. Let cool in pan on a cooling rack for 15 minutes. Run a knife around the edges of pans, invert over cooling rack and gently tap until loaves come out.

Northwest Blueberry Bars

(Makes about 18 bars)

Many farms sell blueberries at local markets in July and August. Rent's Due Ranch in Stanwood has some of the biggest, sweetest blueberries around. You can find the Rent's Due booth at Lake City and the University District farmers markets. Though fresh is always the first choice, you can also make these bars with frozen, thawed berries.

Crust:
1/2 cup butter
3/4 cup maple syrup
1 1/2 cups whole-wheat pastry flour
1 1/4 cups rolled oats
1/2 teaspoon soda
1/2 teaspoon salt

Filling:
2 cups blueberries
2 to 4 tablespoons Rapadura or organic brown sugar
1/4 cup plus 1 tablespoon water
2 tablespoons arrowroot
2 tablespoons lemon juice
1/4 cup lightly toasted, chopped pecans

Preheat oven to 400º. Combine butter and maple syrup until smooth and creamy. Add flour, soda, oats and salt. Mix well. Pat half of this mixture into a 9X9-inch pan.

Combine blueberries, Rapadura and 1/4 cup water in saucepan. Heat over medium heat. Stir and cook until blueberries are broken. Combine 1 tablespoon water and arrowroot. Stir until arrowroot is dissolved. Add arrowroot to the blueberry mixture. Cook on low heat for about 10 minutes or until mixture is quite thick. Remove from heat. Stir in lemon juice and walnuts. Spread filling onto crust, making sure it is evenly spread. Sprinkle the rest of the crust mixture over blueberries and gently pat the top crust down. Bake 30 minutes or until lightly browned on top. Cool before cutting into bars.

Mocha-Hazelnut Date Bars

(Makes one 9-inch pan)

Toast raw buckwheat in a heavy skillet or buy the toasted variety. If you want to make this bar gluten-free, use 1/2 cup arrowroot instead of rolled oats. Cut the bars while they are still warm.

> 1/2 cup rolled oats
> 1 cup kasha (toasted buckwheat)
> 1 teaspoon baking powder
> 3/4 cup hazelnut butter
> 1/2 cup maple syrup
> 6 tablespoons strong coffee
> 1 ounce melted dark chocolate
> 1 1/2 teaspoons vanilla
> 1/2 heaping cup chopped dates

Preheat oven to 350°. Lightly oil baking pan with coconut oil. With a spice grinder or blender, pulse the oats into flour. Mix oat flour with kasha and baking powder. In another bowl, combine hazelnut butter, maple syrup, coffee, chocolate and vanilla. Mix well. Combine with dry ingredients. Stir in dates. Spread into prepared baking dish. Bake for 30 minutes. Run a knife around the edges and cut into bars while still warm.

Variation:

Chewy Date Bars

An egg gives these bars a different texture. Using part tahini with the hazelnut butter produces a lighter flavor.

> 3/4 cup rolled oats
> 1 teaspoon baking powder
> 1 cup kasha (toasted buckwheat)
> 1/2 cup tahini
> 1/3 cup hazelnut butter
> 1/2 cup maple syrup
> 1/2 cup chopped dates
> 1 egg, beaten
> 1/2 tablespoon vanilla
> 1/2 teaspoon coffee extract.

Follow directions above, except add baking powder to dry ingredients and add the beaten egg to the tahini mixture. Blend wet and dry ingredients together and spread into prepared baking pan. Bake for 35 to 40 minutes. Bars will be lightly browned on top and sides. Cut while warm.

Lemon-Pecan Biscotti

(Makes about 3 dozen cookies)

These biscotti are a treat. Try them for a mid-morning break, or serve them with brunch. Bake them the first time up to a day ahead, then slice and bake again. Using unbleached flour will make a lighter cookie, but it won't be as healthy. The recipe will not make as many cookies using tofu instead of eggs.

1 3/4 cups whole-wheat flour or 2 cups unbleached flour
1 cup whole-wheat pastry flour
1 teaspoon each: baking powder and baking soda
Zest of 1 lemon, finely chopped
1 cup lightly toasted, chopped pecans (see tip on p.31)
1/2 cup butter or coconut oil
1 cup organic sugar
2 eggs, beaten or 1/2 cup silken tofu
Juice of 1 lemon
1/2 tablespoon vanilla extract

Preheat oven to 350º. Combine dry ingredients, including lemon zest and pecans in a large mixing bowl. Set aside. In a separate bowl, cream butter and sugar together, blend in eggs or tofu. *(Hint: If using tofu, blend in with a hand blender.)* Mix in lemon juice and vanilla. Combine the wet and dry ingredients, adding enough flour for a very stiff dough, if necessary.

Divide dough in half and roll into 14-inch logs. Place on an ungreased baking sheet, flatten log top and bake for about 25 minutes. Remove from oven and let cool completely before slicing. Allow at least 1/2 hour between the first and second baking.

Preheat oven to 325º. When biscotti is cool, slice 1/2 inch thick on the diagonal at approximately a 45º angle. Lay flat on a baking sheet or pizza screen. Bake for 25 minutes, until lightly browned. If using a baking sheet, turn halfway through baking to insure even browning.

Cherry-Apple Oatmeal Cookies

(Makes about 45 cookies)

If you don't have dried apples or cherries, substitute raisins and dried cranberries. When using sesame oil, reduce heat to 325° and bake cookies for 20 minutes. Grade B maple syrup works the best in this recipe. Add 1/2 cup chocolate chips instead of apples, for a dessert or snack cookie.

1 1/2 cups old-fashioned rolled oats
1 1/2 cups whole-wheat pastry or barley flour
1/2 cup shredded coconut
1/2 cup Rapadura
1/2 tablespoon baking powder
1/2 cup melted coconut or light sesame oil
1/2 cup maple syrup
1/2 tablespoon vanilla extract
1/2 cup toasted, chopped walnuts or pecans (see tip below)
1/2 cup dried sour cherries
1/2 cup dried apple bits (cut slices into small bits with kitchen scissors)

Preheat oven to 375°. Line a baking sheet with parchment paper. In a large bowl, combine dry ingredients, mixing well to make sure there are no small lumps. Set aside. In another bowl, combine coconut oil, maple syrup and vanilla. Stir wet ingredients into flour mixture. Blend in walnuts and dried fruit.

Scoop up a teaspoon of the dough and form into a ball. (*Hint: if the dough sticks to your hands, oil your hands a bit before rolling the cookies.*) It should be about the size of a large marble. Place the dough on the baking sheet and when the sheet is full, flatten cookies with the bottom of a glass or your hand. (*Hint: oil the glass bottom so it won't stick to the dough.*) Bake for 12 to 16 minutes or until lightly browned. Remove from oven and let cool slightly on baking sheet before removing to a cooling rack. Cookies become crisp as they cool because of the coconut oil.

Tip

Set the oven temperature to 325° to toast raw nuts in the oven. Spread in a single layer on a baking sheet and bake for 10 to 12 minutes. Pine nuts and pecans take less time than walnuts, hazelnuts and almonds. To toast nuts in a heavy skillet, turn the heat to medium. Add nuts, stir and toast until they have a nutty aroma and taste toasted.

Hot and Hearty

There are times when nothing but a filling, hot breakfast will do. If you occasionally get into breakfast doldrums and desperately want out, tempt yourself with some baked sweet potato fries and a tofu sauté, or reheat last night's casserole inside an acorn squash and top with Port Madison goat cheese. Below are a few ideas to consider.

Scrambled Tofu

(Serves 2)

Some years ago, a chef from Vancouver demonstrated an unconventional technique for giving scrambled tofu a more creamy, egg-like consistency. Arrowroot is sprinkled onto the tofu as it cooks and then stirred in. The nutritional yeast, found in natural food stores, lends a cheesy flavor without the cheese.

> 1 pound firm or extra-firm tofu, drained
> 1 tablespoon coconut or light sesame oil
> 1 medium onion, chopped
> 2 cloves garlic, minced or pressed
> 1 cup sliced mushrooms, use button, crimini, shiitake or portabello
> 1 tablespoon nutritional yeast
> 1 tablespoon arrowroot
> 1/4 teaspoon turmeric
> Generous pinch of red pepper flakes or few chopped Mama Lil's Peppers (optional)
> 1/2 teaspoon salt
> 1/4 cup chopped cilantro or parsley

Lay tofu on a plate and place about 5 plates on top to press out excess water. Let tofu sit for about 15 minutes while you prepare the onions and mushrooms.

Heat a heavy skillet over medium heat. Add oil and onions, stir, then cover with a lid, turn heat to low and sweat the onions for about 10 minutes, stirring occasionally. Remove lid and add garlic and mushrooms. Cover and cook until mushrooms are slightly soft and garlic is lightly browned.

Drain water off tofu and crumble tofu over the onions and mushrooms. Sprinkle nutritional yeast, arrowroot, turmeric and pepper flakes over the tofu. Stir in and cook on medium heat for about 7 minutes or until tofu is heated through. Blend in salt and serve sprinkled with chopped cilantro or parsley.

Breakfast Burritos
(Makes 6 burritos)

Nutritional yeast gives these burritos a cheesy taste without the cheese, if you want to leave the cheese out. Make these burritos the night before, and there is no need to heat the tortillas before filling. Simply, leave out the arugula and tomato, and store the burritos in the refrigerator until you're ready for them. Heat burritos for a few minutes in the microwave or 10 minutes at 350° in a conventional oven.

1/2 pound firm or extra-firm tofu, drained
1 tablespoon extra-virgin olive oil
1 small yellow onion, chopped
1/2 medium red or green pepper, chopped
6 whole-wheat tortillas
1 cup chopped zucchini
1 to 2 cloves garlic, pressed
1/2 tablespoon arrowroot
1/2 tablespoon nutritional yeast
2 tablespoon salsa
1 tablespoon fresh or 1 teaspoon dried basil
1/8 teaspoon turmeric
1/4 teaspoon salt
1/2 15-ounce can vegetarian refried beans
1/2 cup grated aged cheese such as Samish Bay Gouda (optional)
1 large tomato, chopped (optional)
Arugula or chopped lettuce (optional)
Salsa to taste

Preheat oven to 350°. Lay tofu on a plate. Place about 5 plates on top of tofu to squeeze out excess water. Set aside. Heat a heavy skillet over medium heat. Add oil, onions and red or green pepper. Reduce heat, cover and sweat onions and peppers for about 5 minutes or until onions are limp.

While vegetables cook, wet a clean kitchen towel (not terry cloth) and lay it on a pie tin. Lay tortillas on the towel, cover with the towel and set in the oven for about 10 minutes. Remove skillet lid, add zucchini and garlic. Stir and cook for one minute. Crumble drained, pressed tofu over the vegetables. Sprinkle arrowroot and nutritional yeast over the tofu, stir and cook on medium heat for a few minutes. Blend in salsa, basil, turmeric and salt. Cook for 5 to 7 minutes or until tofu is heated through. While tofu cooks, heat refried beans on low in a small saucepan for a few minutes.

Remove tortillas from the oven. Lay them flat, and spread 1 heaping tablespoon of refried beans on one side. Top with 3 tablespoons of the tofu-veggie mixture. Add tomato and arugula, if desired. Spoon on salsa to taste. Fold the bottom of the tortilla over the filling, then roll up.

Roasted Chile, Squash and Potato Tacos with Goat Cheese

(Makes 8 tacos)

Homestead Organic Produce (p.5) and Billy's Garden (www.billysgardens.com) are a few of the many farms that sell fresh anaheim chiles at local markets. Port Madison soft goat cheese goes perfectly in these tacos.

4 fresh anaheim chile peppers, green or red
4 tablespoons melted coconut oil, divided equally
1 tablespoon maple syrup
1 medium delicata squash, cut in half lengthwise, seeded and cut into 1/2-inch slices
8 corn tortillas
2 ounces Port Madison goat cheese, crumbled
1 1/2 cups chopped arugula, or baby spinach
Fresh salsa

Place peppers under a broiler and roast until they are slightly blackened and soft. Remove, place in a paper bag. When chiles are cool, seed and slip the skins off. Slice into strips and set aside.

Set oven temperature at 350º. Combine 2 tablespoons coconut oil and maple syrup. Pour mixture over squash slices and stir to coat each slice. Bake for 30 minutes or until squash is soft and slightly browned. Remove from oven. Lay corn tortillas flat on a baking sheet. Lightly, brush both sides of tortillas with remaining coconut oil. Place in the oven for about 5 minutes or until tortillas are warm and soft. Remove from oven, place warm roasted squash and pepper strips on tortilla half. Crumble goat cheese over peppers, sprinkle with arugula and a spoonful of salsa. Fold tortillas over and enjoy.

Chipotle Cranberry Bean and German Butterball Potato Tostadas

(Makes 8 to 10 tostadas)

Chile peppers originated in the jungles along the Amazon River. Potatoes are native to Peru, and beans were used by cliff dwellers in the Southwestern United States. These crops are all grown in Washington now and can be found at farmers markets and natural food stores. For quick preparation, simmer cranberry beans the night before, or use a pressure cooker in the morning.

1 1/2 cups finely grated carrots
1/2 cup finely chopped red or green pepper
2 tablespoons lime juice
1 cup cranberry beans, soaked overnight
3 cups water, approximately
1 tablespoon extra-virgin olive oil
1 large onion, chopped
2 German Butterball potatoes, cut into small chunks
1 clove elephant garlic, peeled and sliced (or use 4 cloves regular garlic, minced)
1/2 teaspoon chipotle chile powder
1/2 cup chopped cilantro (optional)
1/2 teaspoon salt
1 to 2 tablespoons coconut oil
8 to 10 corn tortillas

Combine carrots, pepper and lime juice. Mix well and set aside until tostada filling is ready.

Drain and rinse beans, then combine with water in a medium saucepan. Bring to a boil, reduce heat and simmer, partially covered, for 1 hour or until beans are very tender. When beans are done, drain and mash with a potato masher until they are very thick. Alternatively, you can cook the beans in a pressure cooker using only 1 cup water and a tablespoon of coconut or olive oil for 10 minutes.

While beans cook, heat a heavy skillet over medium heat. Add olive oil and onions. Stir, reduce heat, cover and sweat onions until they are transparent. Remove lid, add potatoes, garlic and chipotle chili powder. Mix well, cover and cook until potatoes are soft, stirring occasionally. You may have to add a little water to keep potatoes from sticking. When vegetables and beans are done, blend together, without mashing the potatoes. Mix in cilantro and salt, keep on low heat until tortillas bake.

Preheat oven to 350°. Lay tortillas flat on a baking sheet. Lightly brush one side of the tortilla with coconut oil. Bake for 10 minutes or until tortillas are crisp. Spread about 1/3 cup filling on each tortilla. Top with carrot-pepper mixture.

Quinoa, Corn and Caramelized Walnuts

(Serves 4)

Walnuts add character to this savory breakfast dish. In the summer, I get walnuts and corn from Homestead Organic Produce.

1 3/4 cups water
1 cup quinoa
1 cup corn, use fresh off the cob or frozen
Pinch of cayenne
1/2 cup walnuts
1 tablespoon melted coconut oil or butter
1 tablespoon Rapadura or maple syrup
Salt to taste

Soak quinoa in water overnight. In a saucepan, bring water, quinoa, corn and cayenne to a boil. Reduce heat and simmer for 15 minutes or until quinoa is done. While quinoa cooks, heat a skillet over medium heat. Add walnuts, stir and toast until lightly browned. Stir in oil and Rapadura. Make sure all nuts are coated. Let the nuts dry out a bit. When quinoa is done, mix in walnuts and corn. Add salt to taste and serve.

Variation:

Quinoa, Corn and Scrambled Eggs With Herbs

(Serves 4 to 6)
Quinoa and corn prepared from recipe above
3 eggs
1 tablespoon soymilk or salsa
1 tablespoon chopped fresh chives
1 tablespoon chopped fresh basil
1 teaspoon coconut oil or ghee (optional)
Salt and freshly ground pepper to taste
1 to 2 ounces crumbled goat cheese (optional)

Beat eggs with soymilk, then add chives and basil. Heat a skillet over medium heat. Add coconut oil and then pour in eggs. Stir and cook eggs until done. Season with salt and pepper to taste, add quinoa and corn and continue cooking until heated through. Garnish with goat cheese, if desired.

Red Lentil Pottage with Kale and Lavender Vinegar
(Serves 4)

Pick up lavender vinegar at a farmers market, or make your own with rice vinegar and lavender (see below). There are many lavender culinary creations available at the Lavender Festival that is held in the Sequim-Dungeness Valley in July. For more information see www.lavenderfestival.com.

1 tablespoon olive oil or ghee
1 small onion, finely chopped
1 cup diced carrots
1 medium to small potato, cut into small chunks
1 Anjou pear, cored and cut into small pieces
2 to 3 cloves garlic, pressed
1 tablespoon chopped bottled peppers, such as Mama Lil's (p.108)
Handful of finely chopped kale
1/2 cup red lentils
1 1/2 cups water
Salt to taste
Lavender vinegar
1 cup croutons — toasted whole-grain bread cut into cubes (p. 61)

Heat a heavy skillet over medium heat. Add onion and carrots. Stir and cook over medium heat until onions are soft. Blend in potatoes, then cover and cook for 5 minutes. Remove cover, stir in garlic and peppers. Add kale, red lentils and water. Bring to a boil, then reduce heat and simmer until lentils are soft — about 25 minutes. Add salt to taste. Drizzle lavender vinegar over the pottage, stir in, then top each serving with croutons.

Tip
To make lavender or herbal vinegar, simmer about 3 cups of vinegar. (I like to use rice vinegar because it is less acidic than wine vinegar.) Pour the vinegar into a quart-size jar over a handful of washed and dried lavender or herbs. Cover and let steep for 2 weeks. Turn the jar upside down once in awhile to distribute the flavors.

Roasted Rosemary Vegetables
(Serves 4 or fills about 8 tacos)

Roasted vegetables are good any time of day. Make them in the morning when you first get up. Pack leftovers for lunch. You can use regular garlic and roast whole cloves if elephant garlic isn't available.

1 large onion, chopped into fairly large pieces
1 head elephant head garlic, cloves separated and sliced
1 1/2 cups cut-up (unpeeled) delicata squash
1 carrot, cut into 3/4-inch slices
1 medium red or green pepper, seeded and cut into strips
3 medium yellow or red potatoes, cut into bite-size pieces
1 to 2 tablespoons melted coconut oil
1 teaspoon chopped fresh rosemary
1/2 teaspoon salt
1/2 teaspoon freshly ground pepper

Preheat oven to 350°. Combine onion, garlic, squash, carrots, potatoes, oil and rosemary. Mix well. Place in a baking dish and bake for 1 hour, removing once to stir. Season to taste with salt and pepper. Vegetables should be fork tender.

Savory Baked Home Fries
(Serves 2)

These are a great alternative to hashbrowns. Serve these home fries with scrambled tofu or eggs and whole-grain bread.

1 pound russet or baking potatoes (2 medium potatoes)
1 medium sweet potato
2 tablespoons ghee or coconut oil, melted
2 teaspoons paprika
Salt to taste

Preheat oven to 400°. Cut potatoes and sweet potato into sticks about 1/2-inch thick. Toss potatoes and sweet potato with oil and paprika. Spread on a lightly oiled or nonstick baking sheet. Bake for 15 minutes, remove from oven, turn, then return to oven for another 15 minutes or until fries are lightly browned. Salt to taste.

Maple-Miso Baked Winter Squash

(Serves 2)

For a savory, substantial breakfast, leave out the maple syrup and fill the squash with leftover dinner grains, refried beans or a scrambled egg with sautéed vegetables.

1 small to medium winter squash (acorn, butternut, sweet dumpling or delicata)
1 teaspoon coconut oil or ghee
1 tablespoon light miso
1 tablespoon maple syrup

Preheat oven to 350°. Cut squash in half, remove and discard seeds. Lightly rub the cut side with coconut oil or ghee and miso. Place flesh side down on a baking sheet and bake for 35 minutes or until squash is fork-tender. Turn upright and drizzle maple syrup over baked squash.

Refried Black Beans

(Makes 2 1/2 cups)

*Try starting the day with these refried beans and roasted vegetables on crisp corn tortillas. Or make **Black Bean and Avocado Tostadas** (p.230) for a casual brunch.*

1 cup dry black beans
1/2 strip kombu (a sea vegetable), cut into pieces
1 tablespoon coconut oil or ghee
1 large sweet onion, chopped
1/4 cup bean cooking water
Salt to taste
1 teaspoon chili powder (optional)

Wash and soak beans overnight or for at least 6 hours. Place beans in a large pot and cover with about 4 cups water. Add kombu, bring to a boil, then reduce heat and simmer for 45 minutes or until skins start to peel and beans are very tender. Alternatively, place beans with 1 cup water and kombu in a pressure cooker, cover, bring to pressure and cook for 10 minutes. Drain, saving at least 1/4 cup water to prepare beans.

Heat a heavy skillet over medium heat. Add oil or ghee and onion, stir, cover and sweat the onions until they are transparent. For a sweeter onion flavor, continue to cook until onions are caramelized. Add water and beans. Heat gently and mash with a potato masher. When most of the beans are mashed, add salt and chili powder, if desired.

Orange French Toast

(Serves 2 to 4)

Use locally made artisan bread for better taste and texture in this recipe.

3/4 cup silken tofu
Juice and zest of 1 small orange (about 1/4 cup)
1/2 tablespoon maple syrup
Pinch of salt
1 tablespoon coconut oil
4 1/2-inch slices of whole-wheat bread

Blend the tofu, orange juice and zest, maple syrup and salt together in a food processor or blender until smooth and creamy. Oil a griddle and heat over medium heat. Cut slices of bread in half diagonally and dip into the tofu mixture. Place on heated griddle and cook until lightly browned – about 2 to 4 minutes. Flip and cook the other side. Serve with fresh seasonal berries or jam.

The Essential Baking Company

In an unpretentious brick building, a block up from Lake Union in the Fremont District, you'll find The Essential Baking Company. Established in 1994 by George DePasquale, a long-time baker, and co-owner Jeff Fairhill, Essential Baking Company had a goal to offer Puget Sound customers quality, rustic breads made with organic ingredients at a price competitive with other artisan breads. Committed to organic farming, the company has shown continuing support for PCC Farmland Fund (p.183).

A glimpse behind the scenes at Essential reveals a labor-intensive production bakery. For a production bakery, everything is remarkably low-tech. Loaves and rolls are kneaded and formed by hand on wooden benches. Everyone who works there eventually takes a turn kneading and shaping the loaves. Human handling, slow rises, Old World baking techniques and hearth ovens are the secrets to bread with incredibly rich taste and texture. Up to 13,000 loaves of bread are produced each day at Essential. In a conventional bakery, sometimes over 100,000 loaves a day are made and not one of them is touched by human hands. Machines run the show, and each loaf looks and tastes as lifeless and dull as every other.

In the Essential Baking Company retail store and bakery, you'll find decadent pastries, savory sandwiches, soup or hand-made pizzas, in addition to a variety of breads. Don't leave without sampling the artisan chocolates. A little bit of heaven, they're food for the soul. Here in the Pacific Northwest, we're fortunate to have excellent local quality when we make food choices

Conventional Problems, Organic Solutions

Conventional agriculture has historically emphasized high yield for market at the expense of those who tend diverse farming ecosystems and build up healthy soil. To boost production in the 1920's, commercial crops grown for market were dusted with lead arsenate, nicotine and lime to kill insects. Soil was routinely sterilized with formaldehyde and hot water. After World War II, farming management included use of chemical fertilizers, herbicides, fungicides and pesticides. With continued chemical abuse, soil dried out and became more porous. As organic matter in the soil decreased, land became less efficient at retaining moisture. Once naturally rich, much of our agricultural land is now worn out and fragile. Soils today are more vulnerable to soil pathogens, nematodes and insects. Methyl bromide, a powerful nerve gas and ozone-depleting chemical, is often applied as a soil fumigant to sterilize the earth before various crops such as strawberries are planted.

Farmland today is also threatened with toxic waste in fertilizers. In 1997, Duff Wilson researched and wrote "Fear in the Fields" for *The Seattle Times*. It was a series of articles about the nationwide practice of recycling toxic waste into fertilizer products. Later, Wilson's book "Fateful Harvest" told the details of the entire story as it was first discovered by Patty Martin, former mayor of Quincy, Washington. State laws still don't require disclosure for fertilizer ingredients. Many of these substances are known carcinogens that leach into groundwater or dry up and blow away with the soil. History has proven that chemical solutions by conventional farms are not reliable.

Sustainable farming, on the other hand, nurtures a delicate balance in the ecosystem. When purchasing food, consider the following:

- Organic growers enhance the environment and build up soil by using compost, mulching and planting cover crops like alfalfa, which fixes nitrogen, an essential nutrient for growing plants.
- Organic crops are rotated to deter insects and prevent soil pathogens and fungi from spreading.
- To block out weeds, farmers often underseed with crops. Sweet clover, legumes, vetch and rye grass, for example, are used to add soil nutrients. These crops are tilled back into the soil.
- To reduce pests, organic farmers grow a variety of crops. Beneficial predatory beetles and spiders accompany mulches and help to control insect problems.
- Flowering plants grown in strategic areas attract beneficial insects to prey on various pests, establishing a natural balance.
- Organic soils are a storehouse of living beneficial organisms. Healthier land means healthier crops, and healthy plants are more resistant to disease and insects.

Everyday Salads

Create Salads With a Variety of Ingredients

Profile: John Huschle, Nature's Last Stand

Vinaigrette Variations and Dressings
Balsamic Vinaigrette
Orange-Sesame
Spicy Creamy Lime
Dulse and Green Onion
Thousand Island
Tofu Mayonnaise
Creamy Cucumber
Lemon-Tahini
Spinach-Basil
Lemon-Pine Nut
Orange-Avocado
Lemon-Pesto

Crunchy Additions
Herbed Croutons
Spicy Toasted Pumpkin and Sesame Seeds
Toasted Sea Palm and Sesame Seeds

Vegetable Based Salads
Spicy Spinach and Red Cabbage Salad
Carrot and Raisin Salad
Parsnip and Carrot Salad
Coleslaw
Balsamic Marinated Beets
Festive Potato Salad

Pasta, Grain and Bean Salads
Sesame Noodles
Pasta Salad with Toasted Pecans
Hot Italian Bean and Pasta Salad with Broccoli
Whole-Grain Salad with Pine Nuts

Rice and Kamut Salad with Lemon-Tahini Dressing
Buckwheat, Rice and Roasted Vegetables with Balsamic Vinaigrette
Curried Rice and Pea Salad
Wild Rice, Barley, Squash and Cranberry Salad
Kamut, Spelt and Quinoa Fruit Salad
Millet, Quinoa and Chickpea Florentine Salad
Black Bean, Corn and Couscous Salad
Lentils and Braised Winter Greens with Lemon-Ginger Vinaigrette
Lentil Salad with Spicy Lime Vinaigrette
Spicy Cranberry Bean and New Potato Salad
Black-Eyed Peas and Collard Greens with Sundried Tomato Dressing
Italian White Bean Salad with Yellow, Red and Green Peppers
Marinated Beans

A Farming Dream at Stoney Plains

Food Choices and Farmland

THINK ABOUT IT

A study published in Environmental Health Perspectives indicated that children who consume conventionally grown produce have six to nine times the levels of pesticides in their growing bodies. Animal studies have shown that increased pesticide levels can damage the nervous and hormonal systems and the thyroid gland. According to The Environmental Working Group (www.ewg.org) a nonprofit research organization, the following produce contains the highest levels of pesticides. If you can't afford all organic produce, at least purchase the following items in organic versions only:

Apples	Raspberries	Celery
Peaches	Strawberries	Hot Peppers
Grapes, imported	Pears	Spinach
Cherries	Potatoes	

Farmers preparing to sell at the Tilth Organic Harvest Festival

Everyday Salads

The beginning of any good salad is an organic farm. Without the best organic ingredients, you'll have nothing more than a mediocre salad. Who wants to live with that?

My mother always served small individual salads. Her concept of salad was simple – chunks of iceberg lettuce, a few slices of tomatoes and some avocado chunks. Bottled dressing was served on the side, but I created my own dressings from an early age. My grandmother's salads were also very basic, but her sweet homegrown tomatoes made them a treat. There is something inherently appealing about seasonal greens tossed with a freshly made vinaigrette and topped with juicy heirloom tomatoes and anything else from the market that you couldn't resist. Spring through autumn, salad is a daily food adventure in our house.

Though I'm crazy about green salads, I also love re-creating traditional salads such as potato salad, coleslaw or pasta salad. When winter comes, the quality of many salad staples is off, so I often make salads with whole grains, pasta or beans and serve them warm. Whole-grain and bean salads make excellent leftovers for weekday lunches. During harvest season, I search my favorite farmers markets for unusual bottled products to use when the weather turns colder. Lavender or raspberry vinegar, spicy red peppers, asparagus spears, pickled garlic, green beans or bread and butter pickles are some of the great market finds.

Whether experimenting or just getting different ideas for additions, it's helpful to know what makes a good salad. First, use high-quality, organic ingredients. Also, be aware of visual appeal and use contrasting colors and textures. Balance five flavors — sweet, sour, pungent, hot or spicy and salty. For sweetness, add grated carrots, steamed winter squash, chopped dried apricots or raisins. An acidic taste is something all salads have in common. Try adding raspberry, ume plum, rice or balsamic vinegar, for example. Pungent flavors can be anything from garlic or ginger to the addition of bitter greens, grated turnips or rosemary. Add spicy or salty ingredients according to your own taste. Let your imagination guide you. Salads made with fresh ingredients are the spark of life that gets us through each day.

Create Salads With A Variety of Ingredients

Use a variety of produce, beans and grains for your salads. In the spring, summer and fall, check out a farmers market where you'll find unusual and heirloom varieties of vegetables like tomatoes, squash or beets. If you're unsure about what a particular vegetable is or how to prepare it, ask a farmer. They enthusiastically share tips and recipe ideas. For additional ideas and information, a great resource book is *The Victory Garden Cookbook* by Marian Morash. The following are some ingredients you can include in your salads.

Leafy greens

Everybody is familiar with the ubiquitous crunchy iceberg lettuce, favored by large-scale growers because it is easily packed for long-distance travel. It keeps well, but lacks nutrients. Dark leafy greens such as romaine, arugula, mizuna and chicory outshine head lettuce in taste as well as nutritional qualities. You can find various heirloom greens at a farmers market from local organic farmers.

If you enjoy salad at the end of your meal, include bitter greens such as dandelion greens, endive and radicchio. They are good digestive aids. If bitter greens seem intense, incorporate them a little at a time to sample various tastes of wild, bitter, pungent and spicy varieties.

Arugula (rocket): A spicy, peppery green that has long been popular in Europe, especially Italy. The spicy flavor is refreshing in salads. I'm always on the lookout for it at the market in the summer. Use it within a few days because it is delicate and doesn't keep well.

Belgian endive, curly endive or chicory: These are all technically chicory but are different varieties. Belgian endive is a decidedly bitter, pale-yellow green that is mostly grown in Belgium. Curly endive and other endives are also a light yellow-green color and are grown by some farmers. Chicory, however, grows wild and is darker in color. It can be found at farmers markets during the summer months. Blanching these greens takes the edge off the bitter flavor.

Bib lettuce: With small, loose-leaf heads, bib lettuce is a mildly sweet lettuce. Often, loose-leaf lettuce such as bib is grown locally since it doesn't keep or travel as well as iceberg lettuce.

Chard: This is also known as Swiss chard and is related to beets. It is often cooked, added to minestrone soup and casseroles or braised by itself. It has a mild flavor, reminiscent of beets, and can be finely chopped and added to salads. You can also braise it with onions, and add it to warm salads. Look for baby chard leaves, which are often in gourmet salad mixes.

Dandelion greens: Though you can find these in natural food stores and at farmers markets, you can also forage for this green in your own pesticide-free yard. A decidedly bitter green, it is considered a good tonic for the kidneys and liver, among its many health benefits.

Escarole: A broad-leafed variety of chicory, escarole bunches are made up of separate, curly-edged green leaves that appear pale yellow in the center. Like chicory, escarole is a bitter green.

Mizuna: A bitter, dark leafy green, mizuna belongs to the cabbage family. Look for it in the early spring when other greens are scarce. It can be braised or steamed as well as chopped and added to salads.

Parsley: A well-recognized herb, parsley, especially flat-leaf or Italian parsley, can be added to salads in small amounts. It also makes a good garnish for bean and grain salads that benefit from parsley's sparkling green freshness.

Purslane: More recognized in Europe than here, purslane is considered a weed in many parts of the United States. With small, crisp, green leaves and a light lemony flavor, purslane is an attractive addition to salads. You can forage for wild purslane but can also find it at farmers markets.

Radicchio: Not really a leafy green, but radicchio is in the same category because it is related to chicory. It has a small, loose-leafed red and white head, that resembles a small cabbage. The leaves are bitter. Radicchio can be braised or sautéed as well as added raw to salads.

Romaine: A green that has gained in popularity over the years, Romaine is almost as popular as iceberg lettuce now. The long, sturdy leaves are crisp in salads and have a slightly bitter flavor.

Sorrel: A dark, leafy sour-tasting green, sorrel can be foraged for or found at farmers markets. In small amounts, it makes an excellent addition to green salads.

Spinach: A popular green, you can find tasty, heirloom varieties of spinach at farmers markets during the summer. Mild with a slight sweetness, it can be added to any green salad.

Tat soi: A relative of bok choy, tat soi looks like a tiny version of its cousin, with dainty leaves on slender stems. Tat soi has a sweet taste. The leaves can be torn, and the stems chopped and added to any salad.

Watercress: A very pronounced bitter taste, slightly reminiscent of mustard greens, watercress has been popular in Europe for decades. The small, fresh, vibrant green leaves are a good addition to salads and sandwiches or used as garnish.

Other raw vegetables to consider

You can add just about anything and make any kind of a salad you're in the mood for these days. Pick up ideas from salad bars or ask farmers at the market about unfamiliar vegetables before trying something new. I always add some raw cruciferous vegetables — one of the most important vegetable families known for its anti-carcinogenic properties. Cabbage, bok choy, broccoli, Brussels sprouts, cauliflower, collards, kale, kohlrabi, rutabaga and turnips are all nutritional powerhouses from the cruciferous family. Add other vegetables such as carrots, beets or red pepper for a variety of vitamins and color. Try cutting diagonals, fine dice, julienne strips or batons for different salads.

Beets: These can be sliced if they are young baby beets. Larger beets can be grated and tossed with a little lemon juice and sprinkled around the side of your salad.

Broccoli: The florets can be an attractive addition to a salad, but don't throw those stems away, especially if your broccoli is from Willie Greens Organic Farm (see p.245). Some varieties of broccoli are sweeter and tastier than broccoli available from the grocery store. Peel the stems with a paring knife and dice or slice them into matchsticks for your salad.

Cabbage: Try using Napa (also called Chinese cabbage) or Savoy, both of which are sweeter than the more familiar cabbage. Since cabbage is tougher than lettuce, use a sharp knife and thinly slice or shred cabbage before tossing in with your greens.

Carrots: From tiny baby carrots to large, clumsy-looking versions, carrots come in all sizes, in spite of the uniformity you often see at supermarkets. Though some people think the small versions are sweeter, this isn't necessarily so. Some of the sweetest carrots I've ever tasted are grown by Nash Huber. They are the biggest carrots in the produce department at PCC Natural Markets. Smaller organic farms often use heirloom seeds, which are more expensive and make the produce cost more, but these priceless carrots have an unforgettable sweetness. Grate them or slice them into matchsticks or coins. Any way you cut carrots, get them into your salad!

Cauliflower: A cruciferous family member, cauliflower is available year-round. It is the sweetest during the summer months. Look beyond the usual cauliflower and try different varieties found at farmers markets, such as Romanesco — a beautiful light-green, solid head, that looks like a spiraling flower. There is also a type called broccoflower that looks like a green cauliflower.

Celery: Celery is sold year round and is fairly tasteless, but you'd be surprised how much flavor celery has at the markets during the summer months. Use the entire stalk, as well as the leaves. It's hard to go back to the supermarket variety after a taste of "the good stuff" from local farmers.

Cucumber: Like tomatoes, cucumber is at the peak of flavor during summer months. While you can find one or maybe two varieties at the grocery store, you'll see a number of different cucumbers at the farmers market.

Fennel: A round bulb with feathery leaves at the top of the stalks, fennel has a mild licorice flavor and a crisp, celery-like texture. Dice or finely chop the fennel bulb and use the leaves for garnish in your salad.

Kohlrabi: A member of the cabbage family, kohlrabi is an odd-looking vegetable that looks like a root, but is actually a swelling on the plant's stem with the leaves protruding out from the bulb. It tastes like a mild turnip with cabbage overtones. It can be shredded or diced and added to salads.

Onions: Whether you use green, red or finely chopped sweet onions, they are a good addition to any salad. The common yellow onions have a strong, hot flavor and are better cooked than raw in salads.

Parsnips: Parsnips taste sweeter after the weather freezes. Try freshly grated parsnips tossed with a bit of lemon or lime as a refreshing salad topping.

Peas: Enjoy early peas when the season starts in June or July. Peas from the farmers market are sweet because they were freshly picked. They begin to lose their sweetness quickly. Also try sugar snap peas — slice them on the diagonal for an interesting look.

Peppers: Beyond red, yellow, orange and green peppers, there are numerous varieties of both hot and sweet peppers. Billy Allstot, from Billy's Garden, sells wonderful Washington-grown peppers through Whole Foods Market and at the University District Farmers Market.

Radishes: At farmers markets, there are heirloom purple, red or black radishes, watermelon radishes, golden radishes, icicle, daikon and other types not available in a store. Sliced or grated, they have a peppery, pungent flavor.

Rutabagas and turnips: Though both can be found year-round, the peak season is autumn through spring. Grate or dice them, toss with some lime or lemon juice and toss into your salad. In the spring or summer, you can often find baby turnips with the greens attached. Slice these or leave them whole if they are tiny enough.

Summer squash: An interesting number of varieties, shapes and sizes of summer squash appears in the summer months. Take your pick, they're all good in salads whether they're sliced, diced or grated.

Tomatoes: There are a number of heirloom varieties to choose from, such as sweet Brandywine, black pear, small yellow pear, sweet yellow Sun Gold, Roma Paste, Porter Pink and Green Zebra. Enjoy them all! The season is too short, and tomato lovers all over are sad when the last local tomatoes are gone.

Cooked vegetables and other salad additions

Marinated vegetables, pickles, green beans, pickled beets, olives, or bottled red peppers are tasty options found at farmers markets or in natural foods stores. While some vegetables such as carrots can either be added raw, cooked or marinated, others like winter squash, garlic, corn, or asparagus are better cooked first. Don't overlook any vegetable, grain, bean or even chopped dried fruit when creating a salad.

Artichoke hearts: Be sure to purchase a good quality. Cheap canned versions have too much inedible fiber in them.

Asparagus: Marinated spicy asparagus spears can liven up your salad. Roasted, grilled or blanched spears are another option. To blanch asparagus, bring a large pot of water to a boil. Add asparagus, bring to a second boil and boil for four minutes. Test with a fork for doneness. The spears will be fork-tender. Do not overcook them. As soon as the asparagus is done, plunge the spears into cold water.

Beans, fresh, canned and dried: There is an amazing variety of fresh beans from farmers markets. Cut up fresh green beans are good, but lightly steamed and/or marinated beans lend flavor as well as texture variation. Don't overcook beans or the color will fade and the beans won't be as sweet.

Dried beans can be soaked, cooked, rinsed and sprinkled on top of salads — garbanzos are especially good used this way. With canned beans, be sure to rinse the beans before using them or they will have a canned taste. You can also marinate a combination of dried, soaked, and cooked beans for a few hours or a day and add them to your salad.

Beets: The earthy flavor of beets is great when they are steamed until crisp-tender, then marinated with a high-quality balsamic vinegar for a day or so before adding to a salad. Don't overlook the beautiful Chioggia (pronounced kee-oh-ja), candy-striped beets that are purple on the outside and have rings of red over white flesh on the inside. Try the sweet and mild golden beets, too. Both make great additions to potato salads as well as green salads.

Brussels sprouts: To truly appreciate Brussels sprouts, get them fresh and in season during the fall. The frozen version is inferior-tasting, and they alienate many people from Brussels sprouts. After steaming Brussels sprouts, cut them in half for a salad. Cool the sprouts, then marinate if desired.

Dried fruit: Raisins, blueberries, cherries, cranberries and even chopped apricots are great in salads. Soak and then drain fruit like cranberries or cherries before adding them.

Edible flowers: These are available by themselves or in salad mixes at farmers markets during the summer. Or, you can use some from your own yard. Make sure they are edible before you harvest flowers and top your salad with them. Some the edible varieties include violets, nasturtiums, borage flowers, lemon blossoms, rose petals and acacias.

Garlic: Always good in a salad dressing, you can also add garlic cloves or slices of elephant garlic to vegetables you're going to roast, and when done, add them as a border around a green salad. Marinated or roasted garlic cloves also make an excellent addition to salads. The Seattle Salad Company offers Persian Roasted Pickled Garlic at a number of farmers markets. Contact them at seattlesalad@hotmail.com for more information.

Mushrooms: A mushroom isn't a vegetable, but a fungus that grows in the dark. Mushrooms are especially plentiful during the rainy, autumn months in the Northwest. There are many varieties to choose from, such as portabello, chanterelle, lobster, enoki, crimini, shiitake, angel trumpets, oyster and, of course, the common white button. Raw mushrooms contain hydrazines, phytochemicals that are considered carcinogenic. Cooking inactivates these chemicals, so cook mushrooms before adding them to salads.

Nuts and seeds: A good way to boost the protein and mineral profile of your salad, nuts and seeds are found in many stores that have bulk food sections. Soaking and then toasting improves digestibility and brings out the flavor. To roast your own nuts or seeds see tip on p.31. The Seattle Salad Company sells roasted soy nuts and pepitas (pumpkin seeds) that are quite good on salads (seattesalad@hotmail.com).

Olives: In many grocery stores there are olive bars where you can sample and choose from a wide variety of olives. Kalamata, Greek, Italian, or the large green olives stuffed with cheese, garlic, pimento or jalapeño are all good choices.

Pickles: Whether you like cucumber chips or dill pickles, there are organic versions of each. When you're looking for something with that sweet-tart flavor, consider your favorite pickles. My favorite variety are the bread and butter pickles available from Nature's Last Stand (p.54).

Peppers: Though they are good fresh, peppers really shine when they are roasted. Roasting over an open flame or on a grill lends a smoky flavor, but you can also roast them under a broiler. Watch and turn the peppers until all the skin is blackened. Place them in a paper bag or pan with a lid on top. Let cool and then slip the skins off. Seed and slice before adding to the salad. Or, if you're in a hurry, pick up some freshly roasted peppers from Billy Allstot at the University District Farmers Market during harvest season.

Sea vegetables: These are dried and can be found in natural food stores or Asian markets. Dulse, is quite high in iron and has a very tart salty flavor. It can be washed, torn and added as a garnish. Sea palm can be toasted and crumbled on top. Toasted nori can be cut into small pieces and used as garnish.

Tofu or tempeh: Marinated tofu or lightly steamed or sautéed tempeh can be added in small cubes or crumbled on top of your salad for a different texture variation and extra protein.

John Huschle
Nature's Last Stand

On a Saturday, in mid-December, in a church parking lot behind the Wallingford Dick's Drive-In in Seattle, Farmer John Huschle was adding loaves of organic Tall Grass Bakery bread to his weekly winter vegetable boxes. A few other farmers were selling winter produce selections and eggs. Nigella, John's pitch black, long-coated farm dog, disappeared around the corner at Dick's Drive-In to beg a few french fries from customers. I hoped John had parsnips, celeriac, beets or braising greens for sale. Local pickings were slim. It was that time of year, but there were still good offerings to be found. You just had to know where to look.

Born and raised in Minnesota, John Huschle got a degree in biology at the University of Wisconsin where he studied native plant restoration and bird research. He and Andrew Stout, a good friend, apprenticed together on an organic farm in Minnesota. In 1996, they moved to the Northwest where they founded Full Circle Farm with Wendy Munroe. They acquired a number of choice accounts with restaurants and natural food stores by taking sample boxes around the Puget Sound area. Eventually, John left Full Circle and started his own farm, Nature's Last Stand.

The land that Nature's Last Stand is on was once part of a thriving farm in the 1970's. It was owned and farmed by two friends. One of them, Dan Byers, still owns the land today. Young, articulate and idealistic with a dash of optimism, John, at 34, has been working in organic farming for over ten years now. When the average age of farmers is 54 and only a small percentage are under age 35, it's encouraging to see young farmers like John — passionate about farming and determined to keep it small and locally focused. We desperately need more farmers like John for future generations.

John does most of his direct market sales at the University District Farmers Market, the most lucrative market in the state and one of the most successful markets in the country. At his booth, you can get braising mix, various types of lettuce, collards and other greens, turnips, Savoy cabbage, broccoli, carrots, various types of beets, onions, corn, cauliflower, arugula, parsley root and leeks, among other seasonal selections. Aside from the excellent quality, John's produce is harvested the day before market.

Also good at marketing, each year John does something a little different. One year he offered a "salad card" with which customers could purchase 12 bags of salad mix, a week at a time, and get the 13th mix free. In 2003, he started an innovative produce delivery service that contains an impressive list of seasonal veggies, his own bread and butter pickles (the best around), applesauce, honey or Traffic Jam (his own homemade jam) and locally made organic bread.

John believes one of the big challenges farmers face today is the problem of centralization versus decentralization. Agricultural companies are set up to cater to big farms; everything they sell is designed for high volume sales. Corporate agribusiness manufactures and grows over ninety-five percent of our food, and large organic corporate farms, particularly those in Orange County, California, are changing the face of organic farming today. "Organic farming isn't what it used to be," John told me, "which was diversified, small and local . . . I'd rather not have an [organic] label, but people are attached to the label." When many organic carrots are now grown for shelf life and durability instead of taste, the taste difference between organic carrots from large-scale California farms and conventionally farmed carrots is small.

Focusing on local markets, John grows vegetables for taste and he maintains high quality produce. While many farms have refrigeration on site, Nature's Last Stand doesn't, so what you get at the market has been harvested early that morning or the prior evening. You can't get any fresher than that. Check out John's website at www.natureslaststand.net and take a look at his produce delivery service.

Vinaigrette Variations and Dressings

A good salad dressing completes the salad. Though many cookbooks tell you to stock a variety of oils, you don't need anything more than a good quality flax seed, extra-virgin olive, light sesame and dark sesame oil. For the best quality, it is important that oils in the pantry are unrefined or expeller-pressed and organic. Different vinegars vary the flavor of your salad dressings. Some of my favorites include traditionally aged sherry, balsamic, raspberry, lavender, blood orange and the salty ume plum.

Balsamic Vinaigrette
(Makes enough for 2 large salads)

Cheap balsamic vinegar isn't worth considering for a salad because the quality is so poor. A vinaigrette is only as good as the vinegar used. Invest in a premium quality, imported, aged variety such as FINI to enhance your greens.

> 2 tablespoons extra-virgin olive oil
> 2 tablespoons balsamic vinegar
> 1/2 teaspoon Dijon mustard
> Pinch of Rapadura
> 2 cloves garlic, pressed
> Salt and pepper to taste

Whisk oil, vinegar, mustard, Rapadura and garlic together in a small bowl with a fork. Add a pinch of salt and pepper. Gently toss in with salad.

Citrus Variations:

Orange-Sesame Dressing
2 tablespoons light sesame oil
2 tablespoons orange juice
1 teaspoon finely chopped orange zest
Salt and pepper to taste

Follow directions above.

Spicy Creamy Lime Dressing
2 tablespoons extra-virgin olive oil
2 tablespoon fresh lime juice
1 tablespoon rice vinegar
1 tablespoon aïoli spread or mayonnaise
1 teaspoon honey
Pinch of cayenne
Salt and pepper to taste

Follow directions above.

Dulse and Green Onion Dressing

Dulse can be found with the other sea vegetables in your natural foods store. It comes in packages as well as small shaker bottles.

>2 tablespoons extra-virgin olive oil
>2 tablespoons lemon juice
>1 tablespoon minced onions
>1/2 teaspoon dulse flakes
>1 teaspoon aïoli spread or organic mayonnaise
>Pinch of Rapadura
>Salt and pepper to taste

Follow directions for **Balsamic Vinaigrette**.

Thousand Island Dressing

(Makes 1/2 cup)

Garlic aïoli spread (a garlic mayonnaise) can be found in natural food stores in the refrigerated section, near the cheese or tofu. You can also use regular organic mayonnaise or make your own (see below) instead of aïoli spread.

>4 1/2 tablespoons garlic aïoli spread or mayonnaise
>1 1/2 tablespoons catsup
>1/2 tablespoon lemon juice
>1 1/2 tablespoons finely diced dill pickle, or dill pickle relish
>Freshly ground black or white pepper
>Salt to taste

Blend aïoli spread, catsup and lemon juice together with a fork in a small bowl until creamy. Add dill pickle, black pepper and salt to taste.

Tofu Mayonnaise

(Makes about 1/2 cup)

If you use the tofu in shelf-stable packages, the mayonnaise will not have the beany taste you often get with firm deli tofu.

>1/2 cup firm silken tofu
>1 tablespoon lemon juice
>1 tablespoon extra-virgin olive oil
>1 clove garlic (optional)
>Pinch of salt and pepper

Blend ingredients with a hand blender until creamy. This will keep for about a week in the refrigerator.

Creamy Cucumber Dressing

(Makes about 1 1/4 cups)

Though this recipe makes a lot, it will keep for a week in a covered container in your refrigerator. Put the remainder of the silken tofu in water, then cover, refrigerate and change the water daily. Keep it for up to a week and use it for pureed puddings, smoothies or to thicken soup.

1/2 cucumber, peeled and seeded
1/2 cup silken tofu
Juice from 1/2 lemon
1 teaspoon finely chopped lemon zest
2 tablespoons extra-virgin olive oil
1 teaspoon fresh dill
1 tablespoon raw tahini
Salt and pepper to taste

Combine all ingredients except salt and pepper with a hand blender or use a blender. Puree until smooth and creamy. Thin with water if necessary. Add salt and pepper to taste.

Lemon-Tahini Dressing

(Makes about 1/2 cup)

An all-time favorite dressing, this is good over salads as well as blended in with whole grains for an interesting flavor.

1/4 cup raw tahini
Juice and finely chopped zest from one large lemon
1 tablespoon white miso
2 cloves garlic, pressed
2 tablespoons finely chopped fresh cilantro or parsley
Pinch of cayenne
Water to thin

Blend tahini, lemon juice, miso and garlic together with a fork in a small bowl or with a hand blender. Mix in cilantro or parsley and cayenne. Thin with water to desired consistency.

Spinach-Basil Dressing
(Makes about 1 cup)
With the abundance of spinach available in the summer, make this unusual dressing to top your summer salad.

1 cup packed spinach leaves
1/4 cup packed fresh basil
2 green onions, thinly sliced
3 tablespoons extra-virgin olive oil
1 tablespoon flax seed oil
2 tablespoons brown rice vinegar
1 teaspoon honey or agave nectar
Dash of cayenne
Salt to taste

Place all ingredients, except salt and pepper, in a blender or small food processor and blend until smooth and creamy. Add salt to taste. Chill until ready to serve.

Lemon-Pine Nut Dressing
(Makes about 1 1/4 cups)
Pine nuts are the edible seeds of pine trees. They are high in fat, protein and flavor. After the nuts are soaked in water, they can be blended into this delicious creamy dressing.

1/2 cup pine nuts
1/2 cup water
5 tablespoons lemon juice (juice of one large lemon)
1 teaspoon finely chopped lemon zest
1 teaspoon honey or fruit sweetener
Salt and pepper to taste

Soak pine nuts in water for about 6 hours. Blend pine nuts, water, lemon juice and zest and honey or fruit sweetener in a blender on high for 2 minutes. Add salt and pepper to taste.

Orange-Avocado Dressing
(Makes about 1 cup)

Technically a fruit but considered a vegetable, avocados are good source of vitamin E and contain protein. Leave the cayenne out, add a little ginger and this dressing can bring fruit salads to life.

> 1/2 large, ripe avocado
> Juice of 1 orange
> 1 teaspoon finely chopped orange zest
> 1/4 cup lime juice (the juice of approximately two limes)
> Dash of cayenne
> Salt to taste

Mash avocado in a small bowl. Mix in orange juice, zest and lime juice. Use a hand blender and puree until creamy.

Lemon-Pesto Dressing
(Makes 3/4 cup)

*During the summer, when basil is plentiful and you've made pesto, save some for this delectable dressing. If you need a pesto recipe, see the version in **Angel Hair Pasta with Pesto** (p.219).*

> 1/4 cup pesto
> 1/4 cup fresh lemon juice
> 1/4 cup water
> 1 teaspoon honey or fruit sweetener
> Salt and pepper to taste

Whisk together pesto, lemon juice, water and honey. Add salt and pepper to taste.

FOOD FOR THOUGHT
Organic citrus growers carefully select cover crops that feed nitrogen into the soil. This protects the soil from erosion and enhances the moisture-holding capacity of soil in the orchards. In organic orchards, different varieties of citrus are grown in the same orchard. Ecological diversity of plant and animal life is encouraged on sustainable farms.

Crunchy Additions

Sometimes a salad doesn't seem complete without the crunch of croutons, roasted nuts or seeds. Packaged croutons often taste stale and can contain anchovies or questionable preservatives. The oil they are made with may be poor quality or even rancid. Read the ingredient list before purchasing ready-made croutons. Toasting nuts or seeds ensures they are fresh. Then you'll know they'll go well with your garden-fresh greens. Making your own crunchy additions is always the best choice. It's quick and easy, and they keep in the refrigerator for a week or more.

Herbed Croutons
(Makes about 3 cups)

You can vary the herbs in this recipe. Instead of basil and marjoram, try 1/2 teaspoon sage or crumbled rosemary instead, or simply leave out the herbs and make them with garlic and a little salt and pepper. Use any type of bread you want in this recipe. I like to use locally made artisan bread. Save the crusts to toast and make breadcrumbs.

> 5 slices of bread, hard crusts removed
> 1/4 cup extra-virgin olive oil
> 3 cloves garlic, pressed
> 1 teaspoon dried basil
> 1/2 teaspoon dried marjoram
> 1/4 teaspoon freshly ground pepper
> Pinch of salt

Preheat oven to 300º. Cut bread into small cubes. In a medium bowl, combine oil, basil, marjoram, pepper and salt. Whisk until blended. Add bread and toss until all cubes are coated with oil. Spread on a baking sheet and bake for 10 minutes. Turn cubes and return to oven for about 2 more minutes. Remove and let cool. *(Hint: If you have a pizza screen, croutons can be baked on the screen and will brown without having to turn them.)*

Spicy Toasted Pumpkin and Sunflower Seeds
(Makes 2 cups)

Pumpkin seeds contain omega-3 fatty acids and are a good source of iron and zinc. Sunflower seeds have calcium, iron and several B-complex vitamins. You can find both in bulk bins at your favorite natural foods store.

1 cup raw pumpkin seeds
1 cup raw sunflower seeds
1/2 tablespoon tamari
1 teaspoon chili powder
Generous pinch cayenne

Preheat oven to 300º. In a bowl, combine pumpkin seeds, sunflower seeds, tamari, chili powder and cayenne. Mix well until all seeds are coated. Spread on a baking sheet. Bake for 10 minutes or until seeds are toasted. Cool and store in the refrigerator.

Toasted Sea Palm and Sesame Seeds
(Makes about 2 cups)

Sea palm is rich in calcium as well as all the other minerals of the sea. Use this condiment to sprinkle over whole-grain or bean salads, casseroles, pilafs and soups. Look for a suribachi in Asian and natural food stores.

1 cup brown sesame seeds
1 cup sea palm
1/2 teaspoon cumin
1/2 teaspoon salt
Pinch of cayenne

Preheat oven to 300º. Spread sesame seeds on a baking sheet and bake for 10 minutes or until seeds are browned. Remove from oven, place them in a *suribachi* (Japanese grinding bowl with a wooden pestle) or a spice grinder and let cool. Raise oven temperature to 350º, and spread sea palm on baking sheet. Bake for 2 minutes. Remove from oven and crush sea palm over sesame seeds. Crush or grind to a grainy texture. (*Hint: Grinding half of the mixture at a time in a suribachi is easier than trying to work with all the sesame seeds at once.*) Add the cumin, salt and cayenne. Crush with the seeds and sea palm. Store covered in the refrigerator.

Vegetable-Based Salads

More substantial than green salads, salads like potato salad or coleslaw are comfort foods as well as potluck and picnic favorites. Prepared deli salads often contain inferior ingredients. Even the salads in natural food stores aren't prepared with all organic ingredients. Deli-prepared salads are disappointing for the discriminating salad enthusiast. Search for the best ingredients and you won't be sorry.

Spicy Spinach and Red Cabbage Salad
(Serves 6)

If you're eating light, serve this salad as a main dinner dish. Warm sprouted flour tortillas or whole-grain rolls are all you need for an accompaniment. Toast sesame seeds in a heavy skillet on top of the stove over medium heat. They will smell fragrant and toasted when done.

Dressing:
1/4 cup toasted sesame oil
1/2 cup fresh lemon juice
1 teaspoon honey, Rapadura
1/4 teaspoon crushed chile peppers
1/4 teaspoon salt
1 1/2 tablespoons dried sundried tomato bits
Salad:
1 bunch of spinach, torn in bite-size pieces
1 bunch of arugula, torn into pieces
2 cups finely shredded red cabbage
1/4 cup toasted, crushed sesame seeds
1/4 cup crumbed feta cheese (optional)

Blend dressing ingredients together in a small jar. Let the dressing to sit for about 1 hour while tomatoes rehydrate.

Place spinach, arugula and cabbage in a large salad bowl. Add dressing and toss gently. Sprinkle in sesame seeds and feta cheese, if desired.

Carrot and Raisin Salad
(Serves 4)

It's a toss-up whether my favorite carrots come from Willie Green's Organic Farm in Monroe or Dungeness Farm on the Olympic Peninsula. You can find non-mainstream carrots that just as sweet at your neighborhood farmers market or some local natural foods stores.

Dressing:
1/4 cup garlic aïoli spread or mayonnaise
1 tablespoon honey or fruit sweetener
1 tablespoon white miso
1 teaspoon lemon zest
1/4 teaspoon nutmeg
1/4 teaspoon freshly ground pepper
1/4 cup shredded, toasted coconut
Salad:
3 cups grated carrots
Juice of 1 lemon (about 1/4 cup)
1/3 cup raisins

Mix aïoli spread, honey, white miso, lemon zest, nutmeg and pepper together in a small bowl. Blend until smooth and creamy. In a medium-size salad bowl, combine carrots, lemon juice and raisins. Blend dressing with the carrot-raisin mixture. Serve garnished with toasted coconut.

Variation:

Parsnip and Carrot Salad
Dressing:
1/4 cup garlic aïoli spread or mayonnaise
1 tablespoon honey or fruit sweetener
1 tablespoon white miso
1 teaspoon lemon zest
1/4 teaspoon freshly ground pepper
Salad:
1 1/2 cups each: grated parsnips and carrots
Juice of 1 lemon or lime (about 1/4 cup)
1/3 cup raisins
1/4 cup toasted, crushed sesame seeds (optional)

Follow directions above.

Coleslaw
(Serves 6)

Coleslaw is an old familiar stand-by, but most prepared coleslaw is drowning in so much mayonnaise, you can barely taste the slaw. For a variation, try adding 1 tablespoon freshly grated ginger and squeeze the ginger juice into the dressing. In place of the lemon, use lime and sweeten with a little honey or agave nectar. Savoy or Napa cabbage can be used instead of the standard green cabbage.

Dressing*:*
1/2 cup garlic aïoli spread or mayonnaise
2 tablespoons apple cider vinegar
1 tablespoon catsup
1/2 tablespoon chopped, hot peppers such as Mama Lil's or Italian pepperoncini
Salt to taste

Salad:
2 medium Granny Smith apples, peeled and shredded
2 tablespoons lemon juice
4 to 4 1/2 cups thinly shredded green cabbage
1/4 cup dried fruit such as sour cherries, chopped apricots, figs, raisins or currants

Combine the dressing ingredients in a small bowl and mix well. Toss the shredded apples with the lemon juice. In a large bowl, combine apples, cabbage and dried fruit. Toss and mix well. Blend in dressing. Refrigerate until ready to serve.

FOOD FOR THOUGHT
An ancient vegetable, cabbage has been cultivated for more than 4,000 years and domesticated for about 2,500 years. A popular food crop, cabbage cultivation spread throughout Europe. Cabbage adapted well because it grows in colder climates and could be stored in cold cellars over the winter when people had little else to eat. Compact headed varieties were developed during the Middle Ages. In Japan and Korea, cabbage is often pressed and pickled. Cabbage was brought to the Americas by Jaques Cartier in 1536 and has been grown here ever since.

Balsamic Marinated Beets

(Serves 4)

Although red beets are always good, try using golden or Chiogga beets as well.

2 cups shredded beets
1 or 2 green onions, thinly sliced
2 tablespoon freshly chopped basil
1/2 cup balsamic vinegar
14 teaspoon each: salt and freshly ground pepper

Steam the beets for 5 to 10 minutes or until fork-tender. Combine in a bowl with the other ingredients. Stir, let cool and refrigerate for a few hours before eating.

Festive Potato Salad

(Serves 8)

Nothing says "picnic" like a potato salad. German Butterballs or russets are the best in this recipe. If you don't have enough peppers, use celery, fennel or blanched green beans instead.

Salad:
2 pounds potatoes, cut into bite-size chunks (4 cups)
1 1/2 cups mixed green, yellow and red peppers, finely chopped
1/4 cup thinly sliced green onions
1/3 cup finely chopped parsley
Paprika for garnish
Dressing:
1/2 cup garlic aïoli spread or mayonnaise
1/4 cup white miso
1/4 teaspoon celery seed
4 tablespoons raspberry vinegar, divided
2 teaspoons Dijon mustard with horseradish or wasabi
3 cloves garlic, pressed
1/4 teaspoon cayenne

Peel potatoes, if necessary. Place in a saucepan and cover with water. Bring to a boil, then reduce to simmer and cook for 5 to 7 minutes, or until fork-tender. Drain and set aside.

Combine dressing ingredients and blend with a fork or hand blender until smooth and creamy. In a medium-large salad bowl, blend together potatoes, peppers and parsley. Gently stir dressing into warm potatoes. Refrigerate until ready to serve. Sprinkle paprika before serving.

Pasta, Grain and Bean Salads

Many of these hearty salads can be a meal on their own. Serve them with side dishes like braised or grilled vegetables and a warm whole-grain roll with goat cheese. Each salad will be different when you use an alternative vinegar, change vegetables, or switch between beans, whole grains and pasta. One-time artistic concepts arranged on a platter or in a bowl, salads change with your mood, pantry supplies and vegetables you have on hand.

Sesame Noodles

(Serves 4)

Years ago, I fell in love with a deli salad at Larry's Market. Inspired, I came up with this version. Soba (Japanese buckwheat noodles) can be found on the Asian food aisle of your local natural foods store.

Dressing:
2 tablespoons dark (toasted) sesame oil
1 1/2 tablespoons light sesame oil
Dash of hot chili oil
2 tablespoons tamari
1/4 cup balsamic vinegar
4 cloves garlic, pressed
1 teaspoon Rapadura

Salad:
12-ounce package soba noodles
1/2 cup chopped green onions (scallions)
1/4 cup minced fresh red pepper or pimento
1/3 cup toasted brown sesame seeds

Combine the dressing ingredients in a small bowl and set aside. Bring a large pot of water to a boil, add the soba noodles and a pinch of salt and boil for 4 minutes. Do not overcook. Plunge the hot noodles into a bowl of ice water to stop the cooking process. When noodles are cool, place them in a bowl and pour the dressing over them. Gently toss so all noodles are coated with dressing. With a large fork, blend in green onions, red pepper and sesame seeds and continue gently mixing until everything is blended. Refrigerate for an hour before serving.

Pasta Salad with Toasted Pecans

(Serves 4)

Garden fresh herbs and toasted pecans make this an all-star standout at family gatherings and picnics. Double all ingredients, except the hot peppers, for a crowd.

Dressing:
1/4 cup garlic aïoli spread, or mayonnaise
2 tablespoons lemon juice
1 tablespoon brown rice vinegar
1 tablespoon white miso
2 cloves garlic, pressed
1 tablespoon chopped fresh basil
1 tablespoon fresh marjoram leaves
1 tablespoon chopped hot, bottled peppers such as Mama Lil's
Salt to taste

Salad:
2 cups shell pasta
1 small carrot, grated
2 tablespoons red onion, finely chopped
2 tablespoons marinated sundried tomatoes
1/4 cup parsley, finely chopped
1/2 cup toasted pecans, coarsely chopped

Blend dressing ingredients, except the salt, together in a small bowl. Add salt to taste. Set aside while you prepare the remaining ingredients.

Bring a large pot of water to a boil. Add pasta and a teaspoon of salt and boil according to package directions. Do not overcook. As soon as pasta is done, drain and rinse with very cold water to stop the cooking process. Mix cooled pasta with carrot, onions, sundried tomatoes and parsley. Gently stir in the dressing. Refrigerate for about one hour before serving. Garnish with toasted pecans.

Hot Italian Bean and Pasta Salad with Broccoli

(Serves 8)

For a quick salad, use canned beans in this recipe. Use one 15-ounce can for each type of bean. Drain and rinse the beans before using.

Dressing:
3 tablespoons lemon juice or red wine vinegar
2 tablespoons extra-virgin olive oil
1 tablespoon water
1 1/2 tablespoons tomato paste
1/2 tablespoon fruit sweetener or honey
1 tablespoon chopped fresh basil, or 1 teaspoon dried basil
1/2 tablespoon fresh oregano, or 1/2 teaspoon dried oregano
1/4 to 1/2 teaspoon crushed red peppers
1 teaspoon fresh thyme, or 1/8 teaspoon dried thyme
Salad:
1/3 cup cannellini beans, soaked overnight and drained
1/3 cup kidney beans, soaked overnight and drained
8 ounces shell pasta
2 cups broccoli florets
1/3 cup chopped marinated sundried tomatoes
2 tablespoons pitted, chopped kalamata olives
1/4 cup sliced green onions
Salt to taste
1/2 cup chopped parsley

Combine ingredients for dressing and set aside. Taste, then add more sweetener if desired.

Place the beans in a saucepan, cover with water and bring to a boil. Reduce heat, partially cover and simmer for one hour. Or, cook soaked beans in a pressure cooker with 1 cup water for about 10 minutes. Omit this step, if you use canned beans. Cook shell pasta according to package directions. Drain and rinse with cold water. Combine beans and pasta with dressing. Set aside.

Cut broccoli florets into bite-size pieces. Bring a large pot of water to a boil. Add broccoli florets and blanch, uncovered, for 3 minutes or until broccoli is brilliant green. Remove from water with a mesh strainer and rinse with cold water to stop the cooking process.

Drain the sundried tomatoes, discard water and cut tomatoes into slivers (or use bottled marinated sundried tomatoes). Add tomatoes to the salad with the broccoli, kalamata olives and green onions. Gently mix. Season to taste with salt. Sprinkle parsley generously over the top before serving.

Whole-Grain Salad with Pine Nuts
(Serves 4 to 6)

An excellent source of protein, lightly toasted pine nuts also add flavor and texture to this savory salad.

Dressing:
1/4 cup garlic aïoli spread or mayonnaise
1/4 cup apple cider vinegar
2 tablespoons tomato paste
1 to 2 teaspoons rice syrup, fruit sweetener or honey
2 cloves garlic, pressed
2 tablespoons chopped fresh basil
Dash of cayenne
Salt to taste

Salad:
2 1/2 cups cooked whole grains (use a combination of spelt, barley, brown rice, wheat berries, or kamut)
1 small golden zucchini or crookneck squash, diced
1 red pepper, seeded and finely chopped
1 cup scallions, thinly sliced
1/2 cup lightly toasted pine nuts

Combine dressing ingredients in a small bowl and set aside. In a large salad bowl, combine whole grains, zucchini, red pepper and scallions. Gently blend in dressing. Right before serving, stir in the toasted pine nuts.

Tip
Cook a variety of whole grains in the morning and it's easy to eat them at every meal. For easier cooking, choose grains that cook for approximately the same amount of time. Longer cooking grains such as hulled barley, brown rice, kamut, spelt, wheat berries and wild rice go together well. Use 1 3/4 cup water to 1 cup grain and simmer for one hour. Shorter cooking grains like millet, quinoa and buckwheat use 1 3/4 to 2 cups water for 1 cup grain and simmer for 15 to 20 minutes. Always check 5 minutes before the grains should be done to see if they require additional water.

Rice and Kamut Salad with Lemon-Tahini Dressing

(Serves 6 to 8)

This salad can change with the seasons if you vary the vegetables. Instead of broccoli, use summer squash in the summer or delicata squash in the fall. Peas and corn are also good in this salad. Both can be lightly steamed or added raw to the salad.

Salad:
2 1/4 cups water
Pinch of salt
1 cup basmati rice
1/2 cup kamut
1 each: red and green pepper, seeded and finely chopped
1 1/2 cups blanched broccoli florets

Dressing:
1/4 cup tahini (raw or toasted)
1/3 cup fresh lemon juice
3 tablespoons tamari
1 clove garlic, pressed
1 1/2 tablespoons fruit sweetener
1 1/2 tablespoons rice vinegar
Salt to taste

Bring water to a boil in a medium saucepan. Add salt, rice and kamut. Cover, reduce heat to a simmer, and cook for 1 hour or until both grains are tender. Check 10 minutes before grains are finished cooking to see if grains require more water. To check, gently pull the grains away from the sides of the pan with a fork. If you don't see any liquid, add about 1/4 cup of water and continue cooking until grains are done. Remove from heat, let grains sit for 5 minutes before fluffing with a fork. When grains have cooled, gently mix in with the peppers and broccoli.

In a small bowl, combine the dressing ingredients, except salt. Add salt to taste. Gently blend dressing in with the rice and vegetables. Cover and refrigerate before serving.

Buckwheat, Rice and Roasted Vegetables with Balsamic Vinaigrette

(Serves 4 to 6)

The assertive flavor of buckwheat blends well with the sweet complex tones of balsamic vinegar and roasted vegetables in this savory salad. This salad is good warm or cold.

Salad:
3 Yellow Finn potatoes, cut into small chunks
8 peeled pearl onions, or 1 medium onion, cut into chunks
2 carrots or parsnips cut into 1/2-inch slices
10 cloves of peeled garlic (about 1 head of garlic)
2 tablespoons melted coconut oil or ghee
2 tablespoons balsamic vinegar
1/2 teaspoon chipotle chile powder
1/2 teaspoon salt
1 cup stock or water
1/4 cup each: basmati rice and toasted buckwheat (kasha)
1/3 cup raisins
2 cups finely shredded green cabbage or carrots (or use a combination of both)
1/2 cup toasted, chopped walnuts or pecans
1/3 cup finely chopped parsley

Vinaigrette:
3 tablespoons balsamic vinegar
2 tablespoons extra-virgin olive oil
1/2 teaspoon Rapadura
2 cloves garlic, pressed
Pinch of cayenne

Preheat oven to 350º. Place vegetables and garlic in a glass baking dish. Stir in melted coconut oil and vinegar. Place in a single layer; sprinkle with chipotle powder. Roast vegetables for 1 hour or until they are fork tender. Stir halfway through roasting. Sprinkle with salt.

Bring stock or water to a boil in a small saucepan. Add rice, reduce heat, cover and simmer for 35 minutes. Bring to a second boil, add buckwheat, stir once, then reduce heat again and simmer, covered, for 20 minutes. Let grains sit 5 minutes after cooking, then fluff with a fork.

Blend vinaigrette ingredients in a small bowl. In a large bowl, combine roasted vegetables, grains, raisins, and cabbage. Toss with vinaigrette. Serve warm or refrigerate and enjoy later. Right before serving, blend in toasted nuts and garnish with parsley. Add salt to taste.

Curried Rice and Pea Salad

(Serves 4)

Willie Green's Organic Farm sells sweet, fresh peas already shelled for your convenience. You can also use blanched sugar snap peas sliced on the diagonal for this pretty salad. In the winter, use carrots or squash instead of peas.

Dressing:
3 tablespoons extra-virgin olive oil
2 tablespoons apple cider vinegar
2 tablespoons tamari
1 tablespoon fresh lemon juice
1 teaspoon Rapadura or organic sugar
1/2 teaspoon salt
1/2 tablespoon freshly grated ginger

Salad:
2 teaspoons ghee or coconut oil
1 red onion, finely chopped
2 teaspoons curry powder
1/8 teaspoon cayenne
1 large red pepper, seeded and chopped
1 3/4 cups water
1 cup dry brown rice
2 cups English or garden peas, hulls removed, and lightly steamed
3 cups shredded Savoy cabbage
1/3 cup chopped dried apricots
1/2 cup toasted almonds
2 tablespoons grated coconut (optional)

Blend the dressing ingredients, except the ginger in a small bowl. Squeeze the juice of the ginger into the dressing and blend in (discard pulp).

Heat a saucepan over medium heat and add ghee or oil, onion, curry powder and cayenne. Stir and cook over medium-low heat for about 5 minutes. Add the red pepper, and stir and cook on low for about 5 minutes. When peppers are beginning to get soft, slowly add the water and bring to a boil. Add rice, reduce heat, cover and cook for 45 minutes or until rice is done. Remove from heat and let sit 5 minutes. Fluff rice and place it in a large salad bowl.

Gently toss in the peas and Savoy cabbage. Blend in the apricots and dressing. Serve warm or refrigerate for later. Just before serving, blend in almonds and garnish with grated coconut, if desired.

Wild Rice, Barley, Squash and Cranberry Salad
(Serves 6 to 8)

This salad is excellent served warm. It makes a great entrée or side dish when company is coming for dinner. Or bring it along for a family holiday gathering.

Dressing:
Juice of 1 orange
2 tablespoons balsamic vinegar
2 tablespoons light sesame or extra-virgin olive oil
1/4 teaspoon crushed red pepper flakes
1/2 teaspoon salt
1 tablespoon grated fresh ginger
Salad:
2 cups water
1/2 cup wild rice
1/2 cup hulled barley
Pinch of salt
1 or 2 tablespoons light sesame or extra-virgin olive oil
1 large onion, chopped
1 medium delicata squash, seeds removed and cut into bite-size pieces
1 1/2 cups grated carrots blended with 1 tablespoon lemon juice
1/3 cup dried cranberries
1/2 cup toasted chopped pecans
1/3 cup finely chopped parsley

Combine dressing ingredients, except ginger. Squeeze the juice of the ginger into the dressing and blend in (discard pulp). The flavors will blend before they are mixed in with the rest of the ingredients.

Bring water to a boil in a medium saucepan. Add wild rice, barley and salt. Reduce heat, cover and simmer for 55 minutes or until grains are done. They will both be slightly chewy. Remove from heat, let sit five minutes, then fluff the grains with a fork.

Heat a heavy skillet over medium heat. Add oil and onion, stir to coat onion, then reduce heat, cover with a lid that fits right over the onion, and sweat the onions until they are very soft. Remove cover and continue to cook until onions are caramelized (browned). While onion cooks, steam the delicata squash until squash is fork-tender — this should take about 7 minutes.

In a large salad bowl, blend the cooked grains, onions, delicata squash, carrots, and cranberries. Gently mix in salad dressing. Right before serving, stir in pecans and parsley.

74

Kamut, Spelt and Quinoa Fruit Salad
(Serves 4 to 6)

Homestead Organic Produce, Grouse Mountain Farm or Mair Farm-Taki are a few farmers at the University District Market who sell sour pie cherries. Dehydrated, these cherries are bursting with flavor and can lull you into a timeless place. Just a few are enough to perk up rainy Pacific Northwest winter days.

Salad:
1 3/4 cups water
1/4 cup kamut
1/4 cup spelt
1/2 cup quinoa
1 large apple, Fuji or other sweet-tart variety
1 large carrot, grated (about 2 cups)
1 to 2 tablespoons lemon juice
1/2 cup dried sour cherries
1/2 cup dried apricots, nectarines, raisins or currants
1/2 cup chopped green onions
Salt to taste
1/2 cup lightly toasted walnuts or pecans
1/2 cup finely chopped parsley, for garnish
Dressing:
1 tablespoon orange zest
1/4 cup orange juice
1/4 cup lemon yogurt
1 to 2 tablespoons balsamic vinegar
2 tablespoons extra-virgin olive oil

Bring water to a boil in a medium saucepan. Add kamut and spelt, reduce heat, cover and simmer for 45 minutes. While grains cook, grate the apple and carrot and blend with lemon juice. Then combine ingredients for dressing and set aside. After 45 minutes, bring water to a second boil, rinse quinoa and add to the pot. Reduce heat and simmer for 15 minutes or until quinoa is done. (*Hint: You may have to add a little more water before quinoa is done.*)

Remove grains from heat. Let them sit 5 minutes before removing lid and fluffing with a fork. Let grains cool slightly, then blend with dried fruit, apple, carrot and green onions. Blend in dressing. Season to taste with salt. Stir in nuts and garnish with parsley right before serving.

Millet, Quinoa and Chickpea Florentine Salad
(Serves 6)

You can make most of this salad ahead of time, then gently stir in the spinach and place the sweet tomatoes around the outside right before serving.

Salad:
1/4 cup brown (unhulled) sesame seeds
1/2 cup millet
1/2 cup quinoa
2 cups water
Pinch of salt
1 cup cooked chickpeas (garbanzos) or drained, canned chickpeas
2 cups grated carrots
1/2 cup thinly sliced green onions
1 small bunch fresh spinach, rinsed well and drained, torn into small pieces
1 1/2 cups chopped tomatoes
Dressing:
Juice and finely chopped zest of 1 lemon (about 1/4 cup juice)
1/4 cup extra-virgin olive oil, or hazelnut oil
3 tablespoons chopped fresh basil
2 cloves garlic, pressed
1/2 teaspoon Rapadura or organic sugar
1/4 teaspoon cayenne
1/2 teaspoon salt

Preheat oven to 325º. Place sesame seeds in a skillet and toast until dry and aromatic. They will be a few shades darker. Remove from heat. When cool, grind the seeds in a suribachi until coarsely ground.

Heat a medium-size heavy skillet over medium heat. After rinsing millet and quinoa, place grains in the skillet. Stir and toast grains until lightly toasted — about 7 minutes. Remove from heat. Bring water and salt to a boil in a medium saucepan. Add grains, stir once, cover and cook for 25 minutes, or until both grains are done and all liquid is absorbed. Check water level at 20 minutes and add a small amount more if necessary. Test to see if grains are done. They will be slightly chewy but tender. Remove from heat and let sit for 5 minutes before fluffing with a fork.

In a large bowl, combine grains, chickpeas, carrots and green onions. Set aside. In a small bowl, mix all dressing ingredients. Stir gently into the whole-grain mixture. Right before serving, blend in the spinach. Place tomatoes around the outside of the salad. Sprinkle crushed sesame seeds over the top.

Black Bean, Corn and Couscous Salad

(Serves 6)

This versatile salad goes well with braised greens and cornbread. If you want less heat in this salad, choose pimento-stuffed olives.

Dressing:
3 tablespoons apple cider vinegar
2 tablespoons extra-virgin olive oil
1 tablespoon lime juice
1 teaspoon Rapadura
2 teaspoons chili powder
1/2 teaspoon cumin
1/4 teaspoon cayenne

Salad:
1 cup whole-wheat couscous
1 cup boiling water
1 1/2 cups freshly cooked or canned, rinsed black beans
1 jalapeño, seeded and finely minced
3 cloves garlic, pressed
1 cup fresh or frozen corn, lightly steamed
1 red onion, finely chopped
1/4 cup sliced jalapeño or pimento-stuffed olives
1/4 cup chopped cilantro

Combine dressing ingredients, mixing well. Set aside. Pour boiling water over couscous. Cover and let sit for 5 minutes. Remove cover and fluff with a fork. In a large bowl, combine beans, jalapeño and garlic, mixing well. Add couscous, corn, red onion and olives and stir. Toss with dressing. Refrigerate for a few hours or serve warm. Garnish with cilantro before serving.

Lentils and Braised Winter Greens with Lemon-Ginger Vinaigrette
(Serves 4 to 6)

A perfect one-dish meal, serve this salad with warm whole-grain rolls.

Dressing:
1 head garlic
1 tablespoon melted coconut oil or ghee
1 tablespoon chopped bottled peppers, such as Mama Lil's
2 tablespoons each: lemon juice, sherry vinegar and extra-virgin olive oil
1 tablespoon each: finely chopped lemon zest and grated ginger
1 teaspoon honey
1/2 teaspoon salt

Salad:
1 cup stock
1 cup water
1/2 cup kamut
3/4 cup French lentils
1/4 teaspoon salt
2 cups cut-up, steamed delicata squash (cut in half and sliced)
1/4 cup dried cranberries
1 tablespoon extra-virgin olive oil
1 medium red onion, chopped
2 cups chopped braising greens
2 to 4 tablespoons water or white wine
1/3 cup toasted hazelnuts

Preheat oven to 350°. Cut off the top of the garlic bulb. With a pastry brush, paint the garlic with coconut oil. Wrap in foil and bake for 45 minutes, or until garlic is very tender. Let garlic cool. Squeeze roasted garlic out into a small bowl. Blend garlic and all the dressing ingredients, except ginger. Squeeze ginger juice in with the other ingredients (discard pulp). Blend dressing until smooth.

In a medium saucepan, bring the stock and water to a boil. Add kamut. Reduce heat, cover and simmer for 20 minutes. Add rinsed lentils, bring to a second boil, then reduce heat and continue to simmer for 40 minutes or until lentils are done, adding more water if necessary. When kamut and lentils are done, strain and combine with steamed squash and dried cranberries. Blend in dressing.

Heat a heavy skillet over medium heat. Add oil and red onion. Stir and cover, cooking on low until onions are tender. Add braising greens and water. Cover and cook until greens are very tender — about 20 minutes. Mix warm greens into the rest of the salad. Sprinkle hazelnuts on top and serve.

Lentil Salad with Spicy Lime Vinaigrette

(Serves 6)

The lime vinaigrette in this salad is even better the second day after the flavors have had a chance to marry.

Vinaigrette:
Juice of 1 lime (approximately 3 tablespoons)
1 tablespoon mirin (sweet rice wine)
1/2 teaspoon salt
1/4 cup sesame or extra-virgin olive oil
1 1/2 teaspoons chili powder
1/4 teaspoon cardamom
1/4 cup chopped cilantro

Salad:
1 heaping cup French lentils, rinsed
3 cups water
1 tablespoon extra-virgin olive oil
1 large onion, chopped
1 red pepper, seeded and chopped
1 jalapeño, seeded and minced
2 cups corn, freshly cut off the cob, or frozen
Salt and ground pepper to taste
1/2 cup finely chopped parsley
1/3 cup toasted sunflower seeds

Combine the vinaigrette ingredients together in a small jar. Shake thoroughly and set aside.

Put water in a medium saucepan. Add lentils, bring to a boil, then reduce heat and simmer for 40 minutes or until lentils are soft, but not overcooked. Drain and run under cold water to stop the cooking process. Heat a heavy skillet over medium heat. Add oil, onion, red pepper and jalapeño. Reduce heat, cover and sweat vegetables until they are tender. Remove cover, and continue to stir and cook until onions are lightly browned. Blend in cooked lentils and corn, cover and cook for about 5 minutes or until corn is tender. Remove from heat and place mixture in a large bowl. Pour dressing over all and blend in. Add salt and pepper to taste. Refrigerate before serving. Right before serving blend in parsley. Garnish with sunflower seeds.

Spicy Cranberry Bean and New Potato Salad
(Serves 6)

New potatoes are the first potatoes of the season, which is mid-summer. Alden Farms from Monroe sells a wide variety of potatoes at farmers markets. If you can't find new potatoes, use small red potatoes. Stoney Plains is one of the local farms that sells cranberry beans. I generally buy enough for the year. Use pinto beans if cranberry beans are not available.

Dressing:
1/2 cup fresh lime juice (about 4 organic or 2 conventional limes)
1/4 cup light sesame oil
1 teaspoon Rapadura or organic sugar
1/2 teaspoon salt

Salad:
3/4 cup dried cranberry beans, soaked
2 1/2 cups new potatoes, cut in half or quartered
1 tablespoon light sesame oil
1 large red onion, sliced in slivers
1 red pepper, seeded and cut into strips
1 teaspoon each: coriander, turmeric, cumin and chili powder
1/4 teaspoon each: cardamom, cinnamon and cayenne
1/8 teaspoon cloves
2 1/2 cups grated carrots
1/2 cup raisins or currants
1/2 cup toasted, chopped walnuts
1/2 cup chopped cilantro

Blend the dressing ingredients together in a small jar, shake and set aside. Place soaked cranberry beans in a large saucepan and cover with about 3 cups of water. Bring to a boil, then reduce heat and simmer, partially covered, for about 1 hour or until beans are tender but still hold their shape. Place beans in strainer and run cool water over them to stop the cooking process.

Steam the new potatoes for about 5 minutes or until they are fork-tender. Remove from heat and run under cool water in a strainer. In a large bowl, combine the beans and potatoes with the dressing, tossing gently so you don't mash the beans or potatoes.

Heat a heavy skillet over medium heat. Add sesame oil, onion, pepper, and spices. Stir and cook on medium low heat until onion and pepper are tender — 5 to 7 minutes. Vegetables should be tender but not wilted and overcooked. Remove from heat and let cool slightly. Add the onions and pepper, carrots and raisins to the salad mixture. Serve slightly warm or refrigerate and serve later. Mix in walnuts and cilantro just before serving.

Black-Eyed Peas and Collard Greens with Sundried Tomato Dressing

(Serves 4 to 6)

If you can't find the dry variety of sundried tomatoes already chopped, use kitchen scissors and cut the halves into small pieces.

Dressing:
1 teaspoon fennel seeds
1/4 cup finely chopped sundried tomatoes
1/4 cup extra-virgin olive oil
2 tablespoons mirin
2 1/2 tablespoons brown rice vinegar
1 tablespoon chopped, bottled hot peppers, such as Mama Lil's
2 or 3 cloves garlic, pressed
1/2 teaspoon salt

Salad:
1 cup dry black-eyed peas
1 large Granny Smith apple, peeled and cored
1 tablespoon lemon juice
1 tablespoon extra-virgin olive oil
1 large onion, chopped
1 large bunch collard greens, removed from stems, rolled tightly and cut into thin strips (a chiffonade)
1 1/2 cups finely chopped celery
1/2 cup crumbled feta cheese or 1/2 cup toasted pine nuts

Heat a skillet over medium heat. Add fennel seeds, stir and toast for 5 minutes or until the seeds are a darker color and are very aromatic. Remove from heat and grind to a fine powder with a suribachi (Japanese grinding bowl). Mix in toasted, ground fennel with the rest of the dressing ingredients in a small bowl or jar. Allow dressing to sit for at least one hour so the sundried tomatoes can rehydrate.

Rinse black-eyed peas and place in a saucepan with 3 cups of water. Bring to a boil. Reduce heat, partially cover and simmer for 45 to 60 minutes. While beans cook, prepare the rest of the ingredients. Grate the apple and blend with the lemon juice. Set aside. Heat a heavy skillet over medium heat. Add oil and onion, stir, reduce heat, cover and sweat the onion until it is transparent and soft. Add the collard greens, stir, cover and cook until greens are very tender. You may have to add a bit of water. When black-eyed peas are done, drain and combine with the other ingredients, including celery and dressing. Garnish with feta cheese or pine nuts. Serve warm or cold.

Italian White Bean Salad with Yellow, Red and Green Peppers

(Serves 4)

Cannelini beans are often used in Italian cuisine. This summer salad uses fresh herbs with yellow, red and green peppers, which add a festive look. I often like the addition of Mama Lil's Peppers blended in, with Port Madison goat cheese crumbled on top.

Salad:
1 cup dry cannelini beans, soaked
2 bay leaves
1 each: red, yellow and green pepper
1/4 cup finely minced red onion
1/4 cup finely chopped parsley
Dressing:
5 tablespoons extra-virgin olive oil
1/4 cup lemon juice
1 1/2 tablespoons tomato paste
1 teaspoon honey or agave nectar
2 tablespoons chopped fresh basil
1 tablespoon fresh oregano
1 teaspoon fresh thyme
1/2 teaspoon salt
Freshly ground pepper

Place cannelini beans and bay leaves in a medium saucepan. Cover with about 3 cups water, bring to a boil, reduce heat, partially cover and simmer for 1 to 1 1/2 hours. Prepare the rest of the salad and dressing while beans cook. Drain beans, remove bay leaves and run cold water over them to stop the cooking process.

Place the three peppers on a screen over a grill and turn them until the skins are charred and blistered. If you don't have a grill, put the peppers under the broiler, turning them frequently until blackened. When peppers are done, place in a paper bag to cool. When cool enough to touch, peel skins, seed and cut into thin strips. Set aside while you prepare the dressing.

With a fork, combine oil, lemon juice, tomato paste, honey, herbs and salt, stirring until tomato paste is well blended. Place them in a bowl and combine with peppers, onion and parsley. Toss with dressing. Add freshly ground pepper to taste. Serve warm or at room temperature.

Marinated Beans

(Makes 2 cups)

These beans make a great side dish. They can also be used to add flavor, texture and protein to green salads. Use beans that hold their shape well, such as garbanzos (chickpeas), kidney beans, Great Northern beans or Scarlet Runners. For bean digestion tips, see p. 298.

Dressing:
3 tablespoons sherry or balsamic vinegar
2 1/2 tablespoons extra-virgin olive oil
1/2 teaspoon organic sugar or Rapadura
2 to 4 cloves garlic, pressed
1 teaspoon fresh, chopped rosemary
1/2 teaspoon salt
Dash of crushed red peppers

Beans:
2 cups cooked and cooled beans, or rinsed canned beans
1/4 cup chopped fresh chives

Combine vinegar, olive oil, sugar, garlic, rosemary, salt and red pepper in a bowl. Mix well. In a medium bowl, stir the marinade and beans together. Marinate for at least one hour. Mix in chives right before serving.

A Farming Dream at Stoney Plains

In 1978, Bob and Particia Meyer started Stoney Plains Organic Farm, a 20-acre farm near Tenino, about 20 miles south of Olympia. Named for the rocky, hard soil, it wasn't easy farming there, but the Meyers knew how to build up organic soil. Now they're doing it for their neighbors. In exchange for acreage, three neighboring families get weekly Stoney Plains CSA veggie boxes (see p.279). The Meyers now farm 45 acres. They've always farmed organically. Patricia says that when raising seven children, they didn't want chemicals on their own food, so it was only natural to farm without pesticides. Today, their son Patrick is the field boss and another son, Tom, works part time at farmers markets. Grandson Justin works at the University District Farmers Market.

Originally from St. Paul, Minnesota, Bob was Union Director of American Federation of State, County and Municipal Employees, but his long-time dream was to be a farmer. In St. Paul, twenty miles across town, there was an old historic farm with plots of land divided up. They advertised plots for growing vegetables every year. The Meyers got a few spaces and began farming. They learned all they could. In 1978, Bob was transferred to the Pacific Northwest where they bought Stoney Plains. Initially, Patricia farmed. The children grew up working on the farm, and Bob squeezed in any farming he could when he wasn't at his union job. When he retired, Bob became a full-time farmer. They've been selling organic produce at the Olympia Market since the late 1970's. Today, they sell at four markets around Seattle (West Seattle, Columbia City, University District and Pike Place Market).

Bob ran the farm until he died from surgery complications 2002. He loved farming. He got up at the crack of dawn, especially if he got a new tractor, and he'd go out in the fields to work. When he finished work each day, he read farming books. Then he tried out new ideas and techniques. He was always willing to listen and give advice to young farmers, and he was such a pleasant presence at the market in his overalls and baseball cap. He had ideas for preparation and storage and was knowledgeable with tips about everything he grew.

Patrick Meyer runs the farm now. Stoney Plains' specialty crop is garlic. They grow ten different varieties of garlic such as silverskin, elephant, Bavarian and Oregon Blue. Patricia finds the most challenging thing about organic farming today is all the bookkeeping required for organic certification according the national standards. They have to keep track of where the seeds come from (traditionally farmers saved seeds for planting), when crops are planted and the yields of everything. A farmer has enough to do without the extensive paperwork involved. Thanks to Patrick taking over as foreman, Patricia has a little extra time for bookkeeping, and maybe she can squeeze a vacation in once in a while.

Food Choices and Farmland

Local food production was once an integrated system, intertwined in our daily lives. In 1900, two out of five Americans lived on farms; now only one out of forty of us is a farmer. Most Americans today have no idea who grows the food they eat. Estranged from local farming systems, many don't realize much of the farmland where our food is grown is being lost at an alarming rate.

For the last fifty years, cities have spread outward, encroaching on farmland. As a result, farmland all over the country is rapidly losing ground to urban sprawl. According to American Farmland Trust, 86 percent of cultivated fruits and vegetables and 63 percent of dairy products in this country come from farmland that is at risk from development. Farmland was sold and developed twice as fast in the 1990's as the 1980's. In Washington alone, between 1992 and 1997, we lost nearly 200 acres of farmland each day – that's about 180 farms a year, an average of 4 farms a week. Once a farm is sold for commercial development, agricultural land is gone forever, replaced with asphalt, housing developments and strip malls as if they're the crops of the future. One local farmer recently remarked "If farmland continues to be developed, we could eventually become a food importing nation."

Environmental, economic and social aspects of farming are important for urban and rural local communities. Here are a few things you can do to become a better farmland protection advocate:

- Buy locally, shop farmers markets, and buy directly from farmers. Support businesses such as produce delivery services that buy locally.
- Eat less processed foods, which take us farther away from food origins. In the stores you frequent, find out where their produce comes from. Encourage stores to buy from local farmers. Shop where local produce is featured.
- Be aware of farmland and development issues in your own community, and voice your support for local farmland protection to local zoning boards, law makers or planning commissions.
- On a national level, contact American Farmland Trust (AFT), an organization dedicated to preserving farmland, www.farmland.org. Farm Aid is another organization working to keeping family farmers on their land. Find out more information about Farm Aid at www.farmaid.org.
- On a local level, PCC Natural Markets created PCC Farmland Fund (p.190), which is generating money to save prime farmland from development. In Skagit Valley, a group called Skagitonians to Preserve Farmland has set up a fund to preserve farmland (p.190). Get involved or contribute to either of these organizations.

Sensational Soup And Bread

Soup for the Season

Profile: Steve and Beverly Phillips, Port Madison Farm

Savory Stocks
   Soup Stock Basics
   Basic Soup Stock
   Garlic-Mushroom Soup Stock
   Rich and Savory Quick Stock

Hearty Soups and Stews
   Curried Lentil
   Creamy Double Garlic-Chipotle Lentil
   Savory Split Pea and Celeriac
   Creamy Black Bean
   Black-Eyed Pea Chili
   Savory Baked Bean Stew
   Yellow Split Pea Dal
   Smoky Bean Soup With Collard Greens
   Autumn Harvest
   Potato, Fennel and Tomato
   Jamaican Red Bean
   Old-Fashioned Navy Bean and Vegetable
   Mushroom Barley Soup with Merlot
   Creamy Potato-Vegetable

Satisfying Lighter Soups
   Spring Tonic
   Creamy Ginger-Pumpkin-Apple
   Spicy Tomato, Corn and Rice
   No-Cream of Mushroom
   Sherried Wild Rice
   Summer Vegetable Soup with Kamut and Spelt
   Cream of Celery and Autumn Root
   Borscht
   Eggplant and Flageolet Bean
   "Creamy" Broccoli
   Garlic-Asparagus

THINK ABOUT IT

About a third of our nation's potato crop comes from Idaho and Washington. Potatoes are very susceptible to fungus, and conventional crops are routinely treated with four or more applications of fungicides during the growing season. Many of these chemicals are human carcinogens. Fungicides and pesticides applied to potato crops often contaminate ground and surface water. On the other hand, organic potato farmers enhance soil quality in a variety of ways. For one thing, they plant potatoes with other crops to improve the soil. They also grow a variety of potatoes and rotate crops to avoid fungus and confuse pests. Organic potatoes are planted in dry soil to avoid fungal problems.

Farm sign near Carnation, Washington

Sensational Soup And Bread

No matter what kind of a day you've had, nothing says comfort like the aroma and taste of homemade soup made with vegetables fresh from the farm.

Ask anyone and they can name their favorite soup. When I was young, my favorite was Campbell's bean soup with carrots added. So many people had switched to canned soups in the 1960's, even my grandmother used the canned variety. Today, people aren't accustomed to making soup, and the whole process can seem mysterious and time-consuming. However, a tasty soup doesn't have to take hours of work. With a few tips and some recipes as guides, anyone can grasp the basics and create great soup. One of my favorite secrets is to sample the soup often as it simmers and think about balancing the flavors. Does it need a hint of sweetness or a squeeze of lemon?

First and most important, use a heavy soup pot, not an old aluminum pot. The bottom of an inferior pan becomes thin in spots over time, making it easier for soup to burn. It's difficult, often impossible, to repair burnt soup. Use a good quality pot from the beginning, and you won't regret it. A crockpot is another option. It can slow simmer soup all day while you're at work. There's nothing like coming home to a rich-tasting, savory soup.

Soup stock gives soup depth, grounding it with a rich base and a layer of flavors. Though stocks aren't hard to make, some cooks don't have the time or inclination to make them. Many simply want homemade taste, easy recipes and shortcuts. Thankfully, if you don't have the time to make soup stock, there are fairly good prepared vegetarian stocks available.

Creating soup is part artistry, part skill and part luck, as leftovers are incorporated with stock, beans, grains and fresh vegetables. Spices and herbs make each soup unique. Before putting soup together, think about the end result you want.   Take a few minutes to consider leftovers to use. Try balancing the soup with five tastes — sweet, sour, pungent, hot or spicy, and salty. If soup is missing one of these components, it can taste flat.   For example, when creating **Creamy Black Bean Soup** (p.102), I pureed together leftover refried black beans and baked squash (sweet). Then I added garlic (pungent), salsa (spicy), and salt to taste, thinning with water to the desired consistency. Something was missing when I sampled it. A simple squeeze of lime (sour) and a sprinkling of cilantro for garnish drew rave reviews. For a finishing touch, sprinkle on some finely chopped vegetables, croutons or grated organic cheese. There are a myriad of variations to create. That's what soup is all about.

Soup For The Season

Though cooking magazines today often give lip service to cooking with the seasons, you can easily find strawberry recipes in February, and sweet potato or pear recipes in July. From an environmental perspective, produce grown out of season is more costly because it's grown farther away and shipping or trucking it uses petroleum products. When our food doesn't have to travel as far, these costs are reduced. In the Northwest, we're fortunate to have a variety of produce that is often just days away from when it was harvested. Pay attention to local and regional produce selections and alter your soup accordingly.

Autumn

As the days grow short and the chill of autumn sets in, warmer, heavier fare becomes more appealing. Add soaked, dried beans and whole grains to soup now. Choose from fall produce such as potatoes, winter squash, sweet potatoes, parsnips, turnips, rutabagas, apples and young braising greens. Onions, garlic, celery and carrots are also plentiful. Though fresh tomatoes are on their way out, use organically grown sundried or canned tomatoes in soups.

Soup during autumn and winter tends to have a thicker base. Add body to any soup by pureeing about a cup of the soup, and stirring it back into the pot. Or blend a leftover baked potato or sweet potato, beans or grains with a hand blender in a small amount of soup, then stir it in. Use a half-cup of beans or grains to puree into the soup. If soup is the center focus of a meal, you only need crusty artisan bread and perhaps a tossed salad as accompaniments. Soup served before a meal or on the side, can take second stage to stuffed, baked squash, roasted winter vegetables or whole-grain pilafs, served with some braised greens on the side.

Winter

Chili and thick, hearty stews and soups are nourishing for your body and soul as the short days give way to cold winter nights. This is the time of year when I love the compelling savory aroma of slow-simmered soup in the crockpot. Served with freshly baked bread and local artisan cheese and you've got the perfect winter meal. Seasonal produce selections are fewer and more defined from December through March. Roots and hearty greens take the chill from your bones and warm you from the inside. New soup creations are inspired with stored winter roots like parsnips, beets and Jerusalem artichokes. Both parsnips and kale improve in flavor after the first frost and are perfect winter soup additions. Onions, garlic, potatoes and squash from the fall harvest can keep well during winter months in a cool, dry storage room. Freezing or otherwise preserving produce accumulated during summer months makes welcome winter meal variations.

If you want an accompaniment to your soup, try **Rosemary-Amaranth Flatbread** (p.139) topped with marinated portabello mushrooms, kalamata olives and Port Madison goat cheese. Roasted vegetables or a stuffed baked squash also go well with soup. For salads, try **Coleslaw** (p.65) or **Parsnip and Carrot Salad** (p.64).

Spring

In between winter and spring, the onions and garlic in storage begin to grow. If you find green shoots in your onion or garlic heads, pull them out and discard them before cooking because the growing shoots have a bitter flavor. Check stored potatoes often. If they begin to sprout, cut out the sprouts and throw them away before you use the potatoes. Commercially grown potatoes at grocery stores are chemically treated so the sprouts don't grow.

In the Pacific Northwest, the first local asparagus means spring is officially here. Artichokes, dandelion greens, fiddlehead ferns, mizuna, nettles and early spring peas are signs the summer crops are just around the corner. Soups lighten up. Thick winter soups give way to creamy, lighter vegetable soups. One of my spring favorites is **"Cream" of Seasonal Greens** (p.126). Make it with young wild greens like nettles and serve with warm tortillas and a bean paté, like **Red Lentil and Olive Spread** (p.186). Though wild greens such as nettles don't usually appear in grocery stores, you can forage for your own. Just remember to wear long sleeves, jeans and gloves to avoid getting stung by the bristly hairs that are on the stems and leaves.

Summer

During the summer, there is such a wide variety of excellent produce to choose from, we often end up eating in abundance. Peas, green onions, baby beets and turnips, tomatoes, peppers, eggplant and summer squash, along with fresh herbs of all kinds, are just some of the market finds you can use. Soups are lighter, with fresh soybeans, beans, grains or pasta added, for a relaxing dinner outside as you enjoy the long summer days. For a refreshing treat on a hot summer day, try the delectable **Cool and Spicy Fruit Soup** (p.129). Make it with apricots, peaches or plums. Garnish with fresh, finely chopped cilantro or edible summer flowers. All of these can be found at farmers markets. You can also top summer soup with a drizzle of Port Madison goat yogurt, roasted red pepper strips or a dab of pesto. I like to serve summer soup with tossed baby and bitter greens such as arugula, mizuna or purslane with sweet tomatoes and a **Balsamic Vinaigrette** (p.56).

THINK ABOUT IT

Every tomato or melon you slice into was hand-picked by a farmworker, one of the lowest paid workers with least benefits in our society. Choosing the cheapest tomatoes, peaches, or melons often supports a system that perpetuates a lifestyle below poverty level. Next time you shop at your favorite natural foods store, ask if they support farmworker unions when purchasing produce, and look for grocery items like coffee and tea labeled "fair trade" to help ensure that farm workers are paid a fair wage for their labor. For more information about the lives of farmworkers check out *With These Hands: The Hidden World of Migrant Farmworkers Today* by Daniel Rothenberg.

Steve and Beverly Phillips
Port Madison Farm

Before I tasted Port Madison cheese, I wondered what the big fuss over goat cheese was all about. Most of the varieties I'd sampled were so strong they could easily overwhelm anything within shouting distance. Chèvre was very overrated in my book, and goat yogurt was not a favorite either – until my first taste of Port Madison goat yogurt. Now I'm sure that tangy taste delight is heaven on earth. If it's not Port Madison, it's hardly worth considering.

Port Madison Farm, owned and run by Steve and Beverly Phillips, is a thirty-minute ferry ride to Bainbridge Island and then a short ride north on Sunrise Drive. With 200 goats (175 of them milking goats), Steve and Beverly are busy year-round, spending two and a half hours each morning and evening milking goats. Beverly has been present at all the goat births as well. "We haven't taken a vacation in years. We don't even go out to dinner. We do brunch," Steve says, without a trace of regret. They do, however, find the time to name each goat. "Every goat has a name because our goats are not numbers . . . Our goats are happy goats," Steve adds emphatically. And that's part of his secret for high quality goat milk.

Initially, Steve and Beverly moved to Bainbridge Island and tried organic farming. Steve says he got into farming after he was completely won over by farm fresh eggs in an omelet. They farmed an acre, but struggled to make it work. The land wasn't really suited for row crops. They had always kept one or two goats for milk. Two soon became four, and eventually a new endeavor was born — a goat dairy farm. That was more than ten years ago. "I think I was a mediocre vegetable farmer, but I'm an excellent goat dairy farmer," Steve says. Beverly came from a family with a farming background.

Her grandfather was a blind dairy farmer in rural Maine. He had six cows, and his wife had a butter route.

The Phillips take great pride in their goats and goat milk. They take exceptional care of their goats. The dairy isn't certified organic, but does use organic principles in farming. Getting high-quality organic alfalfa can be a problem, but Steve gets it when it's available. Organic farming doesn't always guarantee the best product; and only with contented goats and the best food, can you get excellent sweet-tasting goat milk. At least a couple times a year, Steve searches for the best alfalfa he can find. For the nutritional profile of alfalfa to be right for a goat, the alfalfa has to be well fertilized and cut at just the right time before the plant blooms, for maximum nutrition. After Steve locates the right alfalfa, he sends it to a lab to be tested. Then he does the goat taste test. "If they fight over it, I know it's good," Steve says.

Contrary to the stereotypical images of garbage-eating and lawn-mowing, goats are very sensitive about their food. For example, a goat will not eat food if another goat sticks its nose in the alfalfa and pushes it around. If grain spills on the ground, the goats are not interested. When they do eat plants, they choose only tiny, tender leaves. "I thought our good cheese was all due to me, but the quality of the cheese comes from good milk," Steve says. "I tried to make goat cheese out of an inferior milk from another dairy and it just didn't work." If the feed isn't high quality or the goats get stressed, the taste can be off. "Goats are more like deer than cows. They're skittish. If they get scared, the milk can have an adrenaline taste to it," Steve says. Goat milk has a different protein structure than cows' milk. The fat molecules in goat milk are smaller and the membranes around the molecules are more fragile, making it more susceptible to off-flavors.

Steve says his biggest challenge in dairy farming is "putting all the pieces together." In this country, we are geared for high production dairies. Just to get the equipment for a small-scale dairy farm, Steve had to turn to other countries that are geared for smaller production. He finally found the machinery he needed in Israel. He had it shipped over and then had problems getting it to work. Then Steve and Beverly needed a USDA-approved machine that seals the yogurt with a lid. They can make six hundred cups of yogurt in two hours now. That's small-scale compared to the dairy yogurt industry.

You can find Port Madison milk and their other goat dairy products in natural food stores around Puget Sound, including Whole Foods Market and PCC Natural Markets. Steve also sells Port Madison products at local farmers markets including the University District Market. In addition to Chèvre and goat yogurt, they sell spring cheese (a seasonal, hard goat cheese that has a similar taste and texture to a Havarti cheese). Try finishing your soup with goat yogurt drizzled on top, crumbling goat cheese on for garnish, or spreading fresh basil goat cheese on organic sourdough rye bread. You'll be won over immediately.

Savory Stocks

A good stock can improve any soup by providing a background flavor for the ingredients. Imagine or Pacific Foods commercial broth or stock can work in a pinch, but making the real thing doesn't take long. You can be creative when making soup stock while using up vegetable scraps that you have saved. Onion skins, sweet potato peels, mushroom stems, celery tops and other produce discards can be stored in plastic bags in the freezer until you need them. On the weekends or whenever you have time, make soup stock. Then freeze it in pint-size containers until you're ready to use it. Simply thaw it in the refrigerator the day before using it.

Soup stock basics

♦ Save vegetable scraps in labeled plastic bags in the freezer for easy stock-making.

♦ Vegetables from your vegetable bin can be slightly over-the-hill, but nothing moldy or really bad should go into a soup stock.

♦ Roughly cut all vegetables the same size — about 1-inch pieces. This brings out the flavor of the vegetables and strengthens the stock flavor.

♦ Start with about 6 cups of cold water. Add all ingredients, bring to a boil, then simmer for 35 to 40 minutes.

♦ Strain the stock after it has finished cooking. Never let it sit because the stock may turn bitter and cause the soup to have a slightly off taste.

♦ If you want a stronger flavor, after straining, reduce stock by simmering until it reaches the desired strength.

Vegetables, herbs and other additions to soup stocks

♦ **Beans** — Use green beans or leftover cooked dried beans for a hearty flavor. You can also add dry lentils — about 1/4 cup.

♦ **Carrots** — Use the tops as well as bottoms. Carrots give stock a sweet, earthy flavor.

♦ **Celery** — A basic addition to soup stock. If you don't have celery use about 1/2 teaspoon celery seed. You can also use raw celery root pieces and skins or leftover cooked celery root.

♦ **Corn** — Use the inner husks, corncob (cut into 2-inch pieces) and corn (fresh, frozen or leftover). The corncobs add a deep, rich flavor.

Vegetables, herbs and other additions (continued)

- **Dried herbs** — Classic additions include 1 or 2 bay leaves, basil, marjoram, and a pinch of thyme. Other herbs that lend specific flavors include sage, rosemary, cilantro or fennel.
- **Fresh herbs** — Add about three times the amount of fresh as you do dried herbs.
- **Garlic** — Roasted garlic adds a rich, deliciously sweet flavor. You don't have to add many fresh garlic cloves (about 3 or 4).
- **Jerusalem artichokes** — Also called sunchokes, raw or cooked, are always good earthy-flavored additions.
- **Kombu** — This is a sea vegetable that contains essential minerals and enhances flavors. You can either leave it whole or cut it into smaller pieces.
- **Miso** — White miso is better for vegetable and summer soups. It imparts a light sweet flavor. For full-bodied soups, add brown or red miso. Add about 1/4 cup of either variety to soup stock. Since miso is salty, don't add additional salt when adding miso.
- **Mushrooms** — Save the stems and use them for an earthy-flavored stock. You can also add dried mushrooms (about 1/2 to 1 ounce). A few shiitake or porcini give a unique flavor to the soup stock.
- **Pepper** — Black peppercorns, a pinch of cayenne, a jalepeño or just 1/4 teaspoon chipotle chile powder add a bit of spice — any type of pepper can make a good addition.
- **Onions** — Red and yellow onions contribute a sweet flavor to the stock. Onion skins make a nice brown broth, but too many in the stock may leave a bitter taste.
- **Parsley** — Use parsley generously – about a handful for a pot of stock. Parsley is rich in nutrients as well as flavor.
- **Potatoes** — Cooked potatoes can fall apart and cloud the stock, which won't be a problem if you are making a thick, creamy soup, but if you want a clear stock, stick to washed, raw potato skins. Don't use any bad portions of the potato.
- **Salt** —Natural sea salt is less processed and contains more minerals. This is the preferred choice for vegetable stock as well as anything else you prepare.
- **Squash** — Winter squash adds a sweet flavor; summer squash imparts a much lighter taste for summer months.
- **Sweet potatoes and yams** — Both add color and an earthy, deep flavor to stocks. Use the skins as well as raw pieces. Leftover baked sweet potatoes, like potatoes, cloud the stock but are excellent for a rich taste.

Basic Soup Stock
(Makes about 6 cups)

This stock will keep for one week in the refrigerator. Kombu, a sea vegetable, and lentils give the soup stock a deep, savory taste. You can make a richer tasting stock by browning mushrooms and garlic in one tablespoon ghee or coconut oil before adding the water and other vegetables. Dried herbs work better than fresh for soup stock.

6 cups water
1 strip kombu, cut into small pieces
3 stalks celery, cut into pieces
2 carrots, cut-up
1 yellow onion, sliced (for a darker stock, use the onion skins)
1 handful parsley, chopped
4 mushrooms, sliced
1/4 cup lentils, rinsed
1/4 teaspoon thyme
1 teaspoon oregano
1 teaspoon basil
3 to 4 cloves garlic, peeled and sliced
6 peppercorns
Generous pinch of sea salt

Combine all ingredients in a large soup pot. Bring to a boil. Reduce heat and simmer for about 30 minutes. Strain (discard cooked vegetables) and cool. Good in soups, stews or as a cooking liquid for grains.

Options:
♦ Add seasonal vegetables such as corn, squash, celeriac or parsley root, leeks, bell peppers, tomatoes, parsnips, turnips, fennel or pea pods.
♦ Use vegetable scraps such as carrots, carrot tops, potato or parsnip skins, corn cobs, mushroom stems and squash seeds. You can also add leftover cooked vegetables.
♦ Vary the herbs according to your own tastes.
♦ Add about 1/4 cup white, brown or red miso instead of salt.

Garlic-Mushroom Soup Stock

(Makes about 6 cups)

A rich tasting savory stock, this also makes an excellent cooking liquid for whole grains. Foragers and wild food gatherers sell fresh and dried mushrooms at local markets. These can be more economical than the packaged dried mushrooms found in specialty grocery stores.

6 cups water
1 onion, chopped
3 stalks celery, cut into pieces
2 heads garlic, cloves separated, peeled and crushed
1 ounce dried porcini mushrooms
1 cup cut-up winter squash with seeds
1/2 tablespoon tomato paste
1/2 teaspoon rosemary
1 teaspoon basil
1/4 teaspoon cayenne
1/2 teaspoon salt or 1/4 cup brown miso

Combine all ingredients in a large soup pot. Bring to a boil. Reduce heat, then simmer for 30 minutes. Strain and cool.

Rich and Savory Quick Stock

(Makes 4 cups)

When I'm in a hurry, I put this stock together and simmer it while I sauté the vegetables for my soup or pilaf.

4 cups water
1 onion and skin, roughly cut
3 cloves garlic, sliced
1/2 teaspoon each: sage, rosemary and thyme
2 tablespoons brown or barley miso
1/4 teaspoon pepper

Combine all ingredients in a large pot. Bring to a boil, then reduce heat, partially cover and simmer for 20 minutes. Strain and use as desired.

Hearty Stews and Soups

Substantial enough to stand on their own, with a simple tossed salad or just some crusty bread, these soups are comfort food during cooler winter months. You can also enjoy these recipes in the spring using seasonal produce selections. The soups in this section progress from quick cooking legumes to longer cooking beans. Vegetable and grain-based soups follow.

Curried Lentil Soup

(Serves 4)

Make this quick, tasty soup faster using red lentils. They only take 20 minutes to cook. The spices are better when freshly ground. If you don't have all the spices for this, substitute 2 1/2 teaspoons curry powder and 1/8 teaspoon cayenne.

> 1 tablespoon extra-virgin olive oil
> 1 teaspoon each: coriander, turmeric, cumin, chili powder
> 1/4 teaspoon each: cardamom, cinnamon
> 1/8 teaspoon each: cloves, cayenne
> 1 large onion, chopped
> 1 stalk celery, chopped
> 1 carrot, sliced
> 3 or 4 cloves garlic, minced or pressed
> 1 heaping cup brown or green lentils, rinsed
> 4 to 5 cups stock or water
> 2 medium-large potatoes, cut into small chunks
> 1 large baked sweet potato, skin removed, or 1 cup winter squash
> Salt to taste
> Juice of 1 large lemon (about 1/3 cup)
> 1/3 cup finely chopped cilantro

Heat a heavy soup pot over medium heat. Add oil and spices and sauté for 1 minute. Stir in onion, reduce heat, cover and cook until onion is translucent. Blend in celery, carrot and garlic. Stir and cook for a few minutes. Add lentils and water. Bring soup to a boil. Reduce heat and simmer, partially covered for 30 minutes. Add chopped potatoes, cover and simmer for another 30 minutes, or until potatoes are soft.

Puree 1 cup of soup with the sweet potato in a blender or with a hand blender. Return to pot and add salt to taste. Cook for about 5 more minutes. Remove from heat, stir in lemon juice. Serve garnished with cilantro.

99

Creamy Double Garlic-Chipotle Lentil Soup

(Serves 4)

Red lentils, roasted garlic and sliced sautéed garlic blend with smoky chopotle chiles to create this smoky-flavored, warming hearty soup. Elephant garlic is a mild garlic cousin more closely related to leeks than garlic. You can get good local garlic from Stoney Plains Organic Farm (p.84).

2 heads garlic
2 tablespoons melted coconut or extra-virgin olive oil, divided
1 large onion, chopped
3 cloves elephant garlic, peeled and sliced
1 cup red lentils
1 or 2 medium carrots, sliced
3 medium potatoes, cut into small chunks
3 chipotle chile peppers
28-ounce can diced tomatoes
4 cups water
Salt to taste
1/2 cup chopped flat-leaf parsley or cilantro

Preheat oven to 350º. Cut the tops off of both heads of garlic. Lay garlic on a piece of tin foil. Drizzle 1 tablespoon oil over the garlic heads. Wrap in foil and bake in the oven for 45 minutes or until garlic is fork tender. Let cool before pressing the roasted garlic out into a small bowl to use in the soup.

Heat a heavy soup pot over medium heat. Add oil and onions, stir, reduce heat, cover with a lid that fits directly over the vegetables, allowing no air to circulate. Sweat the onions until they are limp. Remove lid, stir in elephant garlic slices. Cook over medium heat for another 7 to 10 minutes, stirring constantly. Onions and elephant garlic should be lightly browned. Rinse lentils very briefly and immediately add lentils, carrots, potatoes, chipotle peppers, tomatoes and water to the soup pot. Bring to a boil, reduce heat and simmer for about 30 minutes. The lentils will be falling apart.

When the roasted garlic is done, gently press out all the garlic. Add it to a cup of soup in a small, steep sided container. With a hand blender, puree the garlic and soup then stir it back into the soup pot. Season to taste with salt. Remove chile pods before serving. Garnish with parsley or cilantro.

Savory Split Pea and Celeriac Soup

(Serves 6)

With the texture of potatoes and the taste of celery, celeriac or celery root adds an earthy character to autumn and winter soups. It used to be a fairly common vegetable and is still used quite a bit in Europe. Once cut and peeled, the root turns brown quickly, so use it quickly or plunge it into water with a little lemon juice or vinegar added.

2 tablespoons extra-virgin olive oil
1 1/2 cups peeled pearl onions, or chopped yellow onions
4 cloves garlic, minced or pressed
1/4 teaspoon cayenne
5 cups soup stock or water
1 bay leaf
1 strip of kombu, cut into small pieces
1 heaping cup split peas, rinsed
1/4 cup brown rice (long or short grain)
3 or 4 stalks celery, chopped
2 medium carrots, sliced
1 medium celeriac (about 3/4 pound)
1/2 tablespoon Rapadura or other sweetener
2 tablespoons lemon juice
Salt to taste
1/3 cup finely chopped parsley

Heat a heavy soup pot over medium heat. Add oil and onions. Stir, reduce heat, cover and sweat the onions until they are soft — about 10 minutes. Add garlic and cayenne. Stir and cook for another 5 minutes. The onions should be caramelized. If not, keep stirring and cooking on medium heat until onions are brown.

Add the soup stock or water, bay leaf, kombu, split peas, rice, celery and carrots. Bring to a boil, then reduce heat and simmer for 30 minutes. Peel celeriac with a paring knife and cut in bite-size chunks. Stir celeriac into the soup with Rapadura. Continue to cook for another 30 minutes or until peas are soft and rice is cooked. Blend in lemon juice and salt to taste. Garnish with chopped parsley.

Creamy Black Bean Soup
(Serves 4)

*If you don't have homemade refried beans for this soup, use the canned organic version. This soup goes well with **Coleslaw** (p.65) or **Carrot and Raisin Salad** (p.64) and warm tortillas with Port Madison goat cheese.*

2 cups refried black beans
1 large baked sweet potato, skin removed or 1 1/2 cups baked
winter squash
3 cups water
2 cloves garlic, pressed
1/4 cup spicy salsa (or more according to taste)
Salt to taste
1 large or 2 small limes, thinly sliced
1/2 cup crushed tortilla chips for garnish

Combine beans, sweet potato, water and garlic in a blender or food processor. Blend until smooth and creamy. Pour into a saucepan and heat over medium heat. Cook on medium heat, stirring occasionally for about 10 minutes. Add 1/4 cup spicy salsa and salt to taste. Add more salsa, if desired.

When soup is hot, serve with a squeeze of lime and a lime slice. Sprinkle with crushed tortilla chips.

FOOD FOR THOUGHT
Legumes are loaded with protein and complex carbohydrates, which digest more slowly than refined carbohydrates. They also help stabilize blood sugar levels. Beans also contain soluble as well as insoluble fiber. The former helps the body handle fats and cholesterol; the later corrects constipation, sweeping the intestines as it moves through.

Black-Eyed Pea Chili
(Serves 4 to 6)

My grandmother and mother both believed that eating black-eyed peas on New Year's day gave good luck for the coming year. Don't wait for New Year's to sample this savory chili! Black-eyed peas don't have to be soaked before cooking, but overnight soaking makes all legumes more digestible.

3 tablespoons ghee or coconut oil
1 large onion, chopped
1 or 2 jalapeños, seeded and finely chopped
1 tablespoon chili powder
1 teaspoon ground cumin
1/2 teaspoon oregano
3 cloves garlic, pressed
4 ounces tempeh, cubed into small pieces
1 carrot, sliced
1 cup dry black-eyed peas, soaked overnight and drained
1/2 cup dried kidney beans, soaked overnight and drained
3 cups water
1 strip kombu, cut into small pieces
15-ounce can diced tomatoes
1/8 cup tomato paste
2 tablespoons brown rice vinegar
1 tablespoon Rapadura
Salt to taste
1/2 cup shredded aged Samish Bay Gouda (optional)
1/2 cup chopped cilantro

Heat a heavy soup pot over medium heat. Add ghee, onions and jalapeños. Stir, cover and cook over low heat until onions are transparent. Remove lid, add chili powder, cumin, oregano, garlic and tempeh cubes. Stir and cook for about 7 minutes on medium heat or until tempeh turns a light brown.

Add black-eyed peas, drained kidney beans, water, kombu, tomatoes and tomato paste. Mix well, bring to a boil, then reduce heat, cover and simmer on low until black-eyed peas are tender — about an hour. When black-eyed peas and kidney beans are tender, add vinegar, Rapadura and salt to taste. Simmer for another 15 minutes. Serve garnished with sharp cheddar cheese (if desired) and chopped cilantro. *(Hint: The longer this soup simmers, the more flavorful it becomes.)*

Savory Baked Bean Stew

(Serves 6)

An heirloom variety, Yellow-Eye beans were used traditionally in baked beans and soups in Maine. I can usually find different varieties of dried beans at DeLaurenti's at Pike Place Market. If you can't find Yellow Eye beans, use Great Northern or white beans. Add different colors of vegetables or garnish with contrasting colors of fresh vegetables such as finely chopped parsley or grated carrots.

1 tablespoon coconut oil
1 large onion, chopped
1/4 to 1/2 teaspoon crushed red pepper flakes (optional)
1 or 2 stalks celery, cut into 1/2-inch pieces
1 carrot, chopped
5 cups water
1 strip kombu, cut into small pieces
1 1/2 cups Yellow-Eye beans, washed, soaked overnight and drained
1 cup acorn squash, baked, skin removed
1/4 cup molasses
1 1/2 tablespoons Dijon mustard
3 tablespoons tamari
4 cups cut-up seasonal vegetables (use potatoes, carrots, corn, winter or summer squash, peas, peppers, parsnips or turnips)
Water, to thin to desired consistency

Heat a heavy soup pot over medium heat. Add oil, onion, pepper flakes, celery and carrots. Stir and cook until onions begin to brown — about 5 minutes. Add water, kombu and Yellow-Eye beans. Bring water to a boil. Reduce heat and simmer for one hour or until beans are tender.

Combine squash, molasses, mustard and tamari in a blender and blend until smooth. Stir into the soup when the beans are tender. Add vegetables and cook for another 15 minutes or until vegetables are fork-tender. Add water to thin if needed.

Yellow Split Pea Dal Soup

(Serves 6)

This soup is perfect with autumn favorites — squash, parsnips, carrots and seasonal greens. Leave out the vegetables except the onions, garlic and rutabagas if you want to make a creamy split pea soup. Puree soup with salt, soymilk and lemon before serving.

> 1 1/2 tablespoons coconut oil or ghee
> 1 large onion, chopped
> 1 jalapeño, seeded and minced
> 2 cloves elephant garlic, peeled and sliced (or 4 cloves regular garlic)
> 2 or 3 medium-size rutabagas or turnips, peeled and sliced
> 1 teaspoon each: turmeric, coriander, and garam masala
> 1 tablespoon Rapadura
> 1 cup yellow split peas
> 4 to 5 cups water
> 2 cups seasonal vegetables, cut into bite-size chunks (optional)
> Salt to taste
> 1 cup vanilla or plain soymilk
> Juice of 1 lemon
> Plain yogurt, goat or cow (optional)
> 1/3 cup chopped cilantro (optional)

Heat a soup pot over medium heat. Add oil, onion, jalapeño and garlic. Stir and cook until onions are soft. Stir in rutabagas, spices, Rapadura and split peas. Stir to coat, then add water and seasonal vegetables, if desired. Cover, bring to a boil, then reduce heat and simmer for 40 minutes. Add salt to taste and stir in soymilk. Remove from heat and stir in lemon. Add a spoonful of yogurt and garnish with cilantro, if desired.

Smoky Bean Soup with Collard Greens

(Serves 4)

Use any beans, except black, in this recipe. (Black beans will turn everything black.) Fakin' Bacon (a smoked tempeh strip) is available in natural food stores. Chipotle chiles in adobo sauce can be found in grocery stores in the international section.

1 to 2 tablespoons extra-virgin olive oil
1 onion, chopped
1 green pepper, chopped
4 cloves garlic, pressed
3 strips Fakin' Bacon, cut into 1-inch pieces
1 cup white beans, soaked overnight
2 cups soup stock
2 cups water
1 strip kombu, cut into small pieces
1 bay leaf
3 medium red potatoes, washed and cut into bite-size pieces
1 1/2 cups cut-up delicata squash, yams or sweet potatoes
1 chipotle chile in adobo sauce, chopped
15-ounce can diced tomatoes
6 collard leaves, removed from stems and chopped
1 tablespoon red miso
1 cup crumbled Port Madison goat cheese, or croutons

Heat a heavy soup pot over medium heat. Add oil, onion, pepper, garlic and Fakin' Bacon, stir, cover and reduce heat. Cook until the onions are slightly browned. Drain beans, then stir in with stock, water, kombu, bay leaf, potatoes, squash and chipotle chile. Cook for one hour or until beans are soft.

Add diced tomatoes and collard greens. Cook for 10 minutes or until greens are soft. Remove 1 cup of liquid. Puree it with red miso, then stir pureed soup back into the pot. Remove bay leaf. Stir and serve with goat cheese or croutons.

Autumn Harvest Soup

(Serves 6)

In addition to seasonal harvest CSA boxes (p.279), a number of local farms offer subscriptions to winter CSAs that contain a good selection of local produce after the markets close for the season. With winter veggie boxes, it's fun to come up with new great soups. One year, Willie Green's weekly veggies inspired this creation.

1 small sugar pumpkin (about 2 cups cooked pumpkin)
2 tablespoons extra-virgin olive oil
1 large onion, chopped
4 cloves garlic, pressed or minced
1 cup chopped or sliced fennel
3 carrots, sliced
3 turnips, cut into small chunks
3 small potatoes, cut into small chunks
1 1/2 cups cut-up cauliflower
1/2 cup French lentils
28-ounce can tomatoes, use whole, diced, or ground
3 1/2 cups water
2 teaspoons basil
1/4 teaspoon cayenne
1 teaspoon Rapadura
1/2 cup sliced olives (use your favorite)
2 cups cut-up turnip greens
Salt to taste
Feta cheese or Port Madison goat cheese for garnish (optional)

Poke holes into the pumpkin with a fork, place it on a small baking sheet, and bake at 350° for one hour or until tender. Remove from oven and let cool before cutting. While pumpkin bakes, heat a soup pot over medium heat. Add oil and onion. Cover and sweat onion until translucent. Remove cover, add garlic and fennel. Stir and cook for a few more minutes. Blend in carrots, turnips, potatoes, cauliflower, lentils, tomatoes, water, basil, cayenne and Rapadura. Bring to a boil, then reduce heat and simmer for one hour.

Cut pumpkin in half, remove seeds, scraping pumpkin away from skin. Add to soup and stir in with olives and turnip greens. Cook soup until greens are soft. Add salt to taste. Garnish with crumbled feta or goat cheese.

Potato, Fennel and Tomato Soup
(Serves 4 to 6)

An overabundance of fennel in the autumn one year led to this culinary creation. Goat yogurt adds a tangy flavor. Cheese lends a rich texture. In the winter, Willie Greens has the best dried basil around. The aroma alone is worth the price.

2 tablespoons ghee or extra-virgin olive oil
1 large onion, chopped
1 tablespoon chopped peppers such as Mama Lil's (see below)
2 1/2 cups chopped fennel
4 to 5 cloves garlic, minced or pressed
1 tablespoon Rapadura
4 small red potatoes, cut into chunks
1 tablespoon basil
28-ounce can diced tomatoes
2 cups water
6-ounce container Port Madison goat yogurt
1 cup mild grated cheese, such as Samish Bay Young Gouda
Fennel leaves for garnish

Heat a heavy soup pot over medium heat. Add oil, onion and peppers. Stir, cover and sweat onions until they are translucent. Remove cover and add fennel and garlic, stir and cook until fennel is soft. Add Rapadura, potatoes, basil, tomatoes and water. Cook on low for one hour. Blend in goat yogurt and cheese and heat on low for one minute. Garnish with fennel leaves.

Mama Lil's

The best pickled hot peppers are manufactured in our own backyard! Howard Lev started Mama Lil's taking his inspiration from an old recipe that his mother used and a lot of goathorn peppers, grown and harvested in Eastern Washington. The peppers are sorted, processed, packed into jars and then sold at markets and in specialty and natural food stores around Puget Sound and other areas of the country. No other processed pickled peppers can compare with the taste of Mama Lil's. They are available in mild or spicy (kick-butt variety). The peppers, Asparagini (pickled asparagus), Pepalilli (pickles in spicy mustard) and pickled green beans can also be found at farmers markets during harvest season. For the whole story about Mama Lil's Peppers and some great kick-butt recipes, check out www.mamalils.com.

Jamaican Red Bean Soup

(Serves 6)

Red beans, hot peppers, coconut and lime combine to make this irresistible soup. Serve it with warm corn tortillas and a simple salad of mixed baby greens and pickled beets.

        2 tablespoons ghee or extra-virgin olive oil
        1 large onion, chopped
        1 habañero or jalapeño pepper, seeded and chopped
        1 cup red beans, soaked overnight
        5 cups water or stock (or 2 1/2 cups of each)
        1 strip kombu, cut into small pieces
        2 medium red or yellow potatoes, cut into small chunks
        10 cloves garlic, peeled and pressed
        1 teaspoon cumin
        1 teaspoon oregano
        1 cup cooked short grain brown rice
        1 tablespoon red wine vinegar
        1 cup coconut milk (fresh or canned)
        Juice of 1 lime
        Salt to taste

Heat a soup pot over medium heat. Add oil, onion and pepper. Stir and cook until onions are lightly browned. Add beans, water, kombu, potatoes, garlic, cumin and oregano. Bring to a boil, reduce heat, partially cover and cook for at least one hour, or until beans are done.

When the beans are tender, remove 1 cup of the soup and purée until creamy. Stir back into the soup, along with rice, red wine vinegar and coconut milk. Cook until rice is warm — 5 to 10 minutes. Remove from heat and stir in lime juice and salt.

Tip

Fresh coconut milk is infinitely better than canned. To open a coconut, use an ice pick to pierce the "eyes" or the soft spot at the top of the coconut. Drain out the liquid. Then you can tap all around the edges with a hammer until the shell falls off the coconut meat. The flesh can be eaten raw or grated and made into milk. In a 1:1 ratio, combine grated coconut and hot water and let it sit for at least 20 minutes. Strain through cheesecloth, squeezing all the liquid out. This fresh milk should be used within a few days.

Old-Fashioned Navy Bean and Vegetable Soup

(Serves 6)

To make soup in a crockpot, add all the ingredients except miso and greens and cook on a high setting for about an hour. Then cook the soup on low for 8 hours. Add the greens 20 minutes before serving. Just before serving, blend the miso into 1 cup of the soup, then stir it back into the soup.

1 cup navy beans, sorted, rinsed, soaked and drained
6 cups water or vegetable stock
1 strip kombu, cut into small pieces
2 to 4 cloves garlic, pressed
2 teaspoons each: basil and oregano
1 teaspoon fennel
1/4 to 1/2 teaspoon crushed red peppers
1 bay leaf
2 carrots, diced
3 stalks celery, chopped
2 small red or white potatoes, cut into small chunks
1 small sweet potato, or 1 cup delicata squash, cut into small chunks (no need to peel either one)
1 tablespoon coconut oil or ghee
1 medium onion, chopped
2 tablespoons barley or brown miso
2 cups seasonal greens, torn into small pieces
Port Madison goat cheese, crumbled

Combine beans, water, kombu, garlic, herbs, red chile peppers, bay leaf and vegetables, except onions, in a large soup pot. Bring to a boil, then reduce heat, partially cover and cook on low for one hour, or until beans are tender.

Heat a heavy skillet over medium heat. Add oil and onion. Reduce heat, cover and sweat onions until translucent. Remove cover, and cook onions until lightly browned. Stir onions into soup and continue to simmer until beans are done. Remove bay leaf. Puree 1 cup of soup from the pot with miso using a hand blender. Return to pot, add greens and cook until tender. Add more water if soup is too thick. Garnish with goat cheese.

Mushroom-Barley Soup with Merlot

(Serves 6)

Try this warming soup on a cool autumn evening. Bragg Liquid Aminos is soy-based flavoring that is bolder than tamari, but you can use tamari instead. Look for both in natural food stores.

6 cups mushroom stock (p.98, or use a commercial stock)
2 or 3 small potatoes, cut into small chunks
1 carrot, sliced
1 parsnip, sliced
1 stalk celery, sliced
1/2 cup hulled barley, rinsed
1/2 teaspoon pepper
2 tablespoons extra-virgin olive oil
1 large onion, chopped
4 cups sliced crimini mushrooms
2 tablespoons flour (whole-wheat, spelt or kamut)
1 cup plain soymilk or cream
3 tablespoons Bragg Liquid Aminos
1 cup Merlot
1 cup finely chopped parsley

Combine mushroom stock, potatoes, carrot, parsnip, celery, barley and pepper in a large soup pot. Bring to a boil, reduce heat, cover and simmer. Prepare the onions and mushrooms while soup cooks.

Heat a heavy skillet over medium heat. Add oil and onion, stir, reduce heat, cover and sweat the onions until they are transparent. Remove lid, add mushrooms, stir and cook until mushrooms are soft and onions are lightly browned. Sprinkle flour over mushrooms and onions. Stir until flour blends in and is completely coated with oil. Gradually blend in soymilk and stir until thickened. Add Bragg Liquid Aminos. Combine onion-mushroom mixture with soup stock. You can pour the soup into a crockpot with the wine and set on low for 8 hours, or cook it on the stovetop and for one hour, until barley is tender. Serve garnished with chopped parsley.

Creamy Potato-Vegetable Soup
(Serves 4)

This is a good way to use up leftover mashed potatoes. You can use a variety of seasonal vegetables. Add cheese, tofu chunks or tempeh near the end of cooking for a main course dinner soup, if desired.

2 cups mashed potatoes
4 to 5 cups water
2 tablespoons white miso
2 tablespoons extra-virgin olive oil or ghee
2 large red onions, chopped
Generous dash of cayenne or chipotle chile powder
2 cups seasonal vegetables, chunks of winter squash, diced carrots, celery, red peppers, corn, broccoli florets, peas or green soybeans
Paprika and parsley sprigs for garnish

Blend potatoes, water and miso until smooth and creamy in a blender or with a hand blender. *(Hint: it's easier to prepare if you do this 2 cups at a time in a blender.)*

Heat a heavy soup pot over medium heat. Add oil, onions and cayenne. Stir and cook until onions are soft, but not overcooked. Add 2 cups vegetables and potato-water-miso blend. Simmer gently over medium heat until vegetables are tender. Serve garnished with paprika and a parsley sprig.

Creamy soup tips
Adding cream or sour cream to soup is an easy way to make soup taste rich. However, you can make creamy soup without the saturated fat in a number of ways.

- ◆ Add 1/4 cup oatmeal to a soup like broccoli or carrot. Puree the soup when vegetables are cooked.
- ◆ Puree 1/2 cup leftover potatoes, sweet potatoes, beans (not black beans) or squash into a small amount of soup. You can also blend 1/2 cup cooked whole grains into 1 cup of the soup. Stir back into the soup pot and serve.
- ◆ Add 1/4 cup raw tahini, cashew butter or silken tofu into one cup of the soup and blend. Then add it to back to the pot and stir in.
- ◆ Simply remove one cup of the soup and puree it. Then stir it back in for a thick soup base.
- ◆ Blend 1 cup nonfat yogurt into the finished soup.

Satisfying Lighter Soups

Whether you want a light soup as the center of your meal or a soup to accompany other dishes, whole-grain and vegetable soups are perfect options. You can enjoy many of these soups when you want something less filling, but you can also create a more substantial soup by adding beans, root vegetables or puréeing a leftover baked potato or sweet potato into the pot for a hearty soup. For a sweet cool treat, make a fruit soup to serve on those hot summer days when spending more time in the kitchen is the last thing on your mind.

Spring Tonic Soup
(Serves 2 to 4)

Burdock root can be found in Asian markets and natural food stores. It is often used in detoxification formulas because it's a liver and kidney tonic and helps cleanse, purify and build the blood. It also supports digestion by eliminating toxins and mutagenic substances such as pesticide residues. After a season of heavier foods or when you aren't feeling well, this soup is an invigorating light meal.

> 1 burdock root, scrubbed and sliced into slivers
> 4 cups water
> 1 strip kombu, cut into tiny pieces
> 1 small carrot, diced
> 1 turnip, diced
> 1/4 cup sliced green onions
> 3 to 6 cloves garlic, pressed
> Generous pinch of cayenne
> 2 cups finely chopped kale
> 2 tablespoons light miso

Soak grated burdock root in acidulated, salted ice water for 20 minutes prior to making soup. Use 2 tablespoons lemon juice and 1 teaspoon salt with 2 cups water. This helps eliminate a bitter aftertaste. Drain and rinse.

Combine all ingredients except kale and miso in a saucepan, bring to a boil, then reduce heat and simmer for about 10 minutes. Add kale and continue to cook until burdock, carrots and turnips are done, but not overcooked. Remove from heat. Take a small amount of the soup out and puree with miso. Then, stir the miso puree back into the pot and serve.

Creamy Ginger-Pumpkin-Apple Soup
(Serves 4)

The easiest way to bake a sugar pumpkin or any other hard squash is to poke a number of holes in it with a fork and bake it whole on a baking sheet at about 350° for one hour. It should be soft inside. Remove the seeds and scoop out pumpkin to use in bread, soup or stew.

1 tablespoon extra-virgin olive oil
1 red onion, chopped
1/2 teaspoon cayenne
1 medium-size rutabaga, chopped
1 cup apple juice
2 to 3 cups water
2 cups cooked sugar pumpkin, skin removed
1 tablespoon grated ginger
1/2 cup silken tofu
Salt to taste
2 tablespoons lemon juice
1/4 cup cilantro

Heat a heavy soup pot over medium heat. Add oil, red onion and cayenne. Stir and cook until onion is soft. Add rutabaga, stir to coat, then add apple juice and water. Bring to a boil, cook for about 10 minutes or until rutabaga is soft. Add pumpkin. Squeeze juice from ginger into the mixture and discard ginger pulp. Cook for another 10 minutes. Puree two cups at a time in a blender with silken tofu. Return to pot, add salt to taste and gently heat. Add more water to thin to desired consistency. When soup is hot, remove from heat, stir in lemon juice and garnish with cilantro.

Spicy Tomato, Corn and Rice Soup
(Serves 6)

Roasted ground fennel and cayenne combine to make this a warming, hearty meal. Fresh corn off the cob is best, but use frozen if fresh corn is not in season. For milder tasting soup, leave out the cayenne.

1/2 tablespoon fennel seeds
1/2 tablespoon coconut oil or ghee
1 large onion, chopped
1/4 to 1/2 teaspoon cayenne
1 or 2 stalks celery, chopped
1 fennel bulb, chopped
1 or 2 carrots, thinly sliced
28-ounce can whole or crushed tomatoes
4 to 5 cups water
1 1/2 cups corn, fresh off the cob or frozen
2 1/2 cups cooked brown rice
2 to 3 tablespoons Bragg Liquid Aminos, or 2 tablespoons red miso
1 cup finely chopped parsley

Heat a griddle over medium heat. Toast fennel seeds, stirring constantly until toasted. Remove from heat and grind with a mortar and pestle or suribachi.

Heat a heavy soup pot over medium heat. Add oil, onion and cayenne and sauté until onion is transparent. Add celery, fennel and carrots and cook until soft, blending in a little water, if necessary. Stir toasted ground fennel seeds, tomatoes, water and corn. Simmer for about 15 minutes, stirring occasionally. Mix in cooked brown rice and Bragg Liquid Aminos, or if you prefer adding red miso, remove 1 cup of soup and blend miso in with a hand blender or fork until well blended, add back into the soup and cook on medium-low for 10 minutes. Garnish with parsley and serve.

Corn tips
- ♦ To remove corn kernels from the cob, place the cob in a shallow bowl to catch the corn kernels and hold the husked cob at a slant. With a sharp knife, slice the corn off the cob.
- ♦ Use the cobs to flavor soup stock or whole-grain cooking liquid. Cut them in half, add them to the boiling water and pour in grains. Remove when grains are done. Quinoa is excellent when cooked in corncob water.

No-Cream of Mushroom Soup

(Serves 6)

This soup makes an excellent base for casseroles, other soups and baked potato dishes. If you have the time, it's worth it to make your own mushroom soup rather than use the processed versions.

1/2 cup dried porcini mushrooms
4 cups boiling water
1 onion, finely chopped
1 tablespoon ghee or extra-virgin olive oil
2 to 4 cloves garlic, pressed or minced
1 tablespoon chopped Mama Lil's Peppers or 1/4 teaspoon crushed red peppers
5 crimini mushrooms, sliced
1 teaspoon basil or 2 tablespoons fresh basil
1 shelf-stable package silken tofu (soft or medium)
Salt to taste
1 tablespoon balsamic vinegar
1/2 to 1 cup finely chopped parsley

Soak porcini mushrooms in water for one hour. While mushrooms rehydrate, heat a soup pot or large saucepan over medium heat. Add onions and ghee or oil, stir and cook until onions are soft but not browned. Add garlic, Mama Lil's peppers and crimini mushrooms, stir and cook until mushrooms get soft. Blend in basil.

Strain mushroom water through cheesecloth. Stir 2 cups of the water into the mushrooms and onions.   Cook for about 5 minutes. Puree soup in a blender or food processor with silken tofu. Add porcini mushrooms and remaining mushroom water to thin. Stir in salt to taste and a tablespoon or more balsamic vinegar. Blend in finely chopped parsley before serving.

Sherried Wild Rice Soup

(Serves 4 to 6)

The sherry, combined with chipotle chile and coconut milk lends a decadent taste to this soup. This soup is perfect for special occasions, yet easy enough to make anytime. German Butterball potatoes are my favorite in this soup but you can also use yellow or red potatoes.

2 tablespoons melted coconut oil or ghee, divided
1 head garlic
1 large onion, chopped
1 1/2 cups sliced mushrooms (crimini, button, portabello, shiitake or a combination of mushrooms)
1 or 2 dry chipotle chile pods
1 or 2 potatoes, cut into very small chunks
1 carrot, medium dice (about 1 cup)
4 cups stock or water
1/2 cup dry wild rice
1 teaspoon dried rosemary, chopped
1/2 cup coconut milk (see tip p.109)
1/2 cup sherry
Juice of 1/2 lemon (2 or 3 tablespoons)
Salt to taste
Parsley for garnish
1/4 cup crumbled Port Madison goat cheese or feta (optional)

Set oven temperature to 350º. Cut off the top of the garlic. Drizzle 1 teaspoon coconut oil or ghee over garlic. Wrap in foil and roast for about 45 minutes, or until very soft. Let cool before squeezing out the garlic.

While garlic roasts, heat a soup pot over medium heat. Add remaining ghee and onion. Stir, then cover with a lid that fits directly over onions and sweat the onions until translucent. Remove cover, add mushrooms, stir and continue to cook until onions are lightly browned. Add chipotle chile pods, potato, carrot, stock, wild rice, rosemary, coconut milk and sherry. Bring to a boil, then reduce heat and simmer for 55 minutes or until wild rice is done. Remove from heat and stir in roasted garlic. Squeeze lemon over the soup and mix in. Remove chiles. Season to taste with salt, and garnish with parsley and cheese, if desired.

Summer Vegetable Soup with Kamut and Spelt

(Serves 6)

Precook the grains to make the soup quickly. To do this, bring 3/4 cup water to a boil in a small saucepan. Add kamut and spelt, reduce heat, cover tightly and simmer for at least one hour, or until grains are tender. The soup cooks in about 30 minutes. Stir in precooked grains at the end of cooking to heat them.

3 tablespoons coconut oil or ghee
1 habañero or jalapeño, seeded and diced
1 red pepper, seeded and chopped
1 large eggplant, ends removed and cut into small, 1/2-inch chunks
1 cup sliced zucchini or crookneck squash
4 cups stock, homemade (p.97) or processed
4 large ripe tomatoes, blanched (p. 161), skinned, seeded and roughly chopped
1 strip kombu, cut into small pieces
1/4 cup each: kamut and spelt
4 cloves garlic, pressed
1 leek, rinsed well and finely chopped
2 stalks celery, chopped
1 carrot, diced
1/4 cup white miso
1 bunch of Swiss chard or collard greens, washed, with leaves chopped and stems cut into thin slices
3 tablespoons fresh basil, chopped
1 tablespoon fresh marjoram
Juice of 1/2 lemon (about 2 to 3 tablespoons)

Heat a heavy soup pot over medium heat. Add oil, hot and red pepper, eggplant and zucchini. Stir and cook until soft, adding a bit of stock to keep vegetables from sticking to the bottom.

Add stock, tomatoes, kombu, kamut, spelt, garlic, leek, celery and carrot. Bring to a boil, then reduce heat, partially cover and simmer for one hour or until kamut and spelt are tender. Remove 1 cup of soup from the pot and purée with miso. Add miso-soup mixture, Swiss chard, basil and marjoram. Cook another 5 minutes or until Swiss chard is soft. Remove from heat. Stir in lemon juice before serving.

Cream of Celery and Autumn Root Soup

(Serves 6)

Nothing beats the taste of celery fresh from the farm. Stoney Plains is one farm that has exceptional celery. In late summer and autumn, you can also find celeriac, or celery root, and rutabagas. Peel, chop, then plunge celeriac into about 2 cups acidulated water (add a little lemon or vinegar). This soup goes well with **Corn Biscuits** *(p 23).*

2 tablespoons melted coconut oil or ghee
1 sweet onion, chopped
3 cloves elephant garlic, or 6 cloves regular garlic, peeled and sliced
1 jalapeño, seeded and minced
1 bunch celery, tops removed (save in the freezer for soup stock later) stalks cut into 1/2-inch pieces
5 cups water
1 cup chopped celeriac, peeled
1 parsley root, sliced (optional)
1 medium carrot, sliced
1 medium rutabaga, small dice
2 medium red potatoes, small dice
2 cups chopped kale
Salt to taste
1/2 cup sour cream or silken tofu
Juice of 1 lime (about 3 tablespoons)
1/2 cup chopped cilantro

Heat a heavy soup pot over medium heat. Add oil, onion, garlic and jalapeño. Stir to coat. Cover and sweat the onions until translucent but not browned. Stir in celery, continue to cook for a few minutes, then add water. Bring to a boil, then simmer for 20 minutes or until celery is very tender. Puree soup in a blender, 2 cups at a time until soup is smooth and creamy.

Add celeriac, parsley root, carrot, rutabaga, potato and kale. Bring to a boil, then reduce heat and simmer for 20 minutes or until vegetables are tender. Add salt. Remove from heat. Blend lime and sour cream and stir into the soup. Garnish with cilantro and serve.

Borscht

(Serves 4)

A version of this recipe first appeared in Vegetarian Journal in September 2000. Baked potato gives this traditional Eastern European soup a creamy base. Lemon juice lends a wonderful tangy flavor. If you make this recipe in the spring, you can find sweet, delectable baby beets to use.

1 tablespoon coconut or extra-virgin olive oil
1 large onion, chopped
5 cloves garlic, minced
2 stalks celery, chopped
1 or 2 carrots, diced
2 tablespoons tomato paste
5 cups water or vegetable stock (or half of each)
3 cups sliced beets, tops removed, not peeled
1/2 tablespoon fresh dill, or 1/2 teaspoon dried dill
Salt and pepper to taste
1 medium baked potato, skin removed
Juice and finely chopped zest from 1 lemon
1 to 2 tablespoons Rapadura
Sour cream, or plain yogurt (optional)
Parsley sprigs

Heat a heavy soup pot over a medium heat. Add oil and onion, cover with a lid that fits directly over and sweat onions until translucent. Remove lid, add garlic, celery and carrots and cook for 5 minutes, stirring often. Add tomato paste and mix well, continuing to cook for another minute or so.

Gradually add water or stock, beets and dill. Bring to a boil. Reduce to a simmer, then cover and cook for 20 minutes. Add salt and pepper to taste. Remove 1 cup of soup from the pot. Purée in potato, lemon juice and zest. Stir into soup along with Rapadura to taste. Adjust for salt and pepper. Serve with a dollop of sour cream or plain yogurt, if desired. Garnish each serving with a parsley sprig.

Eggplant and Flageolet Bean Soup
(Serves 6)

On lazy summer days, I make this soup first thing in the morning and let it simmer in a crockpot all day. Flageolet beans are tender, immature kidney beans that are often used in French and Italian cooking. You can find flageolet beans at specialty food stores such as DeLaurenti's at Pike Place Market.

2 tablespoons coconut oil or ghee
1 onion, chopped
1 red pepper, seeded and chopped
1 jalapeño, seeded and minced
2 medium eggplants, sliced and cut into bite size pieces
2 cloves garlic, minced or pressed
1 cup flageolet beans, soaked overnight
4 cups stock, or use half water and half stock
1/2 cup Riesling
2 carrots, sliced
1 tablespoon Rapadura
1 bunch Swiss chard, leaves removed from stems and chopped
1/2 cup chopped fresh basil
2 tablespoons balsamic vinegar
Salt to taste

Heat a heavy soup pot over medium heat. Add oil, onion and red and jalapeño peppers. Stir, reduce heat, cover and sweat vegetables for about 10 minutes. Remove lid, stir in eggplant and cook for about 10 more minutes. If the eggplant begins to stick, pour in a little stock and stir. Blend in garlic. After a few minutes, stir in flageolet beans, stock, Riesling, carrots and Rapadura. Bring to a boil, then reduce heat and simmer until beans are tender — about one hour.

Add chopped Swiss chard leaves, basil and balsamic vinegar. Continue to simmer until chard is done — about 8 more minutes. Salt to taste and serve.

"Creamy" Broccoli Soup
(Serves 6)

If you buy broccoli in season from a local farm, like Willie Green's (p. 245), you'll taste the sweetest broccoli you've ever eaten. Winter broccoli from California is another story. It usually has tough, fibrous bitter stems. Peel winter broccoli stems before slicing and using.

2 tablespoons coconut oil
1 onion, chopped
1 jalapeño, seeded and minced
4 cloves garlic, pressed
4 cups water
1 cup coconut milk
1/4 cup rolled oats
8 cups broccoli, stems sliced and florets separated
2 tablespoons raw tahini or cashew butter
1/4 cup light miso
1 corn tortilla, torn into very small pieces
Juice of 1 lemon (about 1/3 cup)
1/2 cup crumbled Port Madison goat cheese or grated, aged cheese such as Samish Bay Gouda

Heat a soup pot over medium heat. Reduce heat, add onion and jalapeño, cover and sweat for 5 minutes. Remove cover, stir in garlic and cook until onions are very soft. Add water, coconut milk, oats and broccoli stems. Bring to a boil, reduce heat and simmer for 12 to 15 minutes. Stems should be very tender. Let cool slightly, then puree, 2 or less cups at a time. *(Hint: Be careful when blending hot liquids since they can spurt out of a blender and burn you.)* Add tahini and miso to the last batch before returning it all to the soup pot.

Cut broccoli florets into small, bite-size pieces and add to the pot with the corn tortilla. Cook on medium heat until broccoli is tender, stirring frequently. This soup thickens as the corn tortilla melts away. Stir in lemon juice before serving. Garnish with cheese.

Garlic-Asparagus Soup
(Serves 4)

Nothing quite says spring is here like the first sight of asparagus at the market. Savor this soup as you savor the transience of the season. If you can't find Port Madison goat yogurt, use low fat plain yogurt and place a dollop on each serving.

1 tablespoon extra-virgin olive oil
1 medium onion, chopped
1 or 2 jalapeños, seeded and minced ,or 1 tablespoon chopped, Mama Lil's peppers
4 cups water
2 pounds asparagus, washed and cut into 2-inch lengths, tips reserved, discard the woody base
1 head garlic, cloves separated, peeled and sliced
1/4 cup oatmeal
1/4 cup white miso
1/4 cup peanut butter
3 medium potatoes, such as Yellow Finn or Yukon Gold, cut into small chunks
1 medium carrot, sliced
3 cups sliced mushrooms, crimini or portabello
2 to 4 tablespoons lemon juice
6-ounce container of Port Madison goat yogurt

Heat a heavy soup pot over a medium heat. Add oil, onions and jalapeños. Stir, cover and sweat the onions until they are soft and translucent. Add water, asparagus stems (reserve tips), garlic, oatmeal and 1 potato. Bring to a boil, then reduce heat and simmer for 15 minutes or until asparagus stems are very soft. Puree 1 or 2 cups at a time in a blender with peanut butter.

Return all but 1 cup of soup to the pot. Add remaining potatoes, carrot, mushrooms and asparagus tips. Simmer for about 15 minutes, stirring occasionally. Blend 1/4 cup miso into the cup of reserved soup. When all the vegetables are tender, remove from heat and stir in the miso mixture and lemon juice. Top each serving with a swirl of goat yogurt.

Asparagus and Lima Soup
(Serves 6)

This is another easy soup to prepare with asparagus while it's in season. You can use 1 1/2 cups canned or frozen lima beans and skip the soaking process. With canned lima beans, the soup will cook in about 20 minutes.

1/2 to 1 tablespoon extra-virgin olive oil or ghee
1 onion, chopped
5 cloves garlic, peeled and sliced
1 tablespoon chopped bottled, hot peppers such as Mama Lil's
3 cups water
1/2 cup dry lima beans, soaked
1/2 strip kombu, cut into small pieces
2 medium potatoes, cut into bite-size pieces
1 medium carrot, sliced
28-ounce can ground tomatoes
1/4 cup chopped fresh basil
Salt to taste
1 bunch asparagus, cut into 1-inch lengths, woody ends discarded

Heat a soup pot over medium heat. Add oil, onion, garlic and peppers, reduce heat, cover and sweat the onions and garlic for about 5 minutes. Add water, lima beans, kombu, potatoes and carrot. Bring to a boil, then reduce heat, partially cover and simmer for 45 minutes, or until lima beans are tender.

Stir in tomatoes, basil, salt and asparagus and continue cooking for another 10 minutes or until asparagus is fork-tender.

Asparagus tip
Freshly picked asparagus deteriorates rapidly. Choose firm, young, green asparagus shoots, and take care when storing asparagus. The longer it's stored, the more sugar is lost from the stalks. Keep asparagus upright in a little water in the refrigerator. Eat it as soon as possible. Don't eat asparagus with slimy tips. It's too far gone.

Smoky Corn Chowder

(Serves 6)

Chipotle chiles infuse this soup with a hot smoky flavor. Buy the best quality corn you can because frozen corn isn't as sweet as fresh corn. New potatoes have just been harvested and are sweet with very tender skins. Enjoy them while you can.

2 tablespoons extra-virgin olive oil or ghee
2 large sweet onions, chopped
2 cloves garlic, minced
1 red pepper, seeded and chopped
2 carrots, sliced
2 small zucchinis, sliced
3 medium new potatoes, cut into bite-size chunks
2 cups water
15-ounce can fire-roasted tomatoes
Corn from 3 ears of corn
4 or 5 dry chipotle chile pods, soaked in 1/2 cup hot water
3/4 cup milk (soy or dairy)
Salt to taste
1/2 to 1 cup grated, aged cheese, such as Samish Bay Cheese
Croutons (optional)

Heat a heavy soup pot over medium heat. Add oil, onions, garlic, and red pepper. Stir and cook until onions are lightly browned. Add carrots, zucchini and potatoes. Stir to coat, then add water, tomatoes, corn and chipotle chile pods in water. Bring to a boil, then reduce heat and simmer for 20 minutes or until all vegetables are tender. Add milk, and continue to cook on low for about 8 more minutes. Add salt to taste. Remove chiles and discard before serving. Garnish with cheese and croutons, if desired.

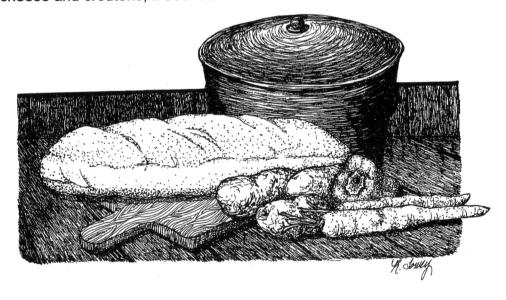

125

"Cream" of Seasonal Greens Soup
(Serves 4)

This is an all-season soup. In the summer, try it with Swiss chard. During autumn and winter, choose kale, collards or braising greens. (At markets and natural food stores this is a mixture of small to medium-size hardy greens that includes kale, collards, and broccoli de rabe.) In the spring, make nettles soup.

1 tablespoon coconut oil
1 large onion, chopped
1/4 to 1/2 teaspoon crushed red chile pepper flakes
4 to 5 stalks of celery, chopped
1 head of garlic, cloves separated
4 cups stock, or half vegetable stock and half water
1 baked potato, skin removed
10 cups of seasonal greens
1/4 cup light miso
1/4 cup cashew butter
1 lemon, cut into wedges
6 ounces Port Madison goat yogurt or low fat yogurt (optional)

Heat a soup pot over medium heat. Add oil, onion and chile pepper flakes. Stir, reduce heat, cover and sweat onions until transparent. Add celery and press garlic cloves into the mixture. Stir and cook for a few minutes. Blend in 3 cups of stock.

Puree the potato into remaining cup of stock. Add it to the soup. Stir in seasonal greens and bring to a boil. Reduce heat and simmer until greens are tender. Puree soup, 2 cups at a time with the miso and cashew butter. Return to pot and heat gently for a few minutes. Serve with a twist of lemon and a dollop of yogurt, if desired.

Tortellini Florentine Soup

(Serves 6)

There are many kinds of tortellini that will work in this soup. Add a few tablespoons balsamic vinegar before serving for an exotic flavor dimension.

2 tablespoons extra-virgin olive or coconut oil
2 medium-large sweet onions, chopped
1/4 teaspoon crushed red chile pepper flakes
1 1/2 cups sliced crimini mushrooms
4 cups water
28-ounce can diced tomatoes
2 stalks celery, chopped
2 or 3 finely chopped carrots
3 cloves garlic, pressed
1/2 cup fresh, chopped basil
12-ounce package dry tortellini
1 bunch spinach (stems removed) rinsed and chopped or 4 cups baby spinach
Salt to taste

Heat a heavy soup pot over a medium heat. Add oil, onions, pepper flakes and mushrooms. Cover, reduce heat and sweat the onions until they are transparent and soft. Remove cover and continue to sauté onions and mushrooms for 5 minutes. Add water, tomatoes, celery, carrots and garlic. Bring to a boil. Add basil and tortellini. Simmer until done. Remove from heat. Stir in spinach. Cook until wilted. Add salt to taste and serve.

Mushroom tips and tidbits

♦ Mushrooms contain glutamic acid, which enhances flavors and makes soup or sauce savory.

♦ Choose mushrooms that are firm and have an earthy, fresh smell. They should never be slimy. The gills shouldn't look matted or damp. Select intact mushrooms rather than broken ones.

♦ Use mushrooms soon after purchasing. Store in a closed paper bag or a perforated plastic bag for up to 6 days in your refrigerator. They need air circulation, so don't crowd them.

♦ Rinse mushrooms quickly under running water, or wipe them off with a damp cloth. To clean wild mushrooms, brush or wipe dirt off before using them.

♦ Remove stems from shiitake or portabello mushrooms before cooking. Shiitake stems can be used for stock. Portabello stems can be cut up and used in various dishes. All others can be cooked with the stems intact. Remove the gills on portabellos with a spoon because the gills can become soggy and bleed a dark liquid over other ingredients.

Fresh Tomato Soup
(Serves 6)

Fresh vine-ripened tomatoes from Eastern Washington are what everyone waits for at the market. The desert heat contributes to their sweetness. Greenhouse raised tomatoes aren't the same.

6 medium, ripe tomatoes (about 2 1/2 pounds, 4 cups chopped)
2 tablespoons coconut oil
1 sweet onion, finely chopped
1 habañero or jalapeño pepper, seeded and minced
3 cloves garlic, pressed
1 1/2 cups finely chopped fresh fennel, or celery
1 carrot, diced
1 teaspoon Rapadura
1 1/2 to 2 cups stock, or water
1/4 cup salsa (use your favorite brand)
1/2 cup cream or pureed silken tofu
2 cups finely chopped arugula
Salt to taste
Port Madison goat cheese, Parmesan, or croutons for garnish

Bring a large pot of water to a boil. To remove the tomato skin, blanch the tomatoes by first cutting a cone shape from the top of each tomato and remove the stem core. Then, plunge tomatoes gently, two or three at a time, into boiling water and let them cook for about 10 seconds. The skin will start peeling back. Very ripe tomatoes will take less time than firm tomatoes. Remove from the pot with a large slotted spoon and plunge them into a bowl of cold water to stop the cooking process. When cool, slip the tomato skins off, squeeze the seeds out, then slice in half and roughly chop. Set aside.

Heat a heavy soup pot over medium heat. Add oil, onions and garlic. Stir, reduce heat and cook for 5 minutes or until onions are soft. Blend in fennel, carrots and Rapadura. Stir to coat fennel and carrots with oil. Add chopped tomatoes and cook for 15 minutes. Pour stock in and simmer, stirring occasionally for another 15 minutes. Add cream and arugula, stirring until barely wilted. Add more stock, if necessary. Season with salt to taste. Garnish with cheese or croutons. Serve with crisp corn tortillas.

Cool and Spicy Fruit Soup
(Serves 6 to 8)

A dairy-free version of this soup first appeared in Vegetarian Journal, July 2000. This soup is great for a first course, and it's just the ticket for cooling off on hot summer days. If you're adventurous and like spice, leave the jalapeño whole before pureeing.

2 cups of any one: pitted plums, peaches, nectarines or apricots (about 1 1/2 pounds)
1 jalapeño, seeded and minced
Juice and finely chopped zest of 1 lemon or lime
1 cup silken tofu
4 cups fruit juice, peach or apricot
1 cup chopped apricots, nectarines or halved cherries
Port Madison goat yogurt (optional)
1/4 cup chopped cilantro

Place 2 cups sliced fruit, jalapeño, lemon or lime juice and zest and silken tofu in a blender and puree until smooth and creamy. Add fruit juice and puree. Chill for 30 minutes or until ready to serve. Mix in chopped fruit. Add a swirl of Port Madison yogurt. Garnish with cilantro before serving.

Sweet and Savory Yeast Breads

There's nothing like kneading bread dough for releasing tension. Pushing and folding in a rhythmic motion, setting the loaf to rise, shaping and finally baking the loaf – this is one of the simple, sensual pleasures of life. When the aroma of freshly baked bread wafts throughout the house, it's heavenly. For people who are new to breadmaking, most of the recipes that follow are made with part unbleached white flour for easier handling. Once you have the technique down and your confidence up, incorporate more whole-grain flour into the dough until you can successfully create a good whole-grain bread.

The basics: yeast bread steps and tips

♦ Buy flour in small amounts or grind your own flour. Use whole-grain flour within a few weeks or store it in the freezer for a few months.

♦ Never use more than 2 teaspoons yeast for a bread recipe. Don't use yeast that is over a year old because it is not as effective. Yeast is alive and is activated by warm water. Dissolve yeast by sprinkling it over warm water (about 105° to 115°). Use a thermometer or a touch test with your finger. If the water is warm but not hot, it should be about right. Stir the yeast in or let it sink into the water.

♦ Add the sweetener right after you put the yeast in water or add it with the flour. Combining sugar with the water will make the yeast work faster. If you do this, watch it carefully. After the yeast begins to bubble up, add the flour and stir.

♦ Don't take the amount of flour in a recipe literally. For a more accurate measure and consistent bread quality, commercial bakers weigh flour to make bread. You can become more confident in bread making skills if you make small quantities (one loaf at a time) and pay attention to the texture of the dough when you add flour. I usually add 1 cup of flour in a recipe and stir well, then gradually add the rest of the flour as needed.

♦ For one loaf of bread, use about 2 1/2 cups of flour (a little less if using whole-wheat flour) for each cup of liquid in your recipe. Mix in the first cup and keep stirring until your arms begin to tire (about 200 strokes). Basic breadmaking always follows the same order of mixing ingredients.

♦ Kneading is tricky when using all whole-wheat flour. It's easier to stir the dough with a wooden spoon because all whole-wheat flour makes the dough very sticky. Don't add too much flour or the bread will have a dry texture. If you're an inexperienced breadmaker, try using kamut flour instead of whole-wheat because it's easier to work with.

- Stirring the dough develops the gluten so bread can rise. Stir for as long as you can, about 200 strokes, then poke and mash with a wooden spoon if using all whole-wheat flour. Ultimately, you're aiming for a smooth and satiny texture. If you add too much flour (the most common beginner's mistake), the bread will be too dry.
- Kneading bread means turning the dough out onto a dry or lightly floured board and turning the far side toward you with a rhythmic, folding motion. Push the dough in a rolling motion each time you turn it. If you oil your hands slightly, kneading is easier. You can add all the oil in this way. If the dough shows creases while you fold, stop adding flour; too much has been added. Knead a few tablespoons of water in if the dough becomes too dry. This takes patience and practice. Aim for a satiny smooth texture. Kneading and rising is often repeated in bread recipes for a lighter loaf.
- Oil a large clean bowl before placing the dough in to rise. The dough will be easier to remove from an oiled bowl.
- Set the bowl with dough to rise in a warm place in your kitchen. Cover with a damp towel or an oiled piece of plastic wrap. Paint olive oil on the plastic wrap to prevent it from sticking to the dough. The ideal temperature for rising is 80°, but bread rises at 75° or even 65°. A slow rise in a cool room over night can develop layers of flavors not present in bread that rises quickly. Use the poke test to determine whether the dough has finished rising. Poke a finger into the dough. If the indentation fills in quickly, the dough needs more rising time. If the indentation remains, the dough is finished rising. It should rise until nearly doubled in bulk.
- Shape dough into a loaf, roll into sticks or rolls, or stretch and flatten it to make focaccia and let it rise again. It will double in bulk again. A second rise takes about half to three-quarters as long as the first rise.
- Slashing or cutting the loaf before baking allows steam to escape. This isn't necessary when putting a loaf in a pan, but when making a peasant loaf on a baking sheet, it may tear at the base if you don't slash it.
- Bake bread until it is slightly browned on top and bottom. Most peasant loaves take 45 to 55 minutes, rolls about 25 minutes and flatbread 15 to 20 minutes. If unsure whether bread is done, remove from the oven and pan. Thump the bottom of the loaf with your fingers. It will sound hollow if it's done. If you aren't sure, return loaf to the oven for another few minutes, remove and thump again.
- Leave bread on cooling rack for 20 minutes after removing from oven. Bread warm from the oven is doughy. It doesn't slice well, but you can still slice and eat it if you like. One unbreakable bread rule is "Eat your mistakes while still warm."

More tips

♦ You can rescue dough that is over-risen. If you forget about your rising dough and it collapses when you poke a finger into it, you let it rise too long. It is still salvageable. Simply gather it up, knead it and give it one more rise. Following this plan, you should still have fairly good bread. Even if you are at the last stage and the loaf is formed and falls, knead it again, and let it rise once more. If you don't, the loaf will have a texture like a brick when baked.

♦ Incorporating nuts, whole grains or fruit into the dough is a fun experiment. One-half cup of cooked whole grains, for example, can be kneaded in. Nuts, seeds, sliced olives and dried fruit are common additions that you can work in during the last kneading. You can also add fresh fruit if the moisture content isn't too high. Apples and pears are perfect for this. Dice the fruit into small pieces. As you knead it in, you will notice the dough becomes wet in places near the fruit. Incorporate a little more flour at this point, and your bread will turn out just fine.

♦ Using applesauce or another fruit puree for part of the liquid ingredients is another idea. Sweet ingredients like these give the loaf a slightly sweet taste. The bread seems to stay fresh longer, too. Whatever your choice for the liquid measurement, make sure it's warm before activating the yeast in it.

♦ Pureed vegetables such as squash, potato, and even roasted red peppers can be used as a starting base in the liquid measurement. When you add pureed vegetables, the bread turns out moist and stays fresh longer.

Basic Bread
(One loaf)

This is an easy beginner's recipe. During the second kneading, you can add about 1/2 cup chopped toasted nuts, dried fruit or olives to the loaf for variation. Experienced bread bakers can use all whole-grain flour (wheat, spelt or kamut) in any recipe.

1 cup warm water (about 105°)
2 teaspoons yeast
1 tablespoon honey, agave nectar, maple syrup or Rapadura
3/4 teaspoon salt
1 tablespoon coconut oil or melted butter
1 1/4 cups whole-wheat, kamut or spelt flour
1 1/4 cups unbleached white flour (approximate measure)
Topping:
2 tablespoons melted butter or coconut oil
1 tablespoon maple syrup

Sprinkle yeast over warm water. Let yeast soften for about 5 minutes. Add sweetener, letting the mixture bubble up. Then, mix in salt and oil. Blend in whole-wheat flour, stirring vigorously, about 150 to 200 strokes, and scraping the sides of the bowl as you mix. Gradually add 1 cup of the unbleached flour. Keep mixing until the sides of the dough pulls away from the bowl. Turn out onto a lightly floured board. Knead until the dough feels smooth and elastic.

Place kneaded dough into a clean, oiled bowl. Cover with a piece of oiled plastic wrap or a wet towel and set aside to rise in a warm place for 1 1/2 hours or until doubled in bulk. While bread rises, combine melted butter with maple syrup for topping. Set aside.

When dough has risen, punch dough down and scrape it out onto a lightly floured counter. Knead again, adding the rest of the flour, if needed. When done, let the dough rest for 5 minutes before forming into loaf. Shape into a loaf. Oil an 8X4–inch pan with oil or butter, and place the loaf in the pan. Let it rise a second time, about one hour. Preheat oven to 400°. Brush top with butter or coconut oil and maple syrup mixture. Bake for 10 minutes, then reduce oven temperature to 325°. Bake for 45 minutes or until golden brown. Remove from oven, let loaf sit in baking pan 5 minutes before removing to cooling rack. Run a knife around the edges of the pan, and invert loaf to a cooling rack. Cool before slicing.

Acorn Squash Bread

(One loaf)

Winter squash adds a taste of sweetness to this bread. You can also use yam or pumpkin puree in this recipe.

1 cup baked acorn or butternut squash
1 cup hot water
2 tablespoons barley malt, maple syrup or molasses
2 teaspoons yeast
1 cup whole-wheat, spelt or kamut flour
1/2 teaspoon salt
1 tablespoon butter or coconut oil
1 1/2 cups unbleached white flour

Puree squash, hot water and sweetener together with a hand blender. Let it cool to warm (about 105°) before sprinkling the yeast over the top. The squash and yeast mixture should sit for about 10 minutes or until it becomes foamy on top from the yeast action. Add all of the whole-wheat flour to squash-yeast mixture and stir for about 100 strokes. Place in a clean oiled bowl, and cover with an oiled piece of plastic wrap. Let dough rise in a warm place for about 1 1/2 hours. You can let it rise in a very cool room overnight (55° to 60°).

Punch dough down, stir again and blending in salt and butter. Add unbleached flour, about 1/2 cup at a time, stirring well after each addition. The dough should begin pulling away from the sides of the bowl before you turn it out onto a lightly floured board. Oil your hands to prevent the dough from sticking as you knead the dough. Knead until smooth yet still slightly tacky. It is the tackiness of the dough that will give your bread a moist, honeycombed, soft texture.

Line a baking sheet with parchment paper. Alternatively, you can oil the baking sheet and dust it with cornmeal. Form the dough into a round peasant loaf and set it on the prepared baking sheet. Cover dough with plastic wrap and let rise again until almost doubled in bulk. Remove plastic and press dough with one finger. If the rise is finished, dough will rebound very slowly from the indentation.

Preheat oven to 450°. Make a diagonal cut with a very sharp knife across the top of the loaf about 1/2-inch deep. Bake for 10 minutes, then lower the temperature to 350° and bake for 35 minutes. Remove loaf from oven. Thump loaf. If it is not done, it will have a dense sound. Return to oven without the baking sheet and bake for a few more minutes until loaf sounds hollow when thumped. For a rich dark crust, brush top with melted butter. Cool before slicing.

Baked Bean Bread

(One loaf)

Next time you have leftover baked beans, try making this savory bread recipe. Beans add moisture as well as fiber, and this bread stays moist and tender for a few days. Chopped toasted pecans make an interesting texture variation in this bread. Add 1/3 cup pecans during the final kneading, if you like.

1 cup baked beans
1 cup hot water
1 1/2 tablespoons molasses
2 teaspoons yeast
1 tablespoon butter or coconut oil
1/2 teaspoon salt
1 cup whole-wheat, kamut or spelt flour
1 1/2 cups unbleached white flour
Topping:
2 tablespoons butter or coconut oil
1 tablespoon maple syrup

Puree beans, hot water and molasses in a blender or with a hand blender until smooth and creamy. When mixture cools to a little hotter than lukewarm, add yeast. Let mixture sit until yeast begins to work — about 5 minutes. Add butter and salt, then mix in whole-wheat flour. Stir vigorously — about 100 strokes, scraping the sides of the bowl often. Add about 1/2 cup of unbleached flour and stir again. Cover bowl with a piece of oiled plastic wrap and place in warm place to rise for one hour or until dough is doubled in bulk. Punch down, stir again, adding more flour about 1/3 cup at a time, until dough begins to pull away from sides of the bowl. Dough will be slightly sticky to the touch.

Turn dough out onto a floured counter or board and knead until smooth, adding flour as needed. Form into a round loaf and place on a parchment lined baking sheet. Place oiled plastic wrap over bread, and set bread to rise in a warm place for about 45 minutes. Preheat oven to 400°. Combine ghee and maple syrup, blending until smooth and creamy.

When dough has risen, slice on the diagonal about 1/2-inch deep all the way across the top of the loaf. Brush maple syrup and ghee on bread, and place in the oven. Bake for 10 minutes. Reduce oven temperature to 350° and bake for 40 minutes. When done, remove from pan and test loaf by thumping on the bottom and listening for a hollow sound. Return to oven without pan, if necessary, for a few more minutes. Cool before slicing.

Blueberry Loaf

(One loaf)

Breads and pastries are always good with the addition of fresh seasonal fruit.

Bread:
1/2 cup hot water
1/2 cup cold vanilla soy or rice milk
2 teaspoons yeast
2 tablespoons honey or fruit sweetener
1 cup whole-wheat flour
1 1/2 cups unbleached white flour
1/2 teaspoon salt
2 tablespoons butter or coconut oil

Filling:
1 1/4 cups fresh blueberries
2 tablespoons fruit sweetener
1 tablespoon arrowroot
1/2 tablespoon lemon juice

Glaze:
1/4 cup orange juice
3 tablespoons Rapadura

Dissolve yeast in warm water and soymilk. When the yeast begins to foam up, add fruit sweetener and mix well. Combine yeast mixture with whole-wheat flour. Stir 100 to 150 strokes. Add salt, butter and 1 cup unbleached flour. Stir 100 strokes, scraping sides of the bowl frequently and adding more flour to make the dough stiff. The dough should begin to pull away from the sides of the bowl. Tip out onto a floured counter and knead until dough is smooth.

Place dough in a clean, lightly oiled bowl. Cover with lightly oiled plastic wrap. Let rise for 1 to 1 1/2 hours. Combine blueberries, fruit sweetener and arrowroot in a saucepan. Mix well. Heat slowly, stirring constantly. Cook 5 minutes. When mixture begins to thicken, stir in lemon juice. Remove from heat and let cool.

When the dough has doubled in bulk, punch it down and turn out onto a lightly floured counter. Knead for 5 minutes. Let it rest for 5 minutes. Pat or roll out to an 8X12-rectangle. Spread cooled blueberry filling to within one inch of the edges. Carefully roll like a jellyroll, starting from the long end. Seal edges and ends by pinching with a little water. Gently roll dough back and forth for a smooth loaf. Transfer to a parchment lined baking sheet. Cover with oiled plastic wrap and let rise for 45 minutes, or until doubled in bulk.

Preheat oven to 350º. When dough has risen, cut three 1-inch slits on the diagonal to let steam escape while baking. Bake 30 to 35 minutes. Whisk orange juice and sugar together to make a glaze. When bread is light golden brown, remove from oven and brush with glaze. Return to oven for 5 to 10 minutes, until deep golden brown and shiny.

Focaccia
(One 14-inch focaccia)

This is a great soup accompaniment. You can also add toppings to make focaccia pizza – a meal by itself. Traditionally made with olive oil, this recipe uses ghee (clarified butter) or coconut oil because high heat alters and damages extra-virgin olive oil.

1 cup warm water (about 105°)
2 teaspoons yeast
1 tablespoon honey, Rapadura or agave nectar
1/2 teaspoon salt
1 tablespoon melted butter or coconut oil
1 1/4 cups whole-wheat, spelt or kamut flour
1 1/4 cups unbleached white flour
Topping:
2 tablespoons melted ghee (clarified butter)
3 or 4 cloves garlic, peeled and sliced
1/2 tablespoon chopped rosemary

Pour warm water into a medium-size mixing bowl. Sprinkle yeast over the top. Let it soften for about 5 minutes. Add honey, let the mixture bubble up, then mix in salt and ghee. Blend in whole-wheat flour and stir vigorously for about 150 strokes, scraping the sides of the bowl as you mix. Gradually add 1 cup of unbleached flour. When dough pulls away from the sides of the bowl, tip out onto a lightly floured counter. Knead until dough feels smooth.

Place in a clean, lightly oiled bowl, cover with a lightly oiled plastic wrap or a wet towel and set aside to rise in a warm place for one hour or until doubled in bulk. While bread rises, combine the garlic and ghee for topping and set aside.

When dough is finished rising, punch down the dough and scrape it onto a lightly floured counter. Oil your hands and knead again, adding the rest of the flour, if needed. Let dough rest for about 5 minutes. Pat into a 14-inch circle. Oil pizza pan and sprinkle with cornmeal. Place the round of dough on the pan. Cover with an oiled piece of plastic wrap again and set aside to rise for about 45 minutes.

Preheat oven to 400°. When dough has finished rising, remove wrap. With the tips of your fingers, poke the surface of the dough until it is covered with indentations about 1/2 inch apart. Brush the garlic infused ghee over the surface of the focaccia. Sprinkle crumbled rosemary over the top. Bake for 20 minutes or until golden brown on top and bottom. Serve with extra-virgin olive oil for dipping.

Variations:

Garlic and Sundried Tomato Focaccia

Add 2 tablespoons chopped, sundried tomatoes to warm water before combining with yeast. Using a garlic press, squeeze 2 to 4 cloves garlic into the water and yeast mixture before mixing with flour.

Follow the directions for basic focaccia on p.137.

Kalamata Olive Focaccia

Add 1/4 to 1/2 cup chopped Kalamata olives during the first kneading.

Follow the directions for basic focaccia on p.137.

Cheese Focaccia

Add 1/4 to 1/2 cup Parmesan cheese to dough during the first kneading.

Follow directions for basic focaccia on p.137.

Pizza

1/2 cup pizza or pasta sauce
Approximately 1 1/2 cups sautéed vegetables (try onions, peppers, eggplant, garlic, mushrooms or summer squash)
8-ounce can pineapple chunks, drained
1/2 cup shredded cheese (optional)

Follow directions for basic focaccia. Remove from oven and let cool. Spread a thin layer of pizza sauce over the top of cooled focaccia. Add vegetables, pineapple and cheese. Place under broiler or in a conventional oven until topping is heated through – about 5 minutes.

Rosemary-Amaranth Flatbread with Roasted Red Peppers
(Four 11X3-inch flatbreads)
Try different toppings on this flatbread for variation, or simply bake the breads with a little grated cheese instead of a topping.

    1 cup plus 1/4 cup water
    1/3 cup amaranth
    1 teaspoon fresh rosemary, chopped
    2 teaspoons yeast
    1 tablespoon honey
    1/2 teaspoon salt
    1 tablespoon melted ghee or coconut oil
    1 1/2 cups kamut flour
    2 red pepppers
    1/2 cup sliced Kalamata olives
    1/2 cup grated aged Samish Bay Gouda

Combine 1 cup water with amaranth in a small saucepan. Bring to a boil, then reduce heat, cover and simmer for 30 minutes or until amaranth is soft. Place amaranth in a large bowl and add 1/4 cup water. Mix well. Sprinkle yeast over the top and gently fold amaranth over yeast. Make sure the yeast is blended in. Let mixture sit until the yeast bubbles up. Add honey, salt and melted ghee. Blend thoroughly. Add 1/2 cup kamut flour. Stir vigorously, scraping the bowl often. Cover and set aside in a warm place for 25 to 30 minutes.

Blend in remaining flour, 1/2 cup at a time, stirring after each addition. When dough pulls away from the bowl, turn out onto a floured board and knead 3 to 5 minutes. The dough should feel slightly sticky. Place dough in a clean, lightly oiled bowl. Cover with an oiled piece of plastic wrap and let it rise in a warm place for one hour or until doubled in bulk.

While bread rises, prepare peppers. Place peppers under the broiler and roast until the outside is charred and blackened. Remove and set in a saucepan, covering with a lid until cool. Peel the peppers and remove the seeds. Cut into strips and set aside.

When dough has finished rising, punch it down. Turn out onto a counter and knead about 5 turns. Set aside for 5 minutes. Preheat oven to 425°. Line a large baking sheet with parchment paper. Divide dough into 4 portions and roll each into a log. Pat or roll to an oval shape about 1/4 to 1/2-inch thick. The ovals should measure approximately 11X3 inches. Place on a baking sheet and top each with red pepper strips, olives and cheese. Bake for 15 to 17 minutes. Gently slide off parchment paper to a cooling rack.

Express Delivery from Pioneer Organics

Pioneer Organics produce delivery boxes are a guilty pleasure. In February, when local braising greens, winter squash, apples and potatoes are beginning to wear me down, a weekly delivered box of organic fruits and vegetables is just what the doctor ordered to boost my sagging seasonal spirits. Those home-delivered boxes can see me through until farmers markets open. Each week I find things like sweet honey tangerines, apples, snap peas, eggplant, baby spinach, green pepper and garlic. About fourteen selections are left in a box on my doorstep.

In 1997, after doing a stint on an organic farm and working in wholesale, Ronny Bell started Pioneer Organics. A New York native and an environmentalist at heart, Ronny started his weekly produce delivery business with only a few customers. He delivered boxes out of the back of his Subaru, gradually growing his business. By the spring of 2004, he was making approximately 2,300 weekly local deliveries, and he has also expanded to the Portland area.

Since its inception, Pioneer Organics has been committed to being an environmentally responsible company. They also offer Fair Trade organic coffee and tea. A number of the delivery vans run on natural gas, which burns 80 percent cleaner than regular gas. In addition to supporting alternative energy fuel, Pioneer recycles and reuses delivery boxes. In the office they use tree-free paper products and the carpet is made from recyled fiber. The company also donates to food banks on a weekly basis, and they contribute to schools, wellness fairs, environmental organizations and community groups. In 2002, Pioneer Organics was awarded the Mayor's Small Business Award for business excellence. That same year, Ronny hosted an open house with featured talks by Annie Schwartz from Blue Heron Farm and Andrew Stout from Full Circle Farm.

Pioneer supports a number of local farmers. "People don't know this, but sometimes I'll pay a few dollars more for an item like spinach when it's available locally," Ronny says. He uses local foods as much as possible. For example, when most natural food stores offer braising greens from Arizona in March, Ronny is able to find a local supply. During his wholesale days, he cultivated relationships with many farmers. Some of Ronny's close farm vendors include Frog's Song Farm, Full Circle Farm, Blue Heron Farm, Sunny Slope, the Alvarez Family Farm and Canales Produce. "Slowly and surely, we're getting better at this," Ronny says.

One of Ronny's biggest challenges is educating the average consumer about why they should eat organic foods. "Whatever brings a person to organics, I support that," Ronny says. Whether or not his customers realize it, they're supporting organic farmers and an environmentally responsible business, as well as helping the local economy. Weekly boxes are available year-round. For more information about Pioneer Organics, check out their website at www.pioneerorganics.com.

The Hidden Cost of Cheap Food

Scan newspaper ads and you can find deals on produce items every week Conventional agriculture's focus on high-yield crops and expansion into the world market gives us continual access to inexpensive food, but the real cost of cheap food isn't found on our grocery store receipts.

Soil, waterway and groundwater pollution, erosion of topsoil, the disappearance of plant diversity, farmworker pesticide exposure and other health costs are worldwide issues we end up paying for in one way or another. In 2003, The Seattle Times ran a story on banned pesticides saturating Cambodia and the health hazards now surfacing as farmers' pesticide use in developing countries grows. Corporate farms are more profitable in other countries where pesticide use isn't regulated and land and farm labor is dirt cheap. Agribusiness agriculture takes advantage of government subsidies and exchange rate swings. They can shift crops from country to country for the highest profits with the lowest cultivation cost.

When considering why organic produce from smaller, local organic farms is preferable compared to less expensive, conventional produce from a grocery store, think about the following issues:

♦ According to the EPA, 60 percent of herbicides, 90 percent of fungicides and 30 percent of insecticides are carcinogenic. According to the World Health Organization (WHO), farmers in developing countries spend three billion dollars a year on pesticides. Inexpensive produce in chain grocery stores is often grown in other countries.

♦ Organic farmers pull weeds or use weed flamers. Labor intensive organic crops can be more expensive to grow and sell, but worldwide cancer rates are on the rise, especially among conventional farm workers and their children who are more consistently exposed to toxic chemicals. Long-term health care becomes part of the bigger picture in the effort to keep the cost of food down.

♦ Wastefully applied synthetic fertilizers from large conventional farms end up in surface runoff in waterways. Nitrogen-rich fertilizers create algae blooms that kill off fish populations. Contaminants from the fertilizers can also leech into and pollute drinking water supplies in rural areas. As taxpayers, we pay for toxic cleanup of waterways. Some of this pollution could be prevented with solid, organic farming methods.

♦ Large agribusiness farms keep retail prices down by holding labor costs down. The minimum wage for farm workers in Washington State in 2004 was $7.01 an hour. Even if a worker is paid by a piece rate, the basis of pay for the week should be the equivalent to minimum wage. Other states and countries have different labor standards, many much lower than in Washington. When we pay a fair price for food, farmers and farm workers can make a living.

Vegetables, Dips And Spreads

A Fresh Vegetable for Every Taste

Profile: Nash Huber, Dungeness Organic Produce

Common and Uncommon Vegetable Side Dishes
> *Roasted Asparagus with Lemon-Garlic Sauce*
> *Orange-Ginger Asparagus*
> *Green Bean and Mushroom Casserole*
> *Roasted Rosemary Beets with Horseradish Sauce*
> *Orange Beet Puree*
> *Spicy Sesame Beets and Greens with Jasmine Rice*
> *Broccoli and Lemon-Saffron Rice*
> *Broccoli with Raspberry Coconut-Butter*
> *Caramelized Onions and Brussels Sprouts*
> *Lemon Brussels Sprouts with Red Onions*
> *Braised Cabbage with Honey-Mustard Sauce*
> *Red Cabbage with Apple and Red Wine Vinegar*
> *Carrots with Fennel and Pecans*
> *Sweet and Sour Carrots with Parsnips*
> *Spicy Corn-on-the-Cob*
> *Balsamic Corn-on-the-Cob*
> *Corn Pudding*
> *Breaded Baked Eggplant*
> *Eggplant Parmesan*
> *Sautéed Fennel, Orange Pepper and Mushrooms with Violets*
> *Lemon-Glazed Jerusalem Artichokes*
> *Simple Braised Kale*
> *Wine-Braised Okra with Basmati Rice*
> *Curried Parsnips*
> *Parsnip and Roasted Garlic Puree*
> *Sesame Peas and Leeks*
> *Peppers Stuffed with Quinoa and Corn*
> *Miso Mashed Potatoes*
> *Buckwheat Potato Balls*
> *Stuffed Potatoes Florentine*
> *Pesto Potatoes*
> *Maple Roasted Rutabagas*
> *Roasted Rutabaga Puree*
> *Curried Rutabaga*

Baked Winter Squash With Sundried Tomatoes
Squash and Potato Gratin with Porcini Mushrooms
Creamy Squash Puree
Squash with Buckwheat and Onions
Sweet Potato Sauté with Caramelized Onions and Red Peppers
Braised Turnips, Squash and Seasonal Greens
Mashed Turnips and Potatoes with Crispy Shallots
Zucchini and Tomatoes with Purslane
Seasonal Vegetable Medley

The Lighter Side of Dips and Spreads
Butternut Squash-Almond Spread
Tom's Guacamole
Spicy Seasonal Greens and Onion Puree
Roasted Eggplant and Pepper Dip
Red Lentil and Olive Spread
Pinto Bean Spread
Black Bean Dip
Pesto White Bean Spread
Spicy Squash and Channa Dal Spread
Red Bean Spread with Sundried Tomatoes
Tofu Patê

Saving Farmland
Skagitonians to Preserve Famland
PCC Farmland Fund

Changes and Choices in the Organic Market

THINK ABOUT IT

Organic farming has traditionally been geared to smaller, more diversified farms. Research has shown that when compared with conventional counterparts per acre over a number of years, smaller organic farms are the most productive farms. Organic farming with a localized focus is a widespread movement. As it gains public acceptance through sales at farmers markets, CSA subscription boxes and natural food stores, it may someday change the face of global farming practices.

Farm stand in Bow, Washington

Vegetables, Dips and Spreads

The Japanese Guidelines for Health Promotion recommend eating 30 or more different kinds of food a day. Without vegetables or fruit, this wouldn't be possible. A variety of vegetables should fill our lives every day.

As a child, I loved vegetables. I couldn't get enough green beans, sweet potatoes, peas, carrots, cabbage and corn. Mom's simple baked acorn squash was one of my favorite treats. In my early 20's, I created vegetable stews simmered in garlic-tomato sauce for my friends. Today, I shop a few farmers markets a week, bringing food home to share with my family and friends. I love getting the best tasting, organic fruit around and finding vegetables I haven't sampled before. Life is close to perfect when there is good food to eat.

In the Northwest, we're fortunate to have an abundant assortment of locally grown produce. During harvest season, visit markets and ask farmers about unfamiliar and heirloom varieties of vegetables. Heirloom usually refers to open-pollinated species that breed and produce plants true to type, year after year. The seed can be saved for the next season's crop. Choose one or two new or different vegetables each week to try. For additional ideas about unusual produce, check out *Vegetables from Amaranth to Zucchini,* by Elizabeth Schneider.

When looking to pair side dishes with entrées, consider the season and how hearty each dish is. Think about the flavors, colors and textures in

145

complimentary dishes. For example, a heavier gratin or casserole entrée would go well with wine-braised seasonal greens and cornbread. An easy bean dish can be served with **Squash with Buckwheat and Onions** (p.180). Balanced vegetarian cooking is the creative art of mix-and-match in any given meal.

A Fresh Vegetable for Every Taste

The most popular vegetable in America today is the potato, usually eaten as french fries. I'm sure if more people sampled produce from local sources, there would be a lot more vegetable enthusiasts. If you aren't exactly a convert yet, try one new vegetable each week. Learn everything you can about it – history, where it grows well, preparation techniques, what can be served with it. If you already appreciate vegetables, peruse the following descriptive list and gather some seeds of inspiration for your next meal.

Artichokes: A Mediterranean native, most of the artichokes found in stores today are grown in California. In the Northwest, they can be purchased from local growers at farmers markets. When selecting artichokes, look for tightly closed leaves, called bracts. Artichokes should be firm with good color. Store them wrapped in a damp paper towel in the vegetable crisper and cook within a few days. Pressure-cooking is the easiest way to prepare artichokes, since it only takes 15 minutes. Steamed on the stovetop, they cook in 50 to 60 minutes. When the artichokes are done, remove from pan and let cool slightly. They are usually served whole. Peel the warm individual leaves away and scrape off a tiny bite with your teeth at the end of the leaf. When you are nearly to the heart, you will see a mass of pale, fuzzy leaves. Pull them off and discard them. Underneath is the heart. This doesn't even need butter to be enjoyed.

Asparagus: You know spring is here when local asparagus is in stores and at farmers markets. An ancient plant, Phoenicians cultivated it in 200 B.C. There are still varieties that grow wild in many parts of the world, and many people prefer it to cultivated asparagus. In Europe, much of the asparagus grown and served in restaurants is white. This is green asparagus that is cultivated in the dark so pigment is not formed. When selecting asparagus, look for bunches that are displayed standing upright in a small amount of water. Choose firm, brittle spears that are tightly closed. If you are not using asparagus within a few days, store it the same way – upright in water in the refrigerator. A rubbery stalk is not a sign of a fresh vegetable. Often when you find asparagus at very low prices, the quality is poor. To prepare it, snap off the ends, discard them, then rinse the stalks. Asparagus can be steamed, stir-fried, roasted or even grilled. It also makes a nice addition to soups or casseroles.

146

Beans (snap): Though snap and dried beans are related, dried beans are heavy and protein rich. You'll find recipes for them in the entrée section. Considered vegetables, not legumes, snap beans are immature and the seeds are barely formed when we pick them. There are quite a few varieties at farmers markets, while grocery stores usually only offer one or two types. When selecting green beans, choose the smaller beans. They are usually more tender. The beans should be firm, have good color and no blemishes. When broken, the seeds inside will be small. Snap beans keep for a few days enclosed in a paper towel and stored in a plastic bag in the refrigerator. Cook them as soon as possible.

Beets: Cultivated for their leaves in prehistoric times, beets add color to your meal. Though you can always find the basic red beet at grocery stores, try farmers markets for cylindrical, albino, golden or Chiogga (candy-striped) beets. Choose beets with greens attached since this is a sign of freshness. The greens will be a deep color and the roots should be firm. The leaves should be cooked within a day or two. The roots will keep for weeks in the refrigerator, stored in a plastic perforated bag in the vegetable bin. The leaves can be sautéed, braised, added to stir-fries, casseroles or soups. The roots are good steamed, sliced and marinated. Try them roasted or grilled.

Bok choy: Also called Chinese cabbage, bok choy is a plant with flat white stalks and green leaves at the top. Used by the Chinese since the fifth century, bok choy is mild-tasting with a cabbage-like flavor. The stems are crisp like celery and the leaves are tender and mild. There are several varieties such as baby, dwarf, mature, Shanghai and Taiwan, and a Japanese variation called tatsoi. Use the stems in salads or stir-fries. The greens go well in salads or soups. Look for fresh undamaged leaves and stalks that are not split or damaged. Plan on using this versatile vegetable within a few days. The leaves wilt fairly quickly like beet greens. Store bok choy in the vegetable crisper in a perforated plastic bag.

Broccoli and broccoli Romanesco: Cultivated by the ancient Romans, broccoli was mostly grown in this country by Italian immigrants until the 1920's. Though you can purchase organic broccoli year-round, some varieties at the markets during the summer have a sweetness that commercial broccoli lacks. Broccoli Romanesco is a beautiful light green, cone-shaped, spiraling head that looks more like cauliflower than broccoli. It is sweet and can be eaten raw or lightly steamed. Pick broccoli that is firm, tightly closed and has a dark green color. If the stems seem tough, peel them before cutting into matchsticks or slices. Use the stems in casseroles or stir-fries or serve them raw with dip. Store broccoli in a perforated bag in the vegetable crisper. Use it within a few days.

Broccoli rabe (broccoli raab, rapini): Closely related to turnips, broccoli rabe or rapini was widely cultivated in California in the 1930's. It is a bitter, assertive green with a mustard-like bite to it. Broccoli rabe adds zest to bland food, casseroles and pilafs. You can make the flavor of it less intense by blanching it briefly in salted water before using it. Broccoli rabe is more perishable than it looks. Refrigerate it in a perforated plastic bag and use as soon as possible. Use the stalk, leaf and flower of the plant.

Brussels sprouts: No one knows if their origin is really Brussels, but Brussels sprouts were originally cultivated in Europe. The miniature cabbage heads are sweeter after the first freeze in autumn. A number of local farmers grow high quality Brussels sprouts well into December. When selecting Brussels sprouts, look for firm, compact heads. They are excellent steamed and tossed with Mama Lil's peppers, organic butter and lemon juice. When steaming, cut the larger ones in half and begin testing for doneness at 4 minutes. Stored Brussels sprouts deteriorate rapidly, losing their sweetness, so use them within a few days. Keep them on the stalk to store them. Cut a little off the base and set it in water in a cool place though it probably won't fit in your refrigerator. You can also store loose sprouts in a perforated bag in the vegetable crisper for a day or two.

Cabbage: Originating along the Northern European coastline, cabbage has been cultivated for about 4,000 years. Though green and red cabbage are the most familiar varieties, you can also find Savoy, Nappa and some Chinese varieties in many markets. Select compact heads that are heavy for their size. Some cabbages, such as Nappa, have looser leaves, but should feel crisp and have a nice light green color. Store cabbage in a perforated plastic bag in the refrigerator for about one week. Sliced cabbage is good in salads, lightly steamed or braised. If you want to make the red stand out when cooking red cabbage, add lemon or vinegar to the water.

Carrots: Cultivated as early as 500 B.C., carrots originated in Afghanistan. Originally purple, after decades of breeding the color of carrots was eventually changed to bright orange. Today you can find carrots in a number of colors at local markets – orange, yellow, red and white. Vibrant color and texture are the best indicators when selecting carrots. If the greens are attached it is a sign of freshness. Keep the greens to use in a stir-fry or to add to soup or stock. Most carrots found in grocery stores in cellophane bags have been stored for months and have lost their sweet flavor. Carrots keep for about a week, sometimes longer, in a perforated bag in your refrigerator. The smaller carrots can be steamed or roasted whole with a small part of the greens attached. Larger carrots can be sliced and sautéed in a little butter or coconut oil.

148

Cauliflower: Cultivated in the Mediterranean for more than 2,000 years, cauliflower is an evolved variety of broccoli and a member of the cabbage family. Cauliflower is grown primarily in Washington, California, Arizona, Colorado and Oregon. Look for solid compact heads with few blemishes. As it gets older, the head develops black spots, which are often cut off in grocery stores. Cauliflower can be cooked in the same ways as broccoli. It can also be pureed into soups or sauces. Refrigerate the head in a perforated plastic bag and store in the vegetable bin for one week.

Celeriac (celery root): There are three forms of celery available – stalk, root and leaf. Celeriac, the root, is a brown knobby vegetable with hairy roots hanging off. It has a concentrated celery taste with a potato-like texture and is quite popular in French cooking. Select small firm roots that are fairly round for easier peeling. Slice off the root end and peel with a sharp knife. Then cut it into slices or chunks and plunge it into lemon water to prevent discoloration. Often served grated, raw in mayonnaise-rich salads, celeriac can be steamed, boiled or braised. You can also mash it separately or with potatoes. Use it in casseroles, soups, or vegetable medleys with a sauce. For storage, trim the stalks, wrap in plastic and refrigerate for one week.

Celery: A member of the carrot family, stalk celery has been cultivated since the ancient Greek and Roman times. Commercial celery is usually a white variety, but when you shop farmers markets, you can find other types with a more pronounced green color and sweet flavor. My favorite celery is grown by Stoney Plains Organic Farm (p.84). If more good celery was available, I'm sure celery salad would still be popular today. Look for crisp, rigid stalks with few blemishes and fresh looking leaves on top. When celery gets soft and rubbery, use it to make soup stock. Celery usually plays a supporting rather than starring role and is good in stir-fries, soups and casseroles. Store celery in a perforated plastic bag in the refrigerator for about one week.

Collards: Collards are an ancient plant and one of the oldest cultivated forms of cabbage. A mild-tasting type of kale, collards are popular in Southern cooking. You can find them at farmers markets in the summer or in grocery stores year round. Collards are high in calcium and worth adding to dishes for nutritional value. Choose deep green leaves, and pass over collards with yellowish leaves; they are old. The smaller leaves are more tender and crisp with a sweet, mild taste. Tiny leaves are often added to braising mixes. Separate the leaves from the stems by sliding them off – hold by the stem with one hand and push the leaf off with the other. The stems can be finely chopped and sautéed. The leaves can be rolled-up in a chiffonade and sliced for steaming or braising or added to soups, stews and casseroles.

Corn: Originating in Mexico over 8,000 years ago, corn is available in many varieties. Some types of corn are ground into cornmeal. You can buy colored flint corn for a decoration in the fall. Popcorn is one of our great snacking foods. The best place to get good sweet corn is the farmers market during the summer. Picked that morning, fresh corn is always the sweetest. The husks should be green, and the cobs filled with firm looking kernels. When pressed, the kernels should spurt a bit of juice. Corn begins to lose sweetness as soon as it is picked, so cook it within a day or two. Store corn in the refrigerator.

Eggplant: Originally cultivated in India, eggplant was transported by Arab caravans to Europe in the 13th century. Like potatoes, tomatoes and peppers, eggplant is a member of the nightshade family. It is available year-round, but there are wonderful and unusual varieties at local markets in the summer. Billy Allstot (www.billysgardens.com) grows a variety of eggplants and sells them at the West Seattle and University District markets. Each type has a slightly different taste and texture. Eggplant is a natural in many entrées and sandwiches because it lends texture as well as flavor. You can bake, roast, grill, or sauté it. In the winter, eggplant transported in from long distances keeps miserably. Use it within a few days. Locally grown eggplant, purchased in season, will keep for about a week in the refrigerator.

Fennel: Cultivated since ancient Roman times, fennel is a parsley relative with a sweet licorice flavor. Fennel is quite popular in the Mediterranean region. It has a crisp texture similar to the crunch of celery. The best time for fennel is in the autumn. Look for firm, white bulbs with green feathery leaves. If the leaves are missing, the fennel may be old. Fennel enhances tomato-based dishes and can be used in almost any recipe that calls for celery. The bulb is often used in recipes, but use the thin stalks in soups and stews and the leaves for garnish. Fennel can be steamed, braised, sautéed or even grilled. Offer it raw, cut in wedges and served with dips. Store fennel in a plastic bag in the refrigerator for up to a week.

Garlic: A member of the lily family that includes onions, garlic has been used for centuries. Spanish roja, Korean red, elephant and California early are among the many kinds you might find at summer markets. Some varieties are mild and others quite hot. Garlic can become milder, sweeter or stronger according to how it is used. Whole roasted garlic and sliced sautéed cloves are remarkably sweet tasting. Pressed or minced raw garlic in sauces and salad dressings can be quite pungent. The mild large bulbs of elephant garlic are more closely related to leeks than garlic. Select firm dry heads. Avoid heads that have soft or black spots when pushed or with green sprouts growing out of the top. Fresh, unblemished garlic heads from autumn months can be stored in a cool, dry cupboard for four months or more. In the early spring, it can be stored for about a month.

Jerusalem artichokes (sunchokes): Native Americans along the East Coast cultivated these odd-shaped tubers long before the Pilgrims arrived. Even when they're in season, these humble earthy tubers aren't supermarket staples. The flavor is uniquely wild with a nutty taste. At their peak during the fall, look for firm, unblemished tubers and use them within a week. Store Jerusalem artichokes in a perforated paper or plastic bag in the refrigerator. Once cut, plunge them into acidulated water (with a little lemon or vinegar added). Then use them in your recipe. They are good roasted with other vegetables, steamed or sautéed with a little coconut oil.

Kale: An ancient relative of cabbage, kale is sometimes referred to as the king of vegetables because it contains so many nutrients. Kale has fiber, folic acid, potassium, vitamin C, K, beta-carotene and a good amount of calcium. Like parsnips, kale is at its peak during winter months, but you can get it year round in grocery stores. When selecting kale, look for crisp, brightly colored leaves. Limp or light-colored leaves might mean that it has been stored too long. If you find the taste of kale too bitter, try adding it to soups or stews, or braise it with caramelized onions, garlic and white wine. Add a squeeze of lemon and a pinch of salt and you've got an excellent side dish. Store kale in a perforated plastic bag in the refrigerator for a week.

Okra: Originating in Ethiopia, okra is most well known in the Southern United States where it is often found in gumbo. The gelatinous texture thickens gumbo and transforms tomato-based dishes. Okra season in the Northwest is mid-summer and it's fairly short. It goes well with tomatoes, peppers, fennel, garlic, sweet onions, corn and peas. Select small specimens, under 3-inches long. It should be crisp and fresh-looking with a uniform color. Okra needs to be super-fresh because it doesn't store well. Keep it for a few days in a perforated bag in the refrigerator. Don't ever purchase the canned variety, buy locally and you'll have more luck with good tasting okra.

Onions: Considered bulbs, not root vegetables, onion flavors are as diverse as the varieties. They can be sweet, pungent or hot with many shades in between. The family includes chives, green onions, leeks, shallots, sweet, red, pearl and storage onions. Always select firm specimens. The green on scallions and chives should be vibrant. Bulbs should be firm with no flaws. Keep green and fresh sweet onions in the refrigerator for about a week. Store dry (storage) onions in a cool dark place (not the refrigerator) away from potatoes. A paper bag in a cupboard is fine for storage. Avoid onions that are beginning to sprout. Like garlic, onions want to grow in the spring, and if they begin to sprout, remove the green sprouts before cooking. If onion fumes bother your eyes while cutting, slice the onion in half, place it in the freezer for 20 minutes and then cut it.

Parsnips: The Greeks and Romans enjoyed wild parsnips, and though it's been cultivated since ancient times, the popularity parsnips once had has declined today. A fair-skinned cousin to carrots, parsnips have an intense and complex flavor. They are best when harvested in the fall after the first frost. The cold weather intensifies their sweet, nutty flavor. Select medium-size, firm roots; larger parsnips have tough cores requiring longer cooking. Store them for up to ten days in a perforated plastic bag in the refrigerator. Steam or sauté parsnips or use them in soups or casseroles. They are also good pureed with a little butter, salt and pepper.

Peas: Though peas are an ancient vegetable, it wasn't until the 17th century that eating fresh peas became popular among the upper class French. When summer produce is at its peak, you can buy English shelling peas, sugar snap or snow peas. Like corn, peas begin to lose their sweetness soon after they are picked. Buying locally and using peas within a day or two is your best bet. Store them in an open plastic bag in the refrigerator.

Peppers: Originating as a New World crop, peppers are now incorporated into cuisines all over the world. There are hundreds of varieties, and as they cross-pollinate, new peppers are created. They range from sweet to very hot, and their colors can be red, green, yellow, orange or chocolate. Peak season is July through October. You can bake, roast, grill, sauté or steam them. Use peppers in salads, stir-fries and pureed in sauces, grilled on sandwiches or added to soups and stews. They store well in a perforated plastic bag in the refrigerator for about a week.

Potatoes: Another New World native, potatoes are popular all over the world. There are two types of potatoes: dry-textured, such as Russets, and thin-skinned, waxy potatoes like Yellow Finn or Yukon Gold. Russets are good for baking, make excellent mashed potatoes and potato salad. Thin-skinned potatoes hold their shape well, and they are great in salads, soups and casseroles. Select firm, unblemished potatoes. If dropped, they become damaged even if they don't show it, so use them soon. Organic potatoes can grow sprouts if you don't eat them within a week or two. The sprouts and green spots contain solanine, which can be toxic. Cut the sprouts out before cooking and never eat green potatoes. Keep potatoes in a cool, dark place (a cool cupboard) away from onions.

Purslane: A short slow-growing herb, purslane has lots of stems and small, lemon-flavored leaves. It grows wild throughout the United States. You can find cultivated and wild varieties at the markets. Often used in salads, it can also be sautéed. Blanching helps set the color and texture. When wild purslane is used, the stems turn a vibrant shade of pink after cooking. The delicate lemon flavor and crisp leaves make a good addition to simple dishes. Store it in the refrigerator in a perforated plastic bag for a few days.

Rutabaga: Developed in the 17th century, rutabagas were often thought of as a turnip hybrid. However, a rutabaga is a mutant, not a hybrid, since the rutabaga contains thirty-eight chromosomes while turnips contain twenty. Yellow-fleshed, the rutabaga is sweeter than the turnip. The season is October through March. Use them as you would turnips. Look for firm, unblemished specimens. Store them unwrapped in the refrigerator for one week.

Soybeans (edamame): Also known as sweet beans, you can find these tasty treats in Asian markets, natural foods stores and farmers markets. Look for bright green pods. At summer markets, some farmers sell them still attached to the branches of the bushes they grow on. Steam or boil the pods for 3 to 5 minutes and then drain. Place the steaming pods in a bowl and squeeze the small, creamy-textured beans out to eat. Alternatively, remove the beans from the cooked pods, and cook as directed in your recipe. Store edamame uncooked in the pods for a day or so in plastic bag in the refrigerator. Cooked edamame keeps for a week in the refrigerator.

Spinach: Cultivated in ancient times where Iran is today, spinach is a mild-tasting, versatile green that is good cooked or raw. Spinach can be found year-round, but is best during the summer months. Look for bright green, firm leaves. Avoid bunches with wilted, damaged or yellow leaves. Store spinach in a perforated plastic bag in your refrigerator vegetable bin for a few days. It takes little cooking, so add it last to whatever you are making. Spinach goes well in pasta and rice dishes, salads and stir-fries.

Squash: Native to the New World, there are many different kinds of squash because, like peppers, squash plants cross-pollinate, creating an endless variety of hybrids. Squash can be divided into two groups — summer and winter. Summer squash has a high water content. Most well known is zucchini, but patty pan, yellow crookneck and Sunburst, along with other varieties are available at markets. When selecting summer squash, look for firm, colorful specimens with no blemishes. Keep them in a perforated bag in the refrigerator and use within a few days. They can be grilled, braised, sautéed or added to other dishes. Winter squash has tougher skin with a colorful yellow to orange, creamy flesh. Select winter squash that is heavy for its size, firm and without soft spots or blemishes. Store it in a cool dry place, not touching other squash or vegetables, for up to five months. Squash can be steamed, boiled or baked. It can also be stuffed with whole grains, beans and vegetables or mashed and used in quick breads or muffins.

Sweet potatoes (and yams): Cultivated in Peru, South America and throughout the Pacific islands, sweet potatoes were a dietary staple by the time Columbus arrived in the West Indies. They belong to the morning glory family. They are not grown in the Northwest because they require eight to eleven months of very warm weather to mature. Sweet potatoes are generally divided into two groups — sweet potatoes and yams — so-called yams in grocery stores are actually varieties of sweet potatoes. True yams are a large, bland, starchy tuber from Africa and are similar to potatoes in texture. Sweet potatoes are dry-fleshed and not as sweet as yams. Yams have more vibrant color and higher water content than sweet potatoes. Look for firm specimens with no soft spots and use them within a few days. Store in a cool, dark cupboard for a few weeks.

Swiss chard: Related to beets, Swiss chard originated in the Mediterranean. Although cultivated in Switzerland, according to Elizabeth Schneider, there isn't any significant reason that it is called Swiss chard. During the summer months, white, red or rainbow chard is available. Chard should be bright-colored, crisp and with no yellow leaves or blemishes. It is mild-tasting and quick cooking, like spinach. Chard makes a good addition to soup, stew, risotto, and casseroles. It is good steamed or braised with onions and peppers. Store chard in a perforated plastic bag in the refrigerator for up to a week.

Tomatoes: A South American native, tomatoes are members of the nightshade family, along with potatoes, eggplant and peppers. There are three basic shapes of tomatoes — round tomato, plum or roma tomato and small cherry tomatoes. In addition to the common garden variety, there are older heirloom tomatoes, many with a unique, deep rich tomato taste. Brandywine, Yellow Pear, Yellow Plum, Stupice and Zebra are among some of unusual varieties of tomatoes available. Tomatoes should be heavy for their size and firm with no soft spots. Though they are more often enjoyed raw, tomatoes can be sautéed, baked or broiled. They can also be stuffed or added to casseroles, soups and stir-fries. Choose firm, unblemished tomatoes that have a slight give when you gently press them. Store them on a kitchen counter or in a fruit bowl until ready to use. Refrigeration drains them of flavor and changes the texture, but if tomatoes are very ripe, they should be refrigerated.

Turnips: With a low reputation, turnips actually have much to be admired. For one thing, they've been around since prehistoric times. They also grow in poor soil, store well and are inexpensive. Nutritional all-stars, turnips contain anti-carcinogenic phytonutrients. The taste is slightly pungent combined with an earthy, sweet flavor. Mash them with potatoes, puree them with other root vegetables, add them to soups, stews or casseroles or roast them with the rest of your vegetables for the week. Young, fresh turnips are excellent grated on fresh green salads. Buy firm, unblemished specimens with vibrant leaves. Store larger turnips in the refrigerator for about a week. Young turnips with greens keep for a few days. Use the greens first. You can cook them like beet greens.

Nash Huber
Dungeness Organic Produce

Nash Huber's farm is in the Sequim-Dungeness Valley on the Olympic Peninsula. With a long growing season and mild climate, this luxurious fertile farmland has one of the best growing environments in Western Washington. Nash Huber is one busy farmer. If you're lucky, you might catch up with him, but don't bet on it during harvest season on the Peninsula, which runs July through December.

On a warm spring day early in the season, I met Nash at the Port Angeles Farmers Market, one of the two markets where he sells produce and vegetable starts. His warmth and passion for growing organic produce is compelling. Nash talked to me about farming as he assisted customers with produce selections, giving them helpful tips. My gaze wandered to Nash's earthy shiitake mushrooms and vibrant Swiss chard. I knew both would go well with basmati rice and lightly toasted hazelnuts for dinner. Nash's attention was focused on a customer who wanted to buy leek starts. He gave her instructions for planting the starts, and talked about tomato varieties and which types grow best on the Peninsula. The market had a small-town feel to it; no one was in a big rush to get going. People strolled by and called Nash by name. Some stopped to chat, share recipes, or ask when his sweet carrots would be in. Nash has been selling his produce every week at this market since 1979.

No stranger to farming, Nash grew up on a farm in Illinois. "Back then we didn't call it organic, that's just how everyone farmed. Farms were about a hundred acres. We planted a variety and rotated crops. Cover crops were planted and compost was used." His relatives are still farming there, but farming has changed since Nash grew up. "There was a drought in '53. That drove a lot of farmers out. Then more farmers left. The farms are big there now; a few thousand acres is a farm."

I asked if farmers in the Midwest are doing well with so much acreage. Nash said, "You have to ask what their gross per acre is. Say you get 100 bushels of corn an acre and [conventionally grown] corn sells for $2.50 a bushel. You get $250 an acre. It costs more to grow it. I can get $4,000 an acre [growing a variety of organic vegetables]. There you have to farm so much more land just to break even. They're leveraged up to their ears." Nash says. Without government subsidies, they might not make it.

When he was a young man, Nash left his family's farm to get a degree in organic chemistry. He worked in that field for awhile and then came to the Dungeness Valley to start farming in 1968. His biggest challenge was getting land. "Land was all locked up, farmers owned it and they passed it on through their family," Nash said. Starting with one acre, he grew hay and did beekeeping. Eventually he acquired more land and by 1979 he was selling organic produce from the back of his '57 Ford flatbed truck at the Port Angeles farmers market. Today, he's got a newer truck and more produce to sell. Although access to land is still one of the biggest issues facing small farmers today, Nash now farms about 200 acres.

Nash has also become an expert on land use laws and issues. He said many of the farmers in the area are passing on their estates, and often heirs see more money to be made by dividing it up and selling it for development. "We've got out-of-town prices here — inflated prices." You can make more money initially, but what about the cost of utilities, transportation and schools, among other things. "I can generate $5,000 an acre a year, every year — forever," Nash says. When the hundred-acre farm near his went up for sale and was slated for development, Nash turned to PCC Natural Markets for help. If our productive farmland goes, we could lose a valuable source for organic produce for future generations. So, PCC and Nash worked together, and PCC set up PCC Farmland Fund to purchase organic farmland. The first farm they purchased with donations and low-interest local business loans was The Delta Farm, next to Nash's land. "The Farmland Fund really came through and saved me," Nash said.

Besides two farmers markets and his own farm stand, Nash sells his produce to seven PCC Natural Markets. Dungeness Organic Produce also has a CSA called "The Farm Share Program" — where local residents can sign up and pay in advance for a weekly box of Nash's best produce for twenty-five weeks. Check out Nash's website at www.nashsproduce.com. His produce is all about quality. "If people want cheap, I tell them Safeway is right down the road," he said, as if he instinctively knew that great locally grown organic taste brings customers back time after time.

Common and Uncommon Vegetable Side Dishes

Stepping out of our food comfort zones is an opportunity to include a wider variety of vegetables in our diets. If you don't know where to start, ask people who work in the produce section of a natural foods store or farmers at the market about different kinds of produce that are new to you. You can also check out books on vegetables at the library. Three interesting books worth taking a look at are A World of Vegetable Cookery *by Alex D. Hawkes,* The Victory Garden Cookbook *by Marian Morash and* The Fruit and Vegetable Stand: The Complete Guide to the Selection, Preparation and Nutrition of Fresh Produce *by Barry Ballister. An excellent local cookbook is* Winter Harvest Cookbook *by Lane Morgan, who shares information about preparing vegetables from our Northwest harvest throughout the winter.*

Roasted Asparagus with Lemon-Garlic Sauce
(Serves 4 to 6)

If your favorite deli has precooked roasted garlic, you can use about 8 whole cloves instead of roasting it yourself. Use virgin coconut oil and the flavor infuses the asparagus in a wonderful way. Try sprinkling a teaspoon of fresh lavender over the asparagus before serving.

> 1 head garlic
> 3 tablespoons melted coconut oil or ghee
> Juice of 1 lemon (about 1/3 cup)
> 1 tablespoon finely chopped lemon zest
> 1 tablespoon minced hot peppers such as Mama Lil's
> 1 teaspoon agave nectar or honey
> 1/2 teaspoon salt
> 2 pounds asparagus

Preheat oven to 350°. Cut off the top of the garlic, so cloves are exposed. Paint the head generously with some of the coconut oil. Wrap garlic in foil and bake for 45 minutes or until cloves are very soft. Remove from oven. Let cool for about 15 minutes before squeezing the soft garlic out and preparing the lemon-garlic sauce. Blend garlic with lemon juice and zest, hot peppers, agave nectar and salt.

Snap off the tough base of the asparagus stalks. Lay asparagus stalks in a shallow baking dish. Drizzle 1 tablespoon of oil over the asparagus. Stir to coat each stalk. Spoon half of the lemon-garlic sauce over the asparagus. Place in oven for 20 to 25 minutes, stirring occasionally. When asparagus is fork-tender remove from oven. Drizzle the remainder of the sauce over the asparagus. Serve warm or let cool and serve with a beautiful spring salad.

Orange-Ginger Asparagus
(Serves 4 to 6)

You can use this orange-ginger sauce for other vegetables like English peas, green beans, broccoli, carrots, Brussels sprout or beets.

4 cups asparagus, cut into 3-inch lengths, tough stems discarded
1/2 cup orange juice
1/4 cup plain or vanilla yogurt
1 tablespoon freshly grated ginger
1 teaspoon honey (optional)
Dash of cayenne
1 tablespoon arrowroot or cornstarch
Salt to taste
1 tablespoon finely chopped orange zest

Blanch the asparagus in a large pot of boiling water for about 3 minutes, then plunge it into ice cold water. The spears should be fork tender. Prepare sauce by combining orange juice and yogurt. Squeeze ginger juice into the mixture (discard the pulp) and blend in honey, cayenne and arrowroot. Heat sauce in a medium-size pan. When it begins to thicken, gently blend in the cooked asparagus. Stir gently until all spears are coated with the sauce. Season with salt to taste. Remove from heat. Garnish with orange zest.

Green Bean and Mushroom Casserole
(Serves 4)

*For the mushroom soup, make **No-Cream of Mushroom Soup** (p.116) or use a commercial non-dairy mushroom soup found in the natural foods section of the grocery store.*

2 tablespoons ghee or coconut oil
1 onion, chopped
1 jalapeño pepper, seeded and minced
1 1/2 cups sliced crimini, shiitake or button mushrooms
4 cloves garlic, minced
2 1/2 cups fresh green beans, cut into 2-inch lengths and blanched
1 cup "creamy" mushroom soup
1 cup toasted breadcrumbs
3/4 cup shredded sharp cheese, or chopped toasted walnuts

Heat a heavy skillet over medium heat. Add ghee, onion and jalapeño pepper. Stir and cook until onion and pepper are soft. Add mushrooms and garlic. Cook until mushrooms are tender, for about 5 minutes, stirring frequently. While vegetables cook, preheat oven to 350º. When vegetables are done, combine beans, vegetables, soup and breadcrumbs in the casserole dish. Mix well. Bake for 25 minutes. Top with cheese and run under the broiler.

Roasted Rosemary Beets with Horseradish Sauce

(Serves 6)

When beets are roasted, the sugar caramelizes making them even sweeter. Add Horseradish Sauce, and the sweet earthy taste is balanced with a perfect blend of flavors. As long as the beets are fresh, leave the skins on for this recipe.

Beets:
6 medium-large beets
2 tablespoons ghee or coconut oil
1/2 to 1 teaspoon dried rosemary, crushed
Dash of salt and pepper

Horseradish Sauce:
1/2 cup soft silken tofu
2 tablespoons lemon juice
1 teaspoon lemon zest, chopped
1/2 tablespoon Dijon mustard
1 teaspoon prepared horseradish
1 teaspoon Rapadura or honey
1 teaspoon extra-virgin olive oil

Preheat oven to 350º. Cut beets into small cubes and combine with ghee and rosemary, blending well. Place in the oven and bake for 35 to 45 minutes or until fork-tender. While beets roast, prepare Horseradish Sauce. Blend all ingredients for the Horseradish Sauce in a blender or with a hand blender until smooth and creamy. When beets are done, serve beets with a dollop of sauce on top.

Orange Beet Puree

(Serves 4)

A sweet side dish, this puree goes well with savory casseroles and steamed greens. This is also a good summer side dish for a picnic.

6 medium beets
Juice and zest of 1 orange
1/2 tablespoon lemon juice
1/4 cup raisins or currants
2 tablespoons toasted, chopped walnuts

Slice beets into 1/4–inch slices. Steam until tender — about 20 minutes. Zest the orange peel and finely chop. Juice orange. Combine orange juice and zest, lemon juice and cooked beets in a blender or food processor and puree until smooth. Mix in currants or raisins, garnish with walnuts and serve.

Spicy Sesame Beets and Greens with Jasmine Rice
(Serves 4)

Brown rice is preferable but if you use refined Jasmine rice, reduce the cooking time appropriately.

1 bunch of beets and greens
1 3/4 cups water
1 cup Jasmine rice, rinsed
Pinch of salt
1/2 tablespoon light sesame or extra-virgin olive oil
1 large onion, small dice or 1 cup chopped shallots
5 cloves garlic
1/4 cup water
2 tablespoons lemon juice
2 1/2 teaspoons tamari
1 teaspoon hot pepper dark sesame oil
2 tablespoons toasted crushed sesame seeds

Separate beets and greens, wash thoroughly. Slice beets about 1/4-inch thick and stems into 1/2-inch lengths. Cut leaves on the diagonal in about 1-inch lengths. Set aside.

In a medium saucepan, bring water to a boil. Add Jasmine rice and a pinch of salt. Bring to a second boil, then reduce heat, cover and cook on low for 45 minutes or until rice is done. If water is not absorbed after 50 minutes, remove lid and continue cooking. (*Hint: if using refined rice, reduce cooking time to about 15 minutes.*) When done, all water will be absorbed. Remove from heat. After 5 minutes, fluff with a fork.

About 15 minutes before rice is done, heat a heavy skillet over medium heat. Add oil and onions. Stir, reduce heat, cover and cook until onions are transparent. Add garlic, stir and continue to cook for another minute. Add sliced beets, stems and 1/4 cup water. Stir, cover and cook until beets are tender — 5 to 7 minutes.

In a small bowl, combine lemon juice, tamari and hot pepper sesame oil. When beets are nearly done, add greens and cook until wilted — about 3 minutes. When both beets and greens are done, blend in lemon-tamari mixture. Serve over hot Jasmine rice and top with toasted sesame seeds.

Broccoli and Lemon-Saffron Rice
(Serves 6 to 8)

Try this dish with baked marinated tofu cutlets or tempeh baked in barbecue sauce. Serve it with a salad that has contrasting colors like **Carrot and Raisin Salad** *(p. 64). Use the stems for another dish. Peel and cut them into matchsticks for dip or stir fry.*

1 3/4 cups water
1 cup basmati rice
2 pinches saffron threads
1 tablespoon finely chopped lemon zest
4 tablespoons lemon juice, divided equally
1/2 tablespoon honey or fruit sweetener
1/2 teaspoon salt
Generous pinch of cayenne
4 cups blanched broccoli florets (see tip below)
1/2 cup thinly sliced green onions
1/2 cup toasted cashews (optional)

Bring water to a boil. Add rice, saffron, lemon zest, 2 tablespoons lemon juice, honey, salt and cayenne. Stir once, bring to a second boil, then reduce heat, cover and simmer for 45 minutes. When rice is done, remove from heat and let sit 5 minutes. Then fluff with a fork, stir in remaining lemon juice and blanched broccoli. Stir in the green onions and garnish with toasted cashews.

Blanching tips

♦ Blanching is a technique used to soften a vegetable or to remove the skins of produce like tomatoes or peaches. Blanching also helps to set color, preserve nutrients and keep the tissues of the vegetable firm. To blanch vegetables, bring a large pot of water to a boil. Some cookbook directions add 1 teaspoon salt to the water, but it isn't absolutely necessary.

♦ For vegetables like broccoli or green beans, cut the vegetables into small, 1/2 to 1-inch pieces. For tomatoes or peaches cut an X on the bottom so the skins will peel off easily. Plunge produce into the water trying not to disturb the boil. How long to blanch is determined by the size, type and degree of ripeness of produce. To prepare broccoli, peel the stems and cut into one-inch lengths. Blanch stems before the tops, which cook more quickly. Blanch the stems for a minute or two, then add the tops. Blanch for one more minute. Vegetables should be fork tender, yet still firm with vibrant color. Whole kale or collard leaves take from 45 seconds to 3 minutes. More mature leaves take longer. Tomatoes and peaches take 30 to 45 seconds. To stop the cooking process, rinse with or plunge into cold water.

Broccoli with Raspberry Coconut-Butter
(Serves 4)

My favorite raspberry vinegar comes from Goebell Hill farm. I can get it at the Machias fruit stand when raspberries are in season. Rent's Due Ranch also sells a tasty raspberry vinegar. You can find it in some grocery stores.

1 1/2 pounds broccoli, peeled stalks cut into1/2-inch slices and florets cut into bite-size pieces
2 tablespoons coconut oil
1/4 cup finely chopped shallots
2 tablespoons raspberry vinegar
Salt and freshly ground pepper to taste

Blanch broccoli stalks in a large pot of boiling water for one minute. Add florets and cook for 1 minute more, or until broccoli turns bright green and is fork-tender. Remove from heat, drain and rinse with cold water to stop the cooking process.

Heat coconut oil in a heavy skillet over medium heat. Add shallots and cook until soft and lightly browned. Stir in raspberry vinegar. Then blend in broccoli. Add salt and pepper to taste.

Caramelized Onions and Brussels Sprouts
(Serves 4)

Although taking the leaves off the sprouts for this recipe takes time, the result is well worth the effort.

1 tablespoon extra-virgin olive oil
1 large onion, sliced
1 pound fresh Brussels sprouts
2 cloves garlic, pressed
1/4 cup stock or water
Pinch of cayenne
Salt to taste

Heat a heavy skillet over medium heat. Add the oil and onion, stir, cover and reduce heat to low. Sweat the onion until it turns translucent. Remove lid and continue to cook onions. When the onions are caramelized, add garlic, stir and cook for 1 minute.

While onions cook, cut the small ends off of the Brussels sprouts and discard. Rinse, then peel off the leaves. When you get to the small head in the center cut it in half. *(Hint: On a larger sprout, there are quite a few leaves. Use your best judgement about when to stop and cut the center in half.)* Set aside.

Add stock to the skillet with Brussels sprout leaves and heads. Cover and cook for 5 minutes or until leaves are tender. Add pinch of cayenne and salt to taste.

Lemon Brussels Sprouts with Red Onions

(Serves 4)

Nash Huber from Dungeness Organic Produce grows some of the sweetest Brussels sprouts I've ever tasted. Though they are sold at PCC Natural Markets, you can find some just as sweet in local winter vegetable CSA boxes (p. 279).

1 pound Brussels sprouts
2 tablespoons coconut oil or ghee
1 medium red onion, chopped
1/4 to 1/2 teaspoon crushed red pepper flakes
1 teaspoon honey or agave nectar
1/2 tablespoon chopped fresh lemon zest
Juice of 1 lemon (about 1/3 cup)
Salt to taste

Cut the Brussels sprouts in half and steam until tender — about 5 minutes. Remove from heat and set aside when done.

Meanwhile, melt coconut oil in a heavy skillet over medium heat. Add onion and pepper flakes, stir and cook until onion is tender. Blend in honey and lemon zest. Combine onions with Brussels sprouts. Mix in lemon juice and add salt to taste.

Braised Cabbage with Honey-Mustard Sauce

(Serves 4)

When I was young, I feasted on steamed cabbage with hot mustard and honey. This is a slightly richer version, but if you want to leave out the fat, steam the cabbage instead of braising it, and add garlic and hot peppers to the honey-mustard sauce.

2 tablespoons extra-virgin olive oil
4 cloves garlic, minced
1 tablespoon chopped hot peppers, such as Mama Lil's
4 cups shredded cabbage
1/4 cup water
1/4 cup spicy Dijon mustard
1/4 cup honey
Salt and freshly ground pepper to taste

Heat a heavy skillet over medium heat. Add oil, garlic and peppers. Stir and cook for about 1 minute. Add cabbage and stir. Add water, cover and cook on low for 5 minutes or until cabbage is soft. While cabbage cooks, blend mustard and honey together. When cabbage is done, mix honey-mustard sauce with the cabbage in a serving bowl. Add salt and pepper to taste.

Red Cabbage with Apple and Red Wine Vinegar

(Serves 6)

I once sampled the best sweet-and-sour cabbage at a vegetarian potluck I hosted. This is my recreation of that heavenly dish.

1 medium tart or sweet-tart apple, peeled and core removed
2 tablespoons lemon juice
2 tablespoons ghee or extra-virgin olive oil
1 large onion, chopped
1 jalapeño, seeded and minced
2 cloves garlic, pressed
3 cups finely shredded red cabbage
1/4 cup red wine vinegar
1/4 cup Rapadura
1/4 cup water
Salt to taste

Grate the apple, toss with lemon juice and set aside. Heat a heavy skillet over medium heat. Add ghee, onion and jalapeño. Stir, reduce heat, cover and sweat onions and pepper until soft. Remove lid, add garlic and stir and cook for a few more minutes. Add shredded apple, cabbage, vinegar, Rapadura and water. Cover and cook on medium-low heat until done — about 10 to 15 minutes. Add salt to taste.

FOOD FOR THOUGHT

The cabbage, or cruciferous, family is one of the most nutritious vegetable groups. Vegetables in this family are high in calcium and magnesium and also contain phytonutrients that are protective against respiratory, colorectal, breast and stomach cancers. They are also high in vitamin C and A. There is something for everyone in the cruciferous family. It includes arugula, bok choy, broccoli, Brussels sprouts, cabbage, cauliflower, collard greens, Daikon, horseradish, kale, kohlrabi, mustard greens, rutabaga, tatsoi, turnip and watercress. For more information about the healing properties of cruciferous vegetables check out *Healing with Whole Foods: Oriental Traditions and Modern Nutrition* by Paul Pitchford.

Carrots with Fennel and Pecans

(Serves 4)

This is a quick side dish that can easily impress company. To toast fennel, heat a skillet over medium heat, then add fennel and toast until fragrant. Use a spice grinder or mortar and pestle to crush the fennel seeds.

2 cups carrots, thinly sliced
1/4 cup water
1 teaspoon toasted, ground fennel
2 tablespoons maple syrup
1 tablespoon cold water
1 tablespoon arrowroot
Dash of salt and freshly ground pepper
2 tablespoons lightly toasted, chopped pecans

Steam or blanch carrots until tender-crisp. Reserve 1/4 cup water or use fresh water. Combine fennel, maple syrup, I tablespoon cold water and arrowroot. Mix in with carrots and water. Gently heat, stirring until mixture thickens and carrots are fork-tender. Transfer to a serving bowl. Add salt and pepper to taste. Garnish with pecans.

Sweet and Sour Carrots with Parsnips

(Serves 4)

Sweet and succulent, carrots and earthy-flavored parsnips naturally go together. This recipe makes a sweet-tart side dish. Always use the best virgin coconut oil (p.viii) because the difference in taste can be pronounced.

3 1/2 cups sliced carrots
1 to 2 tablespoons coconut oil or ghee
1/2 cup finely chopped red onions
1 cup diced parsnips
2 tablespoons red wine vinegar
2 tablespoons maple syrup
Salt and freshly ground pepper to taste

Steam carrots until tender-crisp. Remove from heat and set aside. Heat a heavy skillet over medium heat. Add oil, red onions and parsnips. Stir and cook until onions and parsnips are soft and slightly browned. Add red wine vinegar and maple syrup, and stir to coat vegetables. Mix in carrots. Continue to cook until carrots are heated through. Season to taste with salt and pepper.

Spicy Corn-on-the-Cob

(Serves 4)

Cook corn as soon as possible or the taste becomes bland rather than sweet.

4 ears corn
2 tablespoons coconut oil or butter
1 teaspoon chili powder
1/8 teaspoon each: salt and chipotle chile powder

Steam for 4 to 7 minutes, depending on the size and age of the corn. While corn cooks, blend oil, chili, salt and chipotle powder. Mix well. Brush on freshly cooked corn.

Variation:

Balsamic Corn-on-the Cob

4 ears corn
1 tablespoon extra-virgin olive oil or melted coconut oil
1 tablespoon balsamic vinegar
1 teaspoon mayonnaise or garlic aïoli spread
1 clove garlic, pressed
Dash of salt and cayenne

Follow the directions above.

Corn Pudding

(Serves 4)

The addition of an egg and cheese creates a thick texture and deep flavor.

2 tablespoons ghee or coconut oil
1/2 cup finely chopped onion
1/4 cup diced green pepper
2 garlic cloves, minced or pressed
1 tablespoon barley flour or whole-wheat pastry flour
2 to 4 tablespoons salsa
1 cup soymilk
4 cups of corn, scraped off the cob
1 egg, beaten
1 cup grated sharp Samish Bay cheese

Preheat oven to 325°. Use an ovenproof skillet with a lid (cast iron works well). Heat the skillet over medium heat. Add ghee, onion, green pepper and garlic. Stir and cook for 5 minutes on medium-low heat. Add flour and stir to coat all vegetables. Stir in salsa. Remove from heat and blend in milk. Stir corn with onion-salsa mixture, beaten egg and half the cheese. Cover and place in oven and bake for 45 minutes. During the last 5 minutes of baking, remove cover and top with remaining cheese.

Breaded Baked Eggplant

(Serves 4 to 6)

The season for eggplant is short — late summer through early fall — so get eggplant while it's fresh! For the breading, use Mori Nu tofu in the shelf-stable box. You can make your own breadcrumbs with dry bread ground in a food processor. If you purchase them, buy the kind without partially hydrogenated fat added. There is no need to salt fresh eggplant before baking.

3/4 cup silken tofu
1/4 cup soymilk
3/4 cup toasted breadcrumbs
1 teaspoon dried oregano
1 teaspoon dried basil
1/2 teaspoon freshly ground pepper
1/2 teaspoon salt
1 large eggplant
2 to 4 tablespoons melted coconut oil or ghee

Preheat oven to 350°. With a hand blender, combine tofu and soymilk. Blend to the same thickness as beaten eggs. It should still be thick enough to act as a coating to hold the breadcrumbs onto the eggplant. In another bowl, combine breadcrumbs, oregano, basil, pepper and salt.

Slice eggplant into 1/2-inch slices. With a fork, dip each slice into the tofu mixture and then into seasoned breadcrumbs, patting the crumbs into both sides on each slice. Lay eggplant flat on a lightly oiled baking sheet. Drizzle melted coconut oil over the slices of eggplant. Bake for 15 minutes, then flip eggplant slices over, drizzle with more coconut oil and bake for another 15 minutes with the opposite side up. Serve as a side dish or transform it into an entrée by following the variation below. Serve with whole-grain pasta or crusty Italian bread.

Variation:

Eggplant Parmesan
Approximately 1 cup Parmesan cheese
1 1/2 cups pasta sauce

Follow recipe above. Sprinkle baked eggplant with Parmesan cheese. Run it under the broiler to melt the cheese. Heat pasta sauce over medium heat. Remove eggplant slices from oven, transfer to serving dish and top with pasta sauce.

Sautéed Fennel, Shallots, Orange Pepper and Mushrooms with Violets

(Serves 4)

*A perfect autumn vegetable dish, this goes well with **Fire-Roasted Tomato Bread Pudding** (p.204). Or, use it to top basmati rice and sprinkle with toasted pine nuts for garnish.*

2 tablespoons coconut oil or ghee
1 fennel bulb with leaves, washed, trimmed and thinly sliced
1 cup chopped shallots
1 tablespoon chopped hot peppers such as Mama Lil's
1 portabello mushroom, gills and stem removed and thinly sliced
1 orange pepper, seeded and cut into slivers
1/4 cup cream sherry
1/2 cup plain yogurt
1 teaspoon agave nectar
2 tablespoons lemon juice
Salt to taste
Violets for garnish (optional)

Heat oil in a heavy skillet over medium heat. Add fennel slices, shallots, Mama Lil's peppers, mushroom slices and orange pepper. Stir and cook until fennel and mushrooms begin to get soft and shallots begin to brown. Pull off about 1/4 cup of fennel leaves, mince and set aside. Add sherry to the shallots and mushrooms, stir and cook for about 5 to 7 minutes. Combine yogurt and agave nectar with lemon juice. When vegetables are fork-tender, stir in finely chopped fennel leaves and yogurt. Season with salt, garnish with violets and serve.

Lemon-Glazed Jerusalem Artichokes

(Serves 4)

My favorite recipe for cooking Jerusalem artichokes is inspired from recipes in
The Victory Garden Cookbook.

 3 cups thinly sliced Jerusalem artichokes (1 pound)
 1/4 cup lemon juice, divided (1 lemon)
 2 tablespoons ghee or coconut oil
 Pinch of cayenne
 1 tablespoon finely chopped lemon zest
 1/2 tablespoon Rapadura
 Salt to taste

Plunge the artichokes into about 3 cups water with 2 tablespoons lemon juice.
Heat ghee and cayenne in a skillet over medium heat. Drain chokes and add
them to the skillet. Stir and cook until they are soft and begin to brown. Combine
the remaining lemon juice with lemon zest and Rapadura. Mix in with chokes and
continue to cook for another few minutes. Season to taste with salt.

Simple Braised Kale

(Serves 4)

Braising is a cooking technique using a small amount of liquid in a covered pan.

 1 1/2 tablespoons extra-virgin olive or coconut oil
 1 large onion, chopped
 2 cloves garlic, pressed
 Dash of hot sauce such as Tobascco
 1 bunch kale (lacinato or red Russian kale)
 1/4 cup Riesling
 1/2 teaspoon salt
 2 tablespoons lemon juice

Heat a heavy skillet over medium heat. Add oil and onion, stir, cover and cook
on low until onions are soft. Remove lid and continue to cook until slightly
browned. Stir in garlic and hot sauce; cook a few minutes.

Strip kale from leaves with a knife or use your hand to push the leaves off the
stems. Roll in a chiffonade and thinly slice. Add to the skillet and stir in the wine.
Cover and braise until tender. Add salt and lemon juice before serving.

Wine-Braised Okra with Basmati Rice
(Serves 4)

Use the first okra of the season for this recipe. Tiny okra has a fantastic sweet taste and little of the sticky, slippery texture. The Alvarez Family Farm sells good okra at Columbia City Farmers Market on Wednesday afternoons. To precook rice: boil 1 cup of rice in 1 3/4 cup water with a dash of salt. Cover, lower heat and simmer for one hour.

1/2 cup finely chopped shallots or sweet onions
1 tablespoon ghee or extra-virgin olive oil
1 tablespoon chopped bottled, hot peppers such as Mama Lil's
1 pound whole baby okra, rinsed
1/2 cup red wine (Merlot is a good choice)
2 medium tomatoes, blanched, peeled, seeded and chopped
1 teaspoon maple syrup
Salt to taste
2 1/2 cups cooked basmati rice
1/2 cup grated aged Samish Bay Gouda (optional)

Heat a heavy skillet over medium heat. Add shallots, ghee and Mama Lil's peppers. Stir and cook until shallots are soft. Add okra, stir and cook for a minute or so before blending in red wine, tomatoes and maple syrup. Cover and cook for about 10 minutes. Add salt to taste. When okra is done, mix in cooked rice. Sprinkle 1/2 cup cheese over the top.

Curried Parsnips
(Serves 4)

You can alter the vegetables in this by adding carrots, sweet potatoes, or delicata squash for part of the parsnips. If you use squash, cut it into 1/2-inch slices. You can use your own curry blend, if desired.

1 pound parsnips, peeled and cut into 2-inch matchsticks
1 tablespoon melted ghee or coconut oil
2 teaspoons curry powder
1/8 teaspoon cayenne
1/2 teaspoon salt

Preheat oven to 350º. Place parsnips into a shallow baking dish and toss with ghee and curry powder, making sure curry powder is well distributed. Sprinkle with cayenne. Bake for about 45 minutes or until parsnips are soft and browned. Sprinkle with salt, stir and serve.

Parsnip and Roasted Garlic Puree
(Serves 6)

Instead of mashed potatoes, try this parsnip puree for a change of pace. If you like foods hot and spicy, add chopped Mama Lil's Peppers.

2 heads garlic
2 to 4 tablespoons melted coconut oil or butter, divided
2 pounds parsnips, cut into 1/2-inch lengths
1/3 cup soymilk
1/2 cup chopped chives or green onions
1/2 to1 tablespoon maple syrup
1 to 2 tablespoons lemon juice
Salt and pepper to taste

Preheat oven to 350º. Cut off the tops on the garlic bulbs, lay on tin foil and drizzle with a little melted coconut oil. Wrap tin foil around bulbs, place in oven and bake for about one hour or until garlic is tender. Remove from oven, let cool, then squeeze garlic into a small bowl.

Steam parsnips until very soft. Mash with remaining oil, garlic, soymilk, chives, maple syrup and lemon juice. Continue to mash until smooth and creamy. Add more lemon juice, if desired. Season with salt and pepper to taste.

Sesame Peas and Leeks
(Serve 4)

The delicate sweet flavor of peas is the essence of this simple dish. The leaves of leeks collect soil and grit, so clean them carefully. I usually rinse leeks after I cut them. To toast sesame seeds, see **Toasted Sea Palm and Sesame Seeds** *(p.62). If leeks are not available, use 1 cup minced shallots.*

1 tablespoon light sesame oil
1 leek, cut into thin slices
3 to 4 cloves garlic, minced
2 jalapeños, seeded and minced
1 large red pepper, seeded and diced
1/4 cup water
2 cups shelled peas
2 to 3 tablespoons lime juice (juice of 1 lime)
1/4 cup toasted, ground sesame seeds
Salt to taste

Sauté leeks in sesame oil until soft. Add garlic, jalapeños and red pepper. Stir and cook until peppers get soft, then add water and peas. Cook until peas are barely tender. Add lime juice, toasted ground sesame seeds and salt to taste.

Peppers Stuffed with Quinoa and Corn
(Serves 2)

To make peppers for 4, double everything in the recipe except the hot peppers and salt. Use the pepper tops for decorative effect when serving.

2 large red or green peppers, tops and seeds removed
1/2 cup onions, small dice
1 tablespoon coconut oil or ghee
1/2 tablespoon chopped hot peppers such as Mama Lils
1/4 cup lime juice
1 tablespoon frozen orange juice concentrate or 2 tablespoons orange juice
2 cloves garlic, pressed
1/2 teaspoon salt
1 1/2 cups cooked quinoa (p.291)
1/2 cup corn (fresh or frozen)
1/4 cup currants
1/2 cup shredded sharp cheese such as aged Samish Bay Gouda

Blanch peppers in a large pot of boiling water for 5 minutes. Rinse with cold water and set aside. Preheat oven to 350º. Heat a heavy skillet over medium heat. Add onions, oil and peppers. Stir and cook until lightly browned.

In a small bowl, combine lime and orange juice, garlic and salt. Combine quinoa and corn with onions. Heat gently. Blend lime-orange juice mixture in with quinoa and corn. Add currants. Remove from heat and scoop into peppers and top with cheese if desired. Place tops back on peppers and bake for 20 minutes, or until peppers and filling are heated through.

Miso Mashed Potatoes

(Serves 4)

Making good mashed potatoes without all the added fat can be a challenge. In this recipe, cashew butter, miso and soymilk create a creamy texture. Peeling the potatoes is an individual choice.

2 1/2 pounds peeled russet, red or white potatoes, cut-up
4 shallots, peeled and diced
1/4 cup plain soymilk or soymilk creamer
1/2 tablespoon lemon juice
2 tablespoons cashew butter
2 tablespoons white miso
Freshly ground pepper to taste

Steam the potatoes and shallots together in a large pot until fork-tender — about 10 minutes. When potatoes and shallots are soft, mash together with soymilk, lemon juice, cashew butter and miso, adding more soymilk, if necessary. Add freshly ground pepper to taste. Note: Do not use a food processor to blend.

Options:

♦ For everyday mashed potatoes, use yogurt or buttermilk instead of soymilk, and add butter instead of cashew butter. Omit miso; add salt to taste.

♦ Roast a head of garlic, squeeze the garlic into the potatoes and mash in.

♦ Add Mama Lil's peppers or a dash of chipotle chile powder instead of pepper.

♦ Add 2 tablespoons chopped sundried tomatoes. Use the tomatoes packed in oil or the dried variety. Soak dried tomatoes in a little hot water for at least 1/2 hour, then drain and add. Discard tomato water or use it for another dish.

♦ Mix in 1 or 2 teaspoons curry powder or your favorite curried spice blend for curried potatoes.

♦ For a little sweetness, mash in a cup of baked sweet potato or squash.

♦ Mash in one cup steamed parsley root, celeriac, or rutabaga. Top with freshly grated nutmeg.

♦ Mix in 1/2 teaspoon of sage or finely chopped fresh rosemary.

♦ Add 1/2 cup freshly chopped chives, parsley, basil or cilantro.

♦ Blend in 1/2 cup grated sharp cheese, such as Samish Bay Aged Gouda or use Port Madison Goat cheese. Stir in and let cheese melt into the texture.

Buckwheat-Potato Balls

(Makes about 25 balls)

Put leftover mashed potatoes to good use and prepare these stuffing-like little appetizers. They have a better texture when an egg is used, but tofu can be substituted with satisfactory results. To make soft breadcrumbs, use a fork to pull the bread apart into small pieces.

1/2 cup toasted buckwheat (kasha)
1 cup water
1 tablespoon coconut oil or ghee
1 small onion, small dice
2 stalks celery, finely chopped
2 teaspoons dried sage
1 head roasted garlic (p.171), cooled and pressed from the skin
2 cups mashed potatoes
2 tablespoons chopped hot peppers like Mama Lil's
1/2 teaspoon salt
3 cups soft breadcrumbs (day-old bread works best)
1 egg beaten, or 1/4 cup silken tofu
4 tablespoons melted coconut oil or butter

Bring water to a boil in small saucepan. Add buckwheat; bring to a boil. Cover, reduce heat to a simmer and cook for 15 minutes, or until water is absorbed and buckwheat is soft. If water has not all been absorbed, remove lid and continue to simmer.

Preheat oven to 350°. Line the bottom of a 9X13-inch pan with parchment paper.

Heat a heavy skillet over medium heat. Add oil and onion. Reduce heat; sweat the onions until they are transparent. Remove lid, add celery, stir and cook until onions are browned and celery is soft. Blend in sage.

In a medium to large mixing bowl, combine garlic, mashed potatoes, buckwheat, peppers and salt. Blend in breadcrumbs. Let mixture sit for 10 minutes. Mix in the beaten egg. If using tofu, remove 1/2 of the potato mixture and blend with tofu using a hand blender, then stir back into the buckwheat-potato mixture.

Use an ice cream scoop to form the balls. The mixture will be slightly sticky and hard to handle, but oiling your hands with a little oil prevents the potatoes and buckwheat from sticking to your hands. Form the potatoes into 1-inch balls, and place in the parchment-lined baking dish close together. When the potato balls are in the dish, drizzle with oil. Bake for 45 minutes or until lightly browned.

Stuffed Potatoes Florentine

(Serves 4)

These potatoes can also be used for a main dish. Try out your own creative fillings, but don't add too much liquid or the potatoes will be soupy when done.

2 large russet potatoes
2 tablespoons coconut oil or butter
1 cup chopped crimini mushrooms
6 cloves garlic, peeled and sliced
1 bunch spinach, washed and shredded
2 tablespoons tahini or cashew butter
2 tablespoons plain soymilk or buttermilk
Salt and pepper to taste
1/4 cup shredded sharp cheddar cheese or crumbled feta cheese

Preheat oven to 350°. Rub outside of potatoes with 1 tablespoon oil and pierce the skin with a fork. Bake in a shallow baking dish for one hour or until fork-tender.

Heat a skillet over medium heat. Add remaining oil, mushrooms and garlic. Stir and cook until mushrooms are soft. Mix in the spinach and stir until wilted. Remove from heat, drain off excess liquid and set aside. When potatoes are done, carefully scoop out the inside and place in a mixing bowl. The outside should remain intact. Add the tahini and soymilk to the potatoes and mash together until smooth. Mix in the mushrooms, spinach and garlic. Scoop the mixture back into the potato skins in the baking dish. Top with cheese, if desired. Bake for an additional 5 to 10 minutes or cook under the broiler for a few minutes.

Variation:

Pesto Potatoes

2 to 3 tablespoons pesto
Approximately 2 tablespoons soymilk, add more as needed
Salt to taste
Bottled, chopped hot peppers to taste
1/2 tablespoon ghee
1/2 medium onion, small dice
1/8 cup Parmesan cheese (optional)

Mash the potatoes with pesto and soymilk. Add peppers to taste. Set aside. Heat a heavy skillet over medium heat, add onion and cook for a few minutes. Mix in with the mashed potato mixture. Stuff back into shells, top with Parmesan cheese and bake.

Maple Roasted Rutabagas

(Serves 4)

Maple syrup tames rutabaga's assertive flavor and will quickly covert those who aren't already rutabaga fans.

> 2 pounds rutabagas
> 2 tablespoons coconut oil or ghee
> 2 tablespoons maple syrup
> 1 tablespoon orange juice
> Salt and pepper to taste

Preheat oven to 350º. Peel rutabagas and slice into 1/4-inch slices. Melt coconut oil and combine with maple syrup and orange juice. Lay rutabaga slices flat on a baking sheet. Use a pastry brush to baste with maple syrup-oil mixture. Bake approximately 45 minutes, turning halfway through. Baste frequently using all of the basting liquid. When slices are lightly browned, remove from oven and sprinkle with salt and freshly ground pepper to taste.

Variation:

Roasted Rutabaga Puree

This is a great alternative to mashed potatoes. With a sweet earthy flavor, Rutabagas are also loaded with nutrients that contain antioxidants and anti-cancer properties.

> Roasted rutabagas from recipe above
> Plain soymilk (1/3 cup or more)
> Freshly grated nutmeg to taste

Prepare recipe above. Let rutabagas cool for about 10 minutes. Add soymilk and puree until smooth and creamy. Place in a small casserole dish. Sprinkle with freshly grated nutmeg. Return to oven and bake for about 10 minutes or until heated through.

Curried Rutabaga

(Serves 4)

One of my favorite Indian restaurants used to serve delicious curried turnips. Trying to capture the flavor, I came up with this recipe using rutabagas. Garam masala is a sweet curry blend. Look for it in natural foods stores and ethnic markets.

1 pound rutabagas, cut-up into chunks (about 4 cups)
1 teaspoon garam masala
1 tablespoon Rapadura
Generous pinch of cayenne
2 tablespoons lemon juice
2 to 3 tablespoons coconut oil or butter
Salt to taste

Steam the rutabaga for about 10 minutes, or until very tender. Puree it with remaining ingredients.

FOOD FOR THOUGHT

Rutabagas and turnips are often thrown into the same category. To the novice produce shopper, the two can easily be confused because they are usually right next to each other in the produce department. Turnips have a light skin that is purple and white. Inside, the flesh is white. The taste is sharp and radish like. Rutabagas are sweeter than turnips. They have a purple skin that fades into yellow. In Chinese medicine, both are warming foods when cooked. Raw, they are also good digestive aids. Rutabagas and turnips help detoxify the liver. For an easy dish, sauté rutabagas or turnips in ghee or olive oil with garlic. Cook until slightly browned. Add salt and pepper. Just before serving, squeeze fresh lemon or lime over them.

Baked Winter Squash with Sundried Tomatoes

(Serves 4 to 6)

For a nondairy version, use 1 cup breadcrumbs and combine with 1 tablespoon coconut or extra-virgin olive oil. Brown breadcrumbs in oil in a heavy skillet. Sprinkle on during the last ten minutes of cooking. Stoney Plains Organic Farm (p.84) has the best elephant garlic around, but if it isn't in season use regular garlic.

8 to 10 sundried tomatoes
1/2 cup boiling water
2 tablespoons coconut oil or ghee
1 very large onion, sliced
2 cloves elephant garlic, sliced, or 1 head regular garlic, cloves separated and sliced
1 tablespoon, chopped hot peppers such as Mama Lil's
4 cups delicata squash — seeds removed and sliced into 1/2-inch slices (leave the skin on)
1 to 1 1/2 cups shredded sharp cheese

Pour boiling water over sundried tomatoes. Let sit for 10 to 20 minutes. Drain, reserving liquid, and cut tomatoes into quarters and set aside.

Heat a heavy skillet over medium heat. Add oil, onions and garlic. Stir, cover, reduce heat and sweat the onions and garlic for 10 minutes or until they are very tender. Remove lid, stir and continue to cook until onions are brown — about 15 minutes. Add the reserved tomato liquid and hot peppers.

Preheat oven to 325º. Oil a 1 1/2-quart casserole dish. Layer half the onions and garlic, sundried tomatoes, squash and cheese. Make a second layer, exactly the same as the first. Push vegetables down firmly into the dish. Bake covered, for one hour. Remove cover and continue to bake for 1/2 hour, adding a little water, if necessary. Topping should be nicely browned. If not, run it under the broiler for a few minutes.

Squash and Potato Gratin with Porcini Mushrooms

(Serves 4 to 6)

This is the perfect dish to take the chill away on a cool autumn evening. You can use it as an entrée and serve with braised greens and cornbread.

3/4 cup boiling water
1 ounce dry porcini mushrooms
1 onion, thinly sliced
2 stalks celery, diced
2 tablespoons ghee or coconut oil
2 cloves garlic, minced or pressed
1 tablespoon chopped hot peppers such as Mama Lils
1/2 cup Merlot
1/2 teaspoon salt
2 cups sliced delicata squash
2 cups thinly sliced potatoes
1 1/2 cups shredded aged Samish Bay cheese

Pour boiling water over the mushrooms and let them soften for 30 minutes. Preheat oven to 350º. In a heavy skillet, sauté onion and celery in ghee until soft. Add garlic and hot peppers and cook for a few more minutes. Stir in softened mushrooms with liquid and stir in Merlot. In a 1 1/2-quart casserole dish, layer onion mixture, potatoes and cheese, ending with cheese. Cover and bake one hour. Remove cover and continue baking for 1/2 hour.

Creamy Squash Puree

(Serves 4)

This sweet side dish is a good way to use up leftover squash.

2 1/2 cups baked winter squash (any variety)
Juice of 1 orange (about 1/3 cup)
1 tablespoon lemon juice
3 tablespoons vanilla or pecan amazake
1 teaspoon grated ginger
1/4 teaspoon salt
1/4 cup toasted, finely chopped walnuts

Blend all ingredients, except walnuts, with a hand blender. Add more amazake if desired. Bake at 350º in an oiled small baking dish for 30 minutes. Alternatively, you can heat it gently in a small pan on the stovetop. Top with walnuts and serve.

Squash with Buckwheat and Onions
(Serves 6)

Squash teams up with caramelized onions to tame the assertiveness of buckwheat in this tasty dish. Use sweet potatoes or yams to substitute for winter squash, if you like.

1 tablespoon extra-virgin olive oil
1 large sweet onion, chopped
5 cloves garlic, sliced
1 cup toasted buckwheat (kasha)
1 3/4 cups boiling stock or water
1/2 teaspoon nutmeg
1 medium delicata squash, seeded and cut into bite-size pieces
1/4 teaspoon salt
1/4 teaspoon freshly ground pepper or cayenne
1/4 cup raisins
1/4 cup toasted, finely chopped pecans

Heat a heavy skillet over medium heat. Add oil, onion and garlic. Stir, reduce heat, cover and cook until onions are slightly browned. Remove lid, stir in buckwheat and continue to cook for a few more minutes. Pour in boiling stock, nutmeg, squash, salt and pepper. Stir, bring to a boil, then reduce heat, cover and simmer for 15 minutes or until done. Remove from heat and let sit for 5 minutes. Fluff buckwheat with a fork, then add raisins and toasted pecans.

Sweet Potato Sauté with Caramelized Onions and Red Peppers
(Serves 4)
There is no need to peel organic potatoes or sweet potatoes unless their skins look damaged.

2 tablespoons coconut oil
1 large onion, chopped
1/4 teaspoon crushed red pepper flakes
2 large red peppers, seeded and cut into ribbons
2 medium sweet potatoes or yams, cut into small chunks
2 medium potatoes, small dice
1/2 cup stock (p.97, or use commercial stock)
1/3 cup chopped fresh basil
Salt to taste

Heat a heavy skillet over medium heat. Add coconut oil, onion and peppers. Stir, cover and cook over low heat until onions are transparent. Mix in red peppers and cook until soft and onions are browned. Add sweet potatoes, stir and continue to cook for 5 minutes. Then add potatoes, stock and basil. Cover and cook until potatoes are soft, about 10 minutes. Add more stock, if needed. Stir in salt to taste and serve.

Braised Turnips, Squash and Seasonal Greens
(Serves 4 to 6)
Turnips develop a sweet earthy flavor when sautéed. Delicata or acorn squash are good in this recipe. For variation, try raspberry or lavender vinegar.

2 tablespoons extra-virgin olive oil
1 onion, chopped
3 or 4 cloves garlic, minced
1 chopped fresh jalapeño, seeded and minced
4 medium turnips, thinly sliced
1 cup winter squash, cut into bite-size pieces
4 cups braising greens or finely cut kale or collards
1/3 cup water
Ume plum vinegar

Heat a heavy skillet over medium heat. Add oil, onion, garlic and peppers. Stir, reduce heat, cover and sweat the onions until translucent. Remove lid, add turnips and squash. Stir to coat, then add braising greens. Blend in greens and water, cover again and cook for 15 minutes or until turnips and squash are very tender and greens are soft. Remove from heat. Sprinkle with ume plum vinegar, stir and serve.

Mashed Turnips and Potatoes with Crispy Shallots
(Serves 4 to 6)

Memories of my grandmother's creamy mashed potatoes were the inspiration for this comforting side dish. Use coconut oil or non-hydrogenated margarine in place of butter for a non-dairy recipe.

5 or 6 shallots, peeled and sliced into rings
1 tablespoon coconut oil or ghee
1 pound turnips, roughly chopped
1 pound red potatoes, peeled and roughly chopped
1/2 cup warm soymilk or buttermilk
1 teaspoon lemon juice
1 to 2 tablespoons butter
Salt and pepper to taste

Heat a heavy skillet over medium heat. Add shallot rings and oil. Stir and cook until shallots are crisp but not burned. Set aside. While shallots cook, steam the turnips and potatoes until tender. Combine warm soymilk and lemon juice in a small dish. Mash cooked turnips and potatoes with soymilk-lemon juice mixture. Blend in butter. Add salt and pepper to taste. Top with crispy shallots.

Zucchini and Tomatoes with Purslane
(Serves 6)

I like to serve this dish over Jasmine rice topped with chopped fresh basil or cilantro and Port Madison goat cheese.

1 onion, finely chopped
1 tablespoon coconut oil
3 cloves garlic, pressed
1 to 2 tablespoons chopped Mama Lil's peppers
2 pounds mixed yellow and green zucchini, thinly sliced
15-ounce can diced fire-roasted, diced tomatoes
1/4 cup dry Marsala
2 tablespoons arrowroot
1 tablespoon Rapadura
2 cups roughly chopped purslane (without roots), blanched
Salt to taste

Heat a heavy skillet over medium heat. Add onion and oil. Cover and sweat onions until translucent. Remove lid and add garlic, Mama Lil's and zucchini. Stir and cook until zucchini is tender. Combine tomatoes, wine, arrowroot and Rapadura. Add tomatoes to zucchini and onions and cook until sauce thickens. Stir in purslane. Blend in salt to taste.

Seasonal Vegetable Medley

(Serves 6)

Vegetables in this dish are lightly cooked until succulent, then covered with a savory sauce. As seasons change, use different produce. Use asparagus in the spring. During the summer, try summer squash, cauliflower or green beans. In the autumn and winter, choose kale, parsnips or carrots.

1 or 2 tablespoons extra-virgin olive oil
1 onion, chopped
3 cloves garlic, pressed or minced
1/8 teaspoon crushed red peppers
3 potatoes (yellow or red), cut into small chunks
1 medium sweet potato, cut into small chunks
1 cup creamy mushroom soup, divided (p.116 or use commercial version)
1 tablespoon arrowroot
2 1/2 cups broccoli florets, cut into bite-size pieces and blanched
Salt to taste

Heat a heavy skillet over medium heat. Add oil and onion. Reduce heat, cover and sweat onion until soft. Add garlic and crushed peppers. Stir and cook for a few more minutes. Add potatoes, sweet potatoes and 1/2 cup soup. Cover and simmer for 10 minutes, or until potatoes and sweet potatoes are fork tender.

Blend the remaining soup with arrowroot, stir in bring to a boil, then reduce heat and cook until sauce thickens. Stir in broccoli (or seasonal produce variations) until heated. Add salt to taste and serve.

183

The Lighter Side of Dips and Spreads

Vegetarian dips and spreads in the 1960's were often heavy with sour cream, cream cheese, cheese or nuts. Today, dips have less fat and more vegetables or beans for maximum nutrition and taste. Beans, vegetables, tofu, and soy or nonfat dairy yogurt provide the substance for my favorite spreads and dips. Without the sour cream and cheese, the flavor of the foods shines through. Spreads are a thicker version of dips and have the advantage of making excellent sandwiches.

Butternut Squash-Almond Spread
(Makes 2 cups)

To make a dip for vegetables, leave out the sweet peppers and nuts. Add 1 tablespoon chopped hot peppers such as Mama Lil's or a dash of hot sauce. Thin with a little low fat yogurt or water.

2 cups baked, mashed butternut squash
2 tablespoons almond butter
1 1/2 tablespoon honey, agave nectar or rice syrup
1 tablespoon white miso
Handful of finely chopped red, yellow or green peppers
3 tablespoons finely chopped, toasted almonds

Blend squash, almond butter, honey and white miso together with a hand blender until smooth and creamy. Mix in peppers and nuts and spread on warm flour tortillas.

Tom's Guacamole
(Makes about 1 1/2 cups)

This book would not be complete without my husband Tom's famous guacamole. Leave the seeds from the jalapeño in for a spicy version.

1 ripe avocado
Juice of 1/2 lime (approximately 2 tablespoons juice)
1/2 cup finely chopped red or sweet onion
1/2 jalapeño, seeded and finely chopped
1/2 cucumber, chopped (about 1/2 cup)
1/3 cup finely chopped cilantro
2 tablespoons spicy hot salsa

Mash avocado. Add remaining ingredients blending well. Serve with chips, baked potatoes, for a sandwich spread or add to a pasta salad.

Spicy Seasonal Greens and Onion Puree

(Serves 4)

This is a recipe for those times when you have a surplus of greens and not enough people to eat them all. It's a perfect spread for crisp corn or soft flour tortillas. You can also serve this as a side dish.

2 tablespoons extra-virgin olive oil or coconut oil
1 small red or yellow onion, peeled and chopped
3 to 4 cloves garlic, minced or pressed
1 jalapeño, seeded and finely chopped
6 cups chopped seasonal greens (kale, broccoli rabe, collards, beet greens, or turnip greens) removed from stem and chopped
1/2 cup water, stock (p.97) or dry white wine
Juice of 1/2 lemon
2 tablespoons cashew or peanut butter
2 tablespoons white miso

Heat a heavy skillet over medium heat. Add olive oil, onion, garlic and jalapeño. Stir and cook until onions are soft and garlic is lightly browned. Mix in seasonal greens, stir and add 1/2 cup water. Cover and cook for 20 to 25 minutes, or until greens are very soft. Check every once in awhile to make sure there is enough water. Add only a very small amount if needed. Remove from heat and place in a blender. Then add lemon juice, cashew butter and miso and puree until smooth and creamy.

Roasted Eggplant and Pepper Dip
(Makes about 2 cups)

This dip is even better if you grill the eggplant and pepper. To grill, slice eggplant into 1/2-inch slices and brush with coconut oil. Pierce peppers with a fork and leave whole to grill. Grill eggplant for 5 to 7 minutes on each side and peppers until charred and black. Serve this dip with warm pita bread triangles.

1 large eggplant
1 large red pepper
3 cloves garlic, pressed
2 tablespoons raw tahini, almond or cashew butter
2 tablespoons extra-virgin olive oil
3 to 4 tablespoons lemon juice
Dash of cayenne or chopped hot peppers, to taste
Salt to taste
Finely chopped parsley for garnish

Preheat oven to 375º. Prick eggplant and pepper with a fork in several places. Place in a baking dish and bake for 45 minutes or until both vegetables are blackened and soft. The pepper will be done before the eggplant. Place pepper and eggplant in a paper bag. Let them cool until they are easy to handle, then peel the skins. Seed both vegetables and place in a food processor. Add garlic, tahini, oil, 3 tablespoons lemon juice and dash of cayenne. Blend until smooth and creamy. Add more lemon juice, if desired. Season to taste with salt. This dip thickens after being refrigerated for about an hour. Garnish with parsley.

Red Lentil and Olive Spread
(Makes 2 3/4 cups)

Spread on chapatis and top with tomatoes, green onions and finely chopped cabbage.

1 cup red lentils
2 cups water
1 tablespoon extra-virgin olive oil
1 large sweet onion, chopped
1/4 cup chopped Kalamata olives
2 tablespoons salsa

Place lentils in a medium saucepan with water. Bring to a boil, then simmer, partially covered, for 30 minutes or until lentils are soft and mixture is very thick. Add more water, if necessary. While lentils cook, heat a heavy skillet over medium heat. Add olive oil and chopped onions. Stir and cook until onions are very soft and browned. With a fork, blend lentils with onions, kalamata olives and salsa.

Pinto Bean Spread

(Makes 1 3/4 cups)

As an alternative, you can use red beans or Great Northern beans in this recipe.

1 1/2 cups cooked or canned pinto beans, rinsed
1/4 cup water
2 teaspoons Dijon mustard
2 cloves garlic, pressed
1 teaspoon chili powder
Dash of cayenne (optional)
1/2 cup shredded carrots, finely chopped celery or bell peppers
Salt to taste

Mash beans and water together until smooth and creamy. Add the rest of the ingredients and mix well. Spread inside pita bread. Top with pickles, sprouts and tomato, if desired.

Black Bean Dip

(Makes 2 cups)

This dip always tastes better when you use dried, soaked, slow-cooked black beans rather than the canned variety. Fresh black beans are a real treat and are the most tender. Growing Things sometimes sells them in the autumn.

1 3/4 cups cooked, drained black beans, or canned beans
1/4 cup hot salsa
1 medium red onion, peeled and finely chopped
3 cloves garlic, pressed
Water, as needed, to thin
1/4 cup chopped cilantro
1/3 cup sharp cheddar cheese (optional)

Combine black beans and salsa in a blender or food processor and blend until creamy. Stir in red onion and pressed garlic, and thin to desired consistency with water. Add cilantro and sharp cheddar cheese. Heat in a heavy skillet, stirring until the cheese melts.

Pesto White Bean Spread

(Makes 2 cups)

This spread is great on bagels with a few sprouts, thinly sliced cucumbers and fresh tomatoes.

1 1/2 cups cooked white beans (Great Northern or small white)
1/4 teaspoon crushed red pepper flakes
2 tablespoons water, stock, or bean cooking water
1/3 cup chopped basil
1/2 cup pine nuts or chopped walnuts
1/4 cup extra-virgin olive oil
1 or 2 teaspoons lemon juice
2 green onions, thinly sliced
1 medium-size carrot, grated
Salt to taste

Combine cooked beans, red pepper flakes and water in a bowl and mash until smooth. In a blender, combine basil, nuts, oil and lemon juice. Blend until smooth. Mix in with beans, adding more oil or water, if necessary, for a smooth spread. Stir in green onions and carrots. Season with salt to taste.

Spicy Squash and Channa Dal Spread

(Makes about 1 1/2 cups)

Channa Dal (hulled, split baby garbanzos) are great in this hummus-like spread. They have a creamy texture with a slightly nutty flavor. Look for them in specialty and natural foods stores.

1/2 cup Channa Dal, soaked overnight
1 1/2 cups water
1/2 cup cooked winter squash, butternut or acorn
1/4 cup raw tahini
3 tablespoons extra-virgin olive oil
Juice of 1 lemon
2 garlic cloves, pressed
1 tablespoon chopped Mama Lil's peppers
Salt to taste

Cook Channa Dal in water for about 50 minutes or until done and most of the water is absorbed. The mixture should be fairly dry. Puree channa dal with squash, tahini, oil, lemon juice, garlic and peppers in a blender. Add salt to taste. Serve on warm chapatis.

Red Bean Spread with Sundried Tomatoes

(Makes 3 cups)

Make this spread with garbanzo or pinto beans if you don't have red beans on hand. To cook dried beans see p. 297. Homestead Organic Produce (p.5) sells sweet onions during the summer.

3 cups cooked red beans
1/4 cup chopped, marinated sundried tomatoes
1 1/2 tablespoons extra-virgin olive oil
1 medium-size sweet onion, chopped
1 or 2 jalapeños, seeded and minced
2 cloves garlic, pressed
2 teaspoons chili powder
1/2 teaspoon cumin
Salt to taste
1/3 cup chopped cilantro

Mash beans with sundried tomatoes until smooth and creamy. Heat a heavy skillet over medium heat. Add oil, onion and jalapeños and stir. Reduce heat to low, cover and sweat onions until they are very soft. Remove lid, add garlic, chili powder and cumin. Continue to cook for a few more minutes. Blend onion mixture in with the red beans and sundried tomatoes. Add salt to taste. Stir in chopped cilantro.

Tofu Patê

(Makes about 3 cups)

To press tofu, drain the water off, and lay the whole block on a plate. Place a few plates on top and leave them for 20 minutes. Gently press to get more water out. Serve on crackers or warm pita bread triangles.

1 pound firm tofu, drained and pressed
1/2 teaspoon turmeric
1/2 cup garlic aïoli spread or mayonnaise
4 cloves garlic, pressed
1 tablespoon Mama Lil's peppers, chopped
2 stalks celery, finely chopped
1/2 cup finely chopped parsley
1/2 cup red onion, small dice, or use thinly sliced green onions
1/4 cup salsa
1/4 cup diced fresh pimento or red pepper
Salt to taste

Crumble tofu into a bowl. Add the rest of the ingredients, and mix well with a fork until the patê has a uniform consistency and color. Serve on crackers, as a dip or spread on whole-grain bread for a sandwich spread.

Saving Farmland
Skagitonians to Preserve Farmland
PCC Farmland Fund

Nationwide, farmland is under siege as urban sprawl spreads outward. According to American Farmland Trust, the Puget Sound/Willamette Valley region is the fifth most threatened agricultural area in the United States. When it costs more to raise food than growers bring in, and heirs have little interest in maintaining the farm, it can be attractive, or even necessary, to sell farmland. Once farmland is developed, it's gone forever. Two local advocacy groups are working to change that – Skagitonians to Preserve Farmland and PCC Farmland Fund.

In 1989, Skagitonians to Preserve Farmland (SPF) was formed to keep the Skagit Valley as a working landscape, protecting farmland from encroaching development. By 2002, SPF had helped set aside 4,000 acres in the valley for agriculture. SPF also brings together farm organizations as well as increasing public awareness about the importance of local farming. A locally-grown marketing campaign included the creation of a gold foil label for locally produced foods titled "Skagit's Own." This helps generate community interest about locally produced foods. For information about SPF, check out www.skagationians.org.

In 1999, PCC Natural Markets established PCC Farmland Fund to save prime Washington farmland from development. The land is then put into organic production. Six months after the fund was set up, the first farm was saved. Once slated for development, the Delta Farm, an established 100-acre farm on the Dungeness Delta near Sequim, is now a thriving organic farm. Leased to Nash Huber, the land is part of his apprenticeship program, thanks to the Farmland Fund. Contributions to the fund come from individuals, local and national businesses and voluntary PCC payroll deductions. For more information about current activities The Farmland Fund is involved in, see www.pccnaturalmarkets.com.

Agriculture contributes millions of dollars to our local economy. Money generated from farming percolates throughout our communities, providing jobs on farms and in related businesses. These funds buy farm supplies and equipment. Wholesale brokers, fresh food and crop delivery drivers, feed store employees, warehouse workers and even some grocery store help owe their employment to our agricultural industry. An integral part of our economy, organic farmland benefits generations to come. PCC Farmland Fund and SPF address farm succession and work to raise money for agricultural easements. They encourage environmental stewardship and communicate land use planning strategies to state and federal agencies. Both also support water conservation programs. Skagitonians to Preserve Farmland and the PCC Farmland Fund are nonprofit, tax-deductible organizations.

Changes and Choices in the Organic Market

The organic farming movement started in England in the early 1900's when Sir Albert Howard spoke out against the trend of using chemical fertilizers. Later, in the United States, Robert Rodale became an organic advocate and began publishing *Organic Gardening and Farming Magazine*. Through the 1960's, the organic market was marginal, but it was growing slowly. Small, diversified farms were always at the forefront of the organic movement.

Organic sales climbed steadily through the 1970's. Small health food stores and co-ops thrived. By 1980, total national organic sales reached $178 million. In the same year, Whole Foods Market opened. It started as a mom-and-pop store in Austin, Texas, catering to vegetarians and health-oriented shoppers. At the end of the 90's, total national organic sales reached $7.7 billion. Sales had climbed in double digits annually. In 2003, Whole Foods had grown 900%, with 146 stores across North America. The demand for organic foods was growing faster than conventionally grown and processed foods.

Some organic farms also got larger. The industry was consolidating. Small companies grew and were bought by larger companies. Chiquita, Dole, AJ Heinz, Mars, ConAgra, Smuckers and Kellogs acquired organic farms and companies. On the positive side, as demand grows, more farms are put into organic production, fewer pesticides are used, and organic food can be transported at a lower cost. Lower prices attract more shoppers. Organic food now has mainstream exposure in grocery stores across the country.

As organic production increases, the issues that have plagued conventional farmers for decades now loom over large organic farms. Diversity on larger farms may disappear. To make processed foods, crops are grown for consistency in appearance and taste. Small farmers continue to get squeezed out. Production increases and wholesale prices drop. Overproduction that plagued conventional farmers for decades, may also become a problem for large-scale organic farmers. When price becomes the bottom line, local farmers lose out because they have to compete with retail prices that are lower than the cost of growing a crop.

When considering why purchasing locally grown and produced foods makes a difference, think about this:

♦ Local produce is fresh. Fresh foods have more vitality than foods grown out of season and transported long distances.

♦ Local purchases stimulate the economy where you live.

♦ A strong consumer base means earnings for farmers go up. Prospects for farmland sustainability are enhanced.

♦ Small farms have a better chance for success when they don't have to compete with out-of-state corporate farm prices.

♦ Eating food that originates where you live gives you a sense of being rooted to where you are. It keeps you in touch with the farms that nourish you.

Enticing Entrées

Profile: Michaele Blakely, Growing Things

Creative Casseroles
> *Casserole Preparation Tips*
> *Baked Black-Eyed Peas, Squash and Corn*
> *Rice, Roasted Pepper and Snap Beans*
> *Rum-Spiked Baked Beans and Sweet Potatoes*
> *Wild Rice with Cranberries and Mushrooms*
> *Fire-Roasted Tomato Bread Pudding*
> *Shepherd's Pie*
> *Porcini Mushrooms and Vegetables with Cornbread Topping*
> *Spicy Baked Pasta, Buckwheat and Caramelized Onions*
> *Roasted Eggplant and Red Pepper Lasagna*
> *Red Bean and Quinoa Enchiladas*

Savory Whole Grains and Legumes
> *Easy Spanish Quinoa*
> *Braised Autumn Harvest with Amaranth*
> *Cranberry Beans with Fire-Roasted Tomatoes*
> *Savory Quinoa and Pecan Pilaf*
> *Crispy Tempeh Strips, Basmati Rice and Greens*
> *Squash and Cranberries with Rice and Barley*
> *Smoky Beans with Wild Rice, Leeks and Collards*
> *Black Bean Fiesta Pizza*

Stovetop Pasta
> *Ribbon Noodles with Sweet Onions, Summer Squash and Kale*
> *Orzo with Pearl Onions, Spinach and Pine Nuts*
> *Angel Hair Pasta with Pesto*
> *Fettuccini with Roasted Red Pepper Sauce*
> *Pasta Primavera with Cannellini Beans*
> *Lemon-Tahini Channa Dal over Couscous*
> *Linguini with Fresh Tomatoes and Spinach*

Hot Savory Sandwiches
> *Roasted Onion and Elephant Garlic with Spinach*
> *Coconut-Infused Asparagus with Hummus Sauce and Spinach*

Grilled Eggplant, Caramelized Onions and Tomato
Fried Eggplant
Smoked Tofu in Country Gravy Over Biscuits
Chipotle Joes
Barbecue Tempeh
Tempeh Reuben
Black Bean and Avocado Tostadas
Curried Tempeh Tacos

A Taste of Excellence at Samish Bay Cheese

What's Organic and Who Says So?

THINK ABOUT IT

Heirloom, as defined by Webster's Dictionary, means "something of value, handed down from one generation to another." Often defined as open-pollinated, heirloom varieties date back a half a century or more. Plants from saved heirloom seeds have more genetic vigor, natural disease resistance and regional adaptability than hybrid specimens. Old-fashioned fruit types or heirloom vegetables, there are many kinds of produce grown in the Northwest. Elephant-Heart plums, Stupice tomatoes, Chioggia beets, and Seek-No-Further apples are just a few varieties you can buy. Heirloom plants help provide seed diversity for generations to come. For more information on seed growers' networks and heirloom seeds see www.abundantlife.com or www.seedsofchange.com.

Samish Bay Cheese shop at Rootabaga Country Farm in Skagit County

Enticing Entrées

Taking time to enjoy evening meals with family and friends should be a requirement, not a luxury.

My grandmother was a master at turning a few simple ingredients into savory dishes. A farmwoman from Kansas, she could create a budget-stretching casserole with canned tomatoes, bread and vegetables from her garden and everyone had second helpings. My mother put her creative energy into beautiful watercolors, not food. With simple tastes and little fuss, mom preferred basic meat and salad dinners. Today in our home, I love being creative putting together vegetable, bean or grain-based dinners. I include a much wider variety of ingredients than my grandmother or mother used.

Vegetarian entrées in the past were often heavy with dairy or eggs, but today, most main dishes are lighter with less fat. They draw from a fusion of cuisines around the world. Whether you're vegetarian or not, the main dishes here are designed to fit in with any healthful diet plan. Moving beyond the usual salad-side dish-meat meal plan, there are many ways to create nutritious vegetarian meals. Many people in other countries eat meatless or almost meatless meals on a daily basis. Seitan, a wheat-gluten meat substitute, beans and soy products can take the place of meat in traditional dishes such as stews, casseroles and hot sandwiches.

Beans and soy products, such as tofu or tempeh, make perfect entrée ingredients because they're filling, versatile, nutritious, and supply ample protein without the cholesterol contained in animal products. They easily combine with many foods, spices and herbs, absorbing the flavors with which they are cooked. Beans are low in fat and contain a substantial amount of fiber. For additional savory, low-fat bean entrées, check out *Lean Bean Cuisine* by Jay Solomon. When searching for something with a meaty texture and high protein content to replace meat, use tempeh or look for smoked or marinated tofu in the refrigerated soy section of a grocery store.

Vegetarian entrées today are often easier to prepare and take less time than meatless meals of the past. When I'm in the mood for something warming and comforting, I put together a casserole like **Fire-Roasted Tomato Bread Pudding** (p.204) inspired from my grandmother's kitchen. If I'm pressed for time and want something easy, I get out my pressure cooker for **Smoky Beans with Wild Rice and Collards** (p.216) or take out a frozen pizza crust for **Black Bean Fiesta Pizza** (p.217). Of course, pasta dinners will always be popular for their ease and affordability. There are infinite ways of putting ingredients and pasta together in 30 minutes or less. Warm sandwiches are also fast dinner options. For stay-at-home fast food nights, try **Black Bean and Avocado Tostadas** (p.230), which offer plenty of options for everyone.

When creating entrées, be inventive. Use bold flavors and contrasting textures. Try lining up ingredients that you would like to use, determine what you are drawn to and put together ingredients for complimenting tastes — sour, salty, sweet, pungent and spicy. Combine soft ingredients like beans or tofu with the crunch of celery, toasted nuts or sugar snap peas in a side dish. And if you don't have all the ingredients for a particular recipe, consider substitutes, such as chard or arugula for spinach, fennel for celery, mushrooms for eggplant to name just a few ideas.

THINK ABOUT IT
Even if a farmer does everything right, when it comes to weather, it's a roll of the dice. Early or late frost, hail storms, a rainy spring, a drought that goes on for weeks on end — to us these are passing weather conditions, but to a farmer they could mean a big loss of a season's crop. Continual customer support helps see farmers through difficult times so they can farm the next year and for many years to come.

Michaele Blakely
Growing Things

Drive southeast of Seattle on the Carnation-Duvall Road and you'll find Growing Things, a 50-acre certified organic farm run by Michaele Blakely and her family. Here on the urban edge, Growing Things has the advantage of close proximity to other organic farms and a number of Seattle farmers markets that provide a strong, steady customer base. As the organic market expands, more consumers seek locally grown organic produce and small farmers are supported. The outlook becomes more positive for dedicated organic farmers like Michaele Blakely.

In the late 1980's, the owners of a rundown homestead were looking for someone to lease, manage and farm the property. The condemned old farmhouse and surrounding land had been neglected for some time before Michaele, a friend of the owners, stepped in to restore the old house and set up a farm. No stranger to farming, Michaele grew up on a ranch where she tended the chickens and kept the family garden going. Her grandparents had been farmers in Oregon for most of their lives. On Michaele's farm, only a few acres are actively cultivated, the rest is preserved as open space wildlife habitat. Other farms may have goals of expanding, but the ecological function of the landscape Michaele lives on is important to her. "As long as we have enough to pay the bills, we're doing fine," she says.

Fourteen years after establishing Growing Things, Michaele's enthusiasm for sustainable farming has not dimmed. You can find her produce booth at local farmers markets such as Lake City, Columbia City and University District. Depending on seasonal fluctuations, you'll find familiar as well as unusual and heirloom varieties of vegetables, such as sweet, tiny yellow, red or orange carrots – perfect for grilling or roasting. Baby summer squash with blossoms, a variety of beets, radishes and beans, including unusual shell (fresh dry) beans, cabbage and winter squash are among the wonderful finds at Michaele's perfectly displayed produce booth.

If you eat eggs, this is definitely the place to stop. Michaele's organic eggs have a deep yellow color and a rich flavor. Perhaps it's a sign of content, well-fed chickens. The jumbo-size eggs are larger than any supermarket jumbo eggs I've ever seen. One taste and you'll find yourself back at the Growing Things farm booth time and again for those eggs. Omeletes made with commercial eggs were never this good. You can also find duck eggs and farm raised organic meat. In addition to her market produce, Michaele also offers a CSA subscription(p.279), where you can get a variety of vegetables from her harvest each week from the first of June until the end of October.

One major disadvantage of farming so close to the city is the pressure on farmers to give up farmland for housing, a strip mall or a Wal-Mart. One of the issues Michaele speaks passionately about is how quickly farmland is lost to development. "We're losing farmland worldwide and people don't realize this. When a farm goes, it's gone. That's our food base. Without farmers, we may someday face a food shortage." One of the reasons she chose the old homestead was her belief that we should take care of what we have. Now the restored homestead is a growing business for Michaele and her family.

When you stop at Michaele's farm stand at the market, be sure to select one of her mouthwatering homemade jams – peach, nectarine, raspberry or blueberry. Locally made jam on artisan bread is a perfect way to please visiting out-of-town friends or relatives. While you're there, pick up some baby summer squash, the smallest ones with the flowers attached. When you get home, detach the squash from the flowers and sauté in olive oil with a little garlic and Mama Lil's Peppers. Add a few chopped medium-size tomatoes and cook until the squash is tender. Stir in the flowers last. Season to taste with salt and a squeeze of lemon.

After most of the farmers' markets close for the season in November, Michaele sets up a booth with a few other vendors or farmers in a church parking lot behind Dick's Drive-In on 45th street in the Wallingford district. She sells eggs, jam and produce. Unless the weather is severe, each Saturday from 10 a.m. till noon you can find her there, until the summer markets open again.

Creative Casseroles

These simple, homey, one-dish meals bring to mind potluck suppers, where friends bring their best casseroles and entrées. Good times and local gossip are shared, and favorite recipes are exchanged. Some of the best casserole ideas I've gotten have come from great potlucks. Additional good resources for one-dish meals are old church or PTA recipe booklets. Autumn book sales like Friends of the Edmonds Library, second-hand stores and garage sales are the places to look for these treasures. Many of the recipes naturally favor combinations of beans, grains, pasta and vegetables since they are traditionally budget-stretching meals.

My grandmother often made meatless, dairy-free entrées during the Great Depression to feed three young children on a limited budget. I loved her simple garden-based dishes and fresh salads the best. When I was a teenager, I was inspired by creative efforts of vegetarian friends in their casserole-making endeavors. Today, my baked main dishes aim for healthy ingredients, a minimum of dairy products and great flavors.

Creative casserole tips

- Cook extra beans and grains on the weekend or when you have more time.
- Cut vegetables in very small pieces so they cook faster.
- Have plenty of options in the pantry such as drained pineapple, sauerkraut, raisins, artichokes, pickled green beans, olives, or baby corn.
- Go for simple with only a few ingredients, rather than adding everything you have on hand.
- Imagine how the flavors will blend together before adding things.
- Sauté onions and steam or blanch vegetables before combining.
- Use one cup or more of a fairly thick liquid such as stewed tomatoes, leftover creamy soup or pasta sauce for a rich savory casserole.
- Add foods with different textures and flavors, for example – chopped apples, sliced olives, sundried tomatoes, finely chopped celery, reconstituted dried mushrooms or dried coconut.
- Use leftover pasta with sauce and add some steamed or blanched vegetables. Combine the ingredients and press into a casserole dish. Cover and bake at 350° for 30 minutes.
- Make your casserole ahead and refrigerate to bake later. When you remove it from the refrigerator to bake, add 15 to 20 minutes to the cooking time.

Baked Black-Eyed Peas, Squash and Corn
(Serves 6)

To cook black-eyed peas, use 1 cup dry, sorted and rinsed black-eyed peas. Add 3 cups water to peas in a medium saucepan, and simmer until done – about one hour. Discard water and use the peas. As an alternative, substitute 2 cans drained black-eyed peas.

1/2 cup orange juice
1/4 cup water
1/4 cup sundried tomatoes (chopped, dry pack)
1 medium delicata squash, cut in half, seeded and sliced into 1/2-inch slices
1/4 cup unsulphered molasses
1/2 tablespoon Dijon mustard
1/2 teaspoon salt
1 jalapeño, seeded and minced
1 cup corn
3 cups cooked black-eyed peas
1 red onion, peeled and diced
1 cup crushed red or blue tortilla chips

Combine orange juice, water and tomatoes in a small bowl and set aside. Steam the squash slices until fork-tender. Preheat oven to 350°. Place orange juice-tomato mixture, molasses, mustard, salt and jalapeño in a blender and puree until smooth and creamy. Combine black-eyed peas, squash, corn and onion and mix well. Place the mixture in a 2-quart casserole dish, pressing everything down with the back of a spoon. Pour sauce over beans. Cover and bake 30 minutes or until casserole is bubbling. Top with crushed tortilla chips.

FOOD FOR THOUGHT
Beans contain about 17 to 25 percent protein, which is more than some types of meat. Soybeans contain over 30 percent protein. Beans also have a good supply of calcium, potassium, iron, zinc and B vitamins. They are an excellent source of fiber and are low in fat. If you want to enhance the amino acid profile (protein) in bean dishes, serve them with whole grains or whole-grain tortillas. Round out the meal with fresh vegetables.

Rice, Roasted Red Pepper and Snap Beans

(Serves 6)

*You can make and freeze **Basic Soup Stock** (p.95) or use one of the convenient cartons of vegetarian stock available in natural foods stores.*

2 red peppers
1 cup soup stock
1/2 tablespoon arrowroot
3 cloves garlic, pressed
1 1/2 cups carrots, cut into 1-inch matchsticks
1 pound fresh green snap beans, tips removed and cut into 1-inch lengths
2 1/2 cups cooked brown rice
1/2 cup sliced, jalapeño stuffed green olives
1/2 cup finely chopped parsley

Place both peppers in a shallow pan and broil until their skins turn black and blister. Using long tongs, turn them until all sides are blackened. Put the peppers in a paper bag and close bag. Let peppers cool for about 15 minutes before removing stems, skins and seeds. Slice roasted peppers into thin strips.

Combine stock and arrowroot, mixing well. Add garlic and pour into a saucepan with carrots and green beans. Bring to a boil, then simmer until carrots and beans are cooked and mixture thickens — about 7 minutes. Meanwhile, combine olives and brown rice. Place half in the bottom of an oiled casserole dish. Layer with half of the bean and carrot mixture. Top with half of the red pepper strips. Repeat layers. Cover and bake at 350° for 20 minutes. Remove from oven. Garnish with freshly chopped parsley before serving.

Rum-Spiked Baked Beans and Sweet Potatoes

(Serves 4 to 6)

An easy recipe with hearty beans and a deep rich flavor, this dish will warm you up on cold winter evenings.

> 1/2 cup catsup
> 1 tablespoon Dijon mustard
> 1/4 cup Rapadura
> 1/4 cup molasses
> 1/2 cup dark rum
> 1/2 cup water
> 2 tablespoons coconut oil or ghee
> 2 large onions, peeled and sliced into rings
> Pinch of cayenne
> 2 cloves garlic, pressed
> 1 large sweet potato, cut into very small chunks
> 2 1/2 cups navy beans, cooked, or use canned, rinsed beans

Preheat oven to 350º. Combine catsup, mustard, Rapadura, molasses, rum and water in a saucepan and simmer for 10 minutes. Heat a heavy skillet over medium heat. Add oil, onions and cayenne. Cover and sweat onions until translucent. Remove cover, add garlic, stir and cook until onions are lightly browned. Combine onions and garlic with beans, sweet potato and sauce in a 2 1/2-quart casserole. Mix well. Cover and bake for one hour or more.

FOOD FOR THOUGHT

The tradition of baked beans involves long slow cooking so the beans soak up lots of flavor as they become tender. According to Jaqueline Williams in *Wagon Wheel Kitchens,* emigrants traveling by wagon over the Oregon Trail set bean crocks in Dutch ovens in the coals to cook. Crockpots are used by many cooks today, or place covered baked beans in the oven for an hour or so, until flavors are absorbed. For those who want a smoky campfire flavor, try adding chipotle chile pods — use about 3 or 4, omit the cayenne. Remove the pods before serving.

Wild Rice with Cranberries and Mushrooms
(Serves 6)

*If you can't find any chantrelles, use crimini or portabello mushrooms, but start them earlier in the cooking process because they take longer to cook. Use **No-Cream of Mushroom Soup** (p.116) or look for non-dairy "creamy" mushroom soup on the natural food aisle of your grocery store.*

1 3/4 cups stock or water
1 cup wild rice
2 tablespoons coconut oil or ghee
1 large red onion, finely chopped
1 1/2 cups finely chopped celery
1 medium carrot, diced (1 cup)
2 cloves garlic, pressed
1 teaspoon dried sage
1/4 teaspoon dried marjoram
1/2 teaspoon freshly ground pepper
Salt to taste
2 cups chanterelle mushrooms, cleaned (p.211) and sliced
1 cup cranberries
1 cup cream of mushroom soup
1/2 cup finely chopped parsley
1/2 cup toasted, chopped pecans

In a medium saucepan, bring water to a boil. Add wild rice, cover, reduce heat and simmer for 55 minutes or until rice is done.

Heat a 10-inch heavy skillet over medium heat. Add oil and onions, stir and cook until onions are soft — about 5 minutes. Add celery, carrot, garlic, sage and marjoram. Cover and cook on low until vegetables are soft. Add salt and pepper, mushrooms and cranberries and cook until cranberries are soft, adding a little water, if necessary. Remove from heat. Blend rice with the other ingredients in a 2 1/2-quart casserole dish. Pour the mushroom soup over rice mixture, cover and bake at 350° for 25 to 30 minutes. Remove from oven and stir in parsley. Top with pecans before serving.

Fire-Roasted Tomato Bread Pudding
(Serves 4)

My grandmother called a recipe similar to this "bread and tomatoes." Her version didn't use artisan bread, hot sauce or have mushrooms, but it was one of my favorite meals at her house. Whole-grain artisan bread from local companies like The Essential Baking Company is perfect in this dish.

1 1/2 tablespoons ghee or coconut oil
1 large onion, chopped
3 cloves garlic, minced or pressed
1 portabello mushroom, stem and gills removed, sliced
Dash of hot sauce, such as Brother Bru Brus
4 heaping cups cubed whole-grain artisan bread
28-ounce can diced, fire-roasted tomatoes
1/2 tablespoon Rapadura
1/4 cup fresh basil, chopped, or 2 teaspoons dried basil
1 tablespoon fresh marjoram or 1/2 teaspoon dried marjoram
1/2 teaspoon salt
1 cup grated extra-sharp Samish Bay cheese (optional)

Heat a heavy skillet over medium heat. Add ghee, onions, mushroom and hot sauce. Stir, reduce heat, cover and cook until onions are transparent and mushrooms are soft.

In a large mixing bowl combine bread, tomatoes, Rapadura, basil, marjoram and salt. Mix well. Stir in onions and mushrooms. Place mixture into a 2-quart casserole dish and press down until it is very compact. Let casserole sit for at least 1/2 hour before baking. The tomato sauce will soak into the bread. Preheat oven to 350º. Top with cheese and bake for 30 minutes or until lightly browned around the edges. You can also heat it briefly under the broiler to brown the top.

FOOD FOR THOUGHT
The Essential Baking Company (p.40) makes bread with organic wheat that was grown for taste. Conventional commercial wheat is grown for high-yield capabilities, durability in handling and resistance to disease. Superb taste isn't there. Authentic artisan loaves and rolls at Essential are hand-formed and given slow rises. The bread is baked on a stone in a hearth oven that helps produce a compelling flavorful, rustic crust. Don't settle for cheap machine-produced imitations when purchasing artisan bread. Get the real thing. You won't be sorry.

Shepherd's Pie

(Serves 4)

This recipe uses leftover mashed potatoes for a topping. Instead of white beans, you could use crispy fried tempeh strips (p.214), cubes of smoked tofu (from a natural foods store deli) or chunks of seitan (a high-protein wheat-meat). Prepare different vegetables in this adaptable dish as the seasons change.

2 cups mashed potatoes
1/4 cup salsa
1 1/2 tablespoons coconut oil or ghee
1 small onion, chopped
1 jalapeño, seeded and minced
1 each: small red and green pepper, seeded and chopped
2 cups cauliflower, cut into small pieces
1 carrot, diced
1 to 1 1/2 cups yellow wax, Romano or green beans, cut into 1-inch segments
Corn, from one ear of corn
15-ounce can small white or Great Northern beans, drained and rinsed
3/4 plus 1/4 cup water
1 tablespoon arrowroot
1 tablespoon brown miso or Bragg Liquid Aminos
1/2 cup shredded sharp cheddar cheese (optional)
Paprika

Blend salsa into the mashed potatoes and set aside. Heat a heavy, oven-proof skillet (cast iron works well) over medium heat. Add oil, onion and jalapeño, then stir and cook until onions are soft and lightly browned. Remove lid, add peppers and cook for 5 minutes. Add cauliflower, carrots, yellow beans, corn, white beans and 3/4 cup water, then cover and simmer for 10 minutes.

Meanwhile, combine remaining water with arrowroot and miso. Stir this into the onion-vegetable mixture when vegetables are beginning to soften. Continue to simmer until the sauce thickens. Preheat oven to 350°. Remove pan from heat. In the same pan, gently spread mashed potatoes over the vegetables. Top with cheese and sprinkle paprika on for color. Bake 30 minutes or until mixture is bubbly and top is slightly browned.

Porcini Mushrooms and Vegetables with Cornbread Topping
(Serves 6)

Use a fairly deep cast-iron or an oven-proof skillet for this so it can bake it in the skillet. Get fresh and dried mushrooms from wild food gatherers who have booths at farmers markets or try a natural foods store. Use seasonal vegetable substitutions in this recipe.

Filling:
1/2 ounce dried porcini mushrooms
1 1/2 cups warm mushroom stock (p.98 or commercial variety)
2 tablespoons plus 1/4 cup coconut oil or butter
1 cup diced shallots or onion
Dash of hot sauce
1 porcini mushroom, sliced, or 4 crimini mushrooms
2 cloves thinly sliced elephant garlic or 3 cloves garlic, pressed
3 cups vegetables Romano beans, cut into 1-inch segments
2 carrots, thinly sliced
2 cups chopped kale or collard greens
1 teaspoon sage
15-ounce can red beans, drained
Salt to taste

Topping:
1 cup cornmeal
1 cup whole-wheat pastry flour
1/4 cup Rapadura
1 tablespoon baking powder
1 egg, beaten or egg replacer (p.283)
3 tablespoons melted coconut oil or butter
1 cup soymilk

Pour stock over mushrooms. Let them rehydrate for 30 minutes before using.

Heat a 10-inch skillet over medium heat. Add oil, shallots and hot sauce. Cook until onions begin to soften. Stir in mushroom and garlic. Sauté for 5 minutes. Add Romano beans, carrot, collards, sage and mushrooms with stock. Simmer 10 minutes or until beans and carrots are soft. Season to taste with salt. Remove from heat.

In a medium mixing bowl, combine cornmeal, flour, Rapadura and baking powder. Mix well. Cut in coconut oil or butter with a pastry blender until mixture resembles small granules. Set aside. Combine beaten egg with milk and oil. Add to the flour mixture. Stir until a dough forms. Spread cornbread over the vegetables in the skillet. Bake at 350º for 30 minutes or until the top is lightly browned and the inside is bubbling. Let cool 5 minutes before serving.

Spicy Baked Pasta, Buckwheat and Caramelized Onions

(Serves 6)

The taste of sweet onions, carrots and peas helps tame buckwheat's assertive nature. To make this casserole without eggs, substitute 1/2 cup silken tofu. Puree tofu and salsa with a hand blender then stir in like you would eggs.

2 cups farfalle (bowtie) pasta
1 tablespoon coconut oil or ghee
1 large onion, chopped
2 medium carrots, thinly sliced
1 tablespoon maple syrup
1/3 cup toasted buckwheat (kasha)
1/2 cup soup stock or water
2 eggs, beaten
1/3 cup salsa
1/4 cup soymilk
1 cup toasted breadcrumbs mixed with 1 tablespoon melted ghee or coconut oil

Bring a large pot of salted water to a boil. Add pasta and cook according to package directions. Do not overcook. Drain pasta and let cool.

Heat a heavy skillet over medium heat. Add oil and onions, reduce heat, cover, and sweat onions until soft. Remove cover. Continue to stir and cook until onions are lightly browned. Add carrots and maple syrup. Cook until carrots begin to soften. Stir in buckwheat and add stock, cover and cook 10 minutes or until buckwheat is done.

Preheat oven to 350º. With a hand blender, combine beaten eggs, salsa and soymilk; blend until smooth and creamy. Gently mix eggs and salsa with cooked buckwheat mixture, peas and pasta. Press into a 2-quart casserole dish. Cover and bake 25 minutes or until casserole is steaming. Remove from oven and sprinkle with breadcrumbs. Place casserole under the broiler for about 5 minutes to brown top.

Roasted Eggplant and Red Pepper Lasagna
(Serves 8)

Use 3 cups of hummus for a delicious dairy-free filling option. Use crushed toasted pine nuts for the topping.

Filling:
1 large eggplant (local summer varieties are the best)
2 large red peppers
1 1/2 packages shelf-stable Mori-Nu firm silken tofu
2 tablespoons lemon juice
1 tablespoon extra-virgin olive oil
1/2 cup chopped fresh basil
1/4 teasoon salt.
1 cup shredded mozzerella or provolone
1/2 cup grated Parmesan or Romano
2 cups spinach, torn into small pieces
1 tablespoon chopped hot bottled peppers

Sauce:
2 tablespoons extra-virgin olive oil
1 large onion, chopped
1 green or red pepper, chopped
4 cups sliced mushrooms (1 pound)
2 cups sliced summer squash (3/4 pound)
3 cups pasta sauce (25-ounce jar)
3/4 cup red wine (Cabernet Sauvignon or Merlot) or water
1/2 cup sliced olives
10 to 12 lasagna noodles
1 to 2 cups grated Parmesan or Romano (optional)

Set oven to broil. Prick eggplant and peppers with a fork and set on broiler pan under the broiler. Turn every 5 minutes. When the skins are blackened and vegetables are tender, remove and place in a paper bag to cool. When cool, peel, seed and cut into strips. Reserve juice from eggplant.

Combine tofu, lemon juice, oil, basil and salt with a hand blender. Stir in spinach and hot peppers. Set aside. Heat a skillet over medium heat. Add oil, onion and pepper. Stir, cover and reduce heat. Sweat onion and pepper for 5 minutes. Add mushrooms and squash. Cook 10 minutes. Stir in pasta sauce, wine, eggplant juice and olives. Continue to cook for 20 minutes.

Preheat oven to 350º. Ladle 1/3 of the sauce into a 9X13-inch baking dish. Place dry noodles on top (enough to cover the surface). Spread half tofu-cheese filling over noodles. Lay half of the strips of eggplant and peppers over filling. Repeat – noodles, filling, eggplant – saving the sauce for the top. Sprinkle Parmesan cheese over surface, cover bake for one hour. Remove cover during last 15 minutes of baking.

Red Bean and Quinoa Enchiladas

(Serves 6)

Smoked jalapeños in adobo sauce can be found in the international section in most grocery stores. These are hot, so use your best judgment when adding.

Filling:
7-ounce can chopped green chiles
1 cup cooked quinoa
3/4 cup cooked or canned red beans
1/2 cup baked butternut or acorn squash
1/2 cup corn
1/2 teaspoon salt
1/4 cup chopped cilantro

Sauce:
1 tablespoon coconut oil or ghee
1 medium onion, chopped
1 or 2 chopped canned, smoked jalapeños
2 or 3 cloves garlic, minced or pressed
1/2 teaspoon cumin
1/4 teaspoon coriander
28-ounce can fire-roasted whole tomatoes
1 teaspoon Rapadura
Salt to taste

Tortillas:
12 corn tortillas
2 tablespoons melted coconut oil or ghee
1 1/2 cups grated sharp cheese

Mash half of the chiles and all of the quinoa, beans and squash together in a medium mixing bowl with a potato masher. Blend in corn, salt and cilantro.

Heat a heavy skillet over medium heat. Add oil, onion and jalapeños. Stir, reduce heat, cover and sweat onions until they're transparent. Remove lid, add garlic, cumin, coriander and chipotle chile powder. Stir and cook on medium-low heat for 15 minutes, adding a little water if mixture gets too dry. Remove lid, add tomatoes and Rapadura. Bring to a boil, then reduce heat and simmer for 25 minutes. Let cool while you prepare tortillas.

Preheat oven to 350º. Brush one side of each tortilla with oil. Lay tortillas on a baking sheet and bake 5 minutes. Reverse sides, brush with oil and cook until softened. Pour sauce in a pie tin. Remove tortillas from oven. Dip both sides in the sauce. Spread 3 tablespoons quinoa-squash filling down the middle of each tortilla. Fold the sides over and turn the tortilla over so the seam side is down. Continue with each tortilla. Spread leftover filling over rolled tortillas. Sprinkle tortillas with cheese and remaining chiles. Pour remaining sauce over all. Cover and bake for 25 minutes.

Savory Whole Grains and Legumes

Whole grains and beans are excellent choices for vegetarian main dishes. Whole grains contain carbohydrates, protein, fiber, vitamins and minerals. Refined grains have been stripped of vitamins and minerals during the refining process. Even if the package says "enriched," the grains contain only simple carbohydrates and protein with a few nutrients added back. Beans are a good source of protein, complex carbohydrates and fiber, as well as calcium, iron and other valuable minerals and vitamins.

Rice, corn, barley, oats and wheat are the most commonly used grains. Lentils, split peas, black beans, red beans, white beans and pinto beans are frequently used legumes. Make an effort to include more unusual grains such as quinoa, buckwheat or amaranth. Incorporate a wide variety of beans into main dishes.

Easy Spanish Quinoa
(Serves 6)

With 16 to 20 percent protein content, quinoa stands on its own in entrées. Here, kidney beans also enhance the amino acid profile of this main dish. Fresh corn is always best, but if corn isn't in season use 1 cup thawed, frozen corn.

> 1 ear of corn
> 1 cup canned diced tomatoes with liquid
> 1 cup water
> 1 cup quinoa, rinsed
> 1 teaspoon chili powder
> Generous pinch cayenne
> 3 cloves garlic, pressed
> 15-ounce can kidney beans, rinsed and drained
> 1/4 cup sliced scallions
> 1/4 cup chopped cilantro
> Salt to taste
> 1/2 cup shredded, aged Samish Bay cheese (optional)

Scrape corn from the cob. Cut the cob and place it in a saucepan along with tomatoes and water. Bring to a boil. Add quinoa, chili powder, cayenne, garlic, kidney beans and corn. Cover, reduce heat and simmer for 15 minutes or until quinoa is done. Remove from heat and let quinoa sit for 5 minutes. Discard cob. Fluff quinoa with a fork and stir in scallions and cilantro. Add salt and pepper to taste. Top with cheese, if desired.

Braised Autumn Harvest with Amaranth

(Serves 4)

*Steamed Romano beans with a squeeze of lemon and **Sundried Tomato Biscuits** (p.24) would make great companions for this autumn entrée. Chanterelle mushrooms are available at farmers markets and natural foods stores. To prepare chanterelles, brush off debris with a mushroom brush.*

1 cup water
1/2 cup amaranth
2 tablespoons extra-virgin olive oil
1 onion, chopped
1 head garlic, peeled, cloves separated and sliced
1/2 delicata squash, cut into small chunks
1 potato, cut into small chunks
I carrot, sliced
1/3 cup marinated sundried tomatoes, roughly chopped
1 tablespoon chopped Mama Lil's peppers
3/4 cup mushroom or vegetable stock
1/2 pound sliced chanterelle mushrooms
Salt to taste
1 cup crumbled Port Madison goat cheese

Bring water to a boil in a small saucepan. Add amaranth, cover and simmer for 30 minutes or until amaranth is the consistency of thick porridge. While amaranth cooks, prepare vegetables.

Heat a heavy skillet over medium heat. Add oil, onion, garlic, stir and cook until onions are caramelized. Stir in squash, potatoes, sundried tomatoes, peppers and vegetable stock. Cover and cook until potatoes and squash are tender. Stir amaranth into the vegetables. Gently stir in mushrooms and cook until they are soft and amaranth is blended in. The mixture should be quite thick. Add salt to taste, if necessary. Top with crumbled goat cheese.

Tip

When cooking with acidic ingredients like tomatoes, use a non-reactive metal pan like stainless steel. Tomato-based sauces, vinegar and citrus juices pull metals such as iron and aluminum into the food. This increases the iron you can absorb, but if a tomato sauce is cooked too long in cast iron, it will taste like an iron supplement.

211

Cranberry Beans with Fire-Roasted Tomatoes

(Serves 6)

A number of farms such as Growing Things (p.197) and Stoney Plains Organic Farm (p.84) sell cranberry or flageolet beans in the autumn. Freshly cooked, they practically melt in your mouth like butter.

1 teaspoon fennel
1 tablespoon coconut oil or ghee
1 sweet onion, chopped
1 jalapeño, seeded and minced
1 head garlic, cloves separated and peeled
2 cups corn
1 cup fresh cranberry beans, removed from pods, or soaked, cooked dry beans
1/4 cup millet, rinsed
15-ounce can diced or crushed fire-roasted tomatoes
1 3/4 cups water
2 cups cut fresh green or yellow wax beans, blanched (p.212)
Salt to taste
2 cups cubed artisan bread
1/2 cup crumbled goat cheese, such as Port Madison (optional)
1/2 cup finely chopped parsley

In a heavy skillet on medium heat, toast fennel for 5 minutes. Remove from skillet and grind with a mortar and pestle.

Turn heat to medium and add oil, onion, jalapeño and garlic to the skillet. Stir for a minute, reduce heat, cover and cook for about 5 minutes. Blend in corn, cranberry beans, millet, tomatoes and water. Bring to a boil, reduce heat, cover, then simmer for one hour, or until beans are done. Cooked dry beans will take considerably less time. Add green beans and cook until beans are heated – about 10 minutes. Season with salt to taste. Place artisan bread cubes in serving dishes. Ladle beans over the bread. Garnish with goat cheese and parsley.

Savory Quinoa and Pecan Pilaf
(Serves 6)

An autumn potluck favorite, serve this as a main or side dish. You can find dulse (a red sea vegetable) in the international section of natural foods stores.

1 cup quinoa
1 3/4 cup stock
1 tablespoon fresh or 1/2 teaspoon dried sage
1 tablespoon fresh or 1/4 teaspoon dried marjoram
1/2 teaspoon fresh or 1/4 teaspoon dried thyme
1/4 teaspoon red pepper flakes
1 tablespoon extra-virgin olive oil
1 onion, finely chopped
1 or 2 stalks celery, chopped
1 carrot, diced
4 cloves garlic, minced or pressed
Salt to taste
1/2 cup lightly toasted, chopped pecans
1/4 cup dulse, rinsed and chopped
1/2 cup finely chopped parsley

Rinse quinoa well and dry roast in a heavy skillet over medium heat until the grains have dried and are slightly toasted. Heat stock, sage, marjoram, thyme and red pepper flakes in a medium saucepan. Bring to a boil, add quinoa, reduce heat, cover and simmer for 15 minutes or until quinoa is done.

While quinoa cooks, heat a skillet over medium heat. Add oil, onion, celery and carrot. Stir, reduce heat, cover and sweat for 10 minutes or until vegetables are soft. Remove lid, add garlic, stir and cook until onions are caramelized. When quinoa is done, remove from heat and let sit 5 minutes before fluffing with a fork. Combine quinoa and vegetables. Season with salt to taste. Just before serving, blend in toasted pecans, dulse and parsley.

Crispy Tempeh Strips, Basmati Rice and Greens
(Serves 4)

You can use collards, red Russian kale, chard, beet or turnip greens or broccoli de rabe (rapini) for this dish.

1 peeled, grated, sweet-tart apple
Juice of 1 lime (about 3 tablespoons)
3 tablespoons coconut oil
4 ounces tempeh, cut into thin strips
1 red onion, chopped
1/4 teaspoon crushed red pepper flakes
2 cloves garlic, minced or pressed
1 teaspoon minced fresh rosemary
2 cups finely chopped greens
1/4 cup water or stock
2 1/2 cups cooked basmati rice
Salt to taste

Blend grated apple and lime juice, set aside. Heat oil in a heavy skillet over medium heat. Add tempeh strips and cook until browned on each side. Remove strips when crisp. Add onion, pepper flakes and garlic to the skillet. Stir and cook until onions are soft. Blend in rosemary and greens. Add water, then cover and cook until greens are tender or done to your taste. Stir in cooked rice. Crumble and sprinkle in tempeh strips over the rice, mix well and heat. Add salt to taste. Blend in grated apple and lime.

Squash and Cranberries with Rice and Barley

(Serves 6)

This dish combines tart and sweet flavors in a savory blend. If you don't have cooked rice and barley on hand, bring 2 cups water to a boil, add 3/4 cup brown rice and 1/2 cup hulled barley. Cook for approximately 75 minutes. You can substitute cooked quinoa (p. 291) for the grains in this recipe.

2 tablespoons light sesame or extra-virgin olive oil
1 large onion, chopped
1 jalapeño, seeded and minced
1/4 cup apple juice
1/3 cup currants
1 cup fresh cranberries
2 cups butternut squash, cut into-bite size pieces (about 1 pound)
1/2 teaspoon salt
2 cups cooked brown rice
1 cup cooked hulled or hull-less barley
1 cup finely chopped celery
1/2 cup lightly toasted pecans

Heat a heavy skillet over medium heat. Add oil, onion and jalapeño. Cover and cook for 5 minutes, or until onions are transparent. Remove lid and cook on low, stirring occasionally, until onions are lightly browned. Add apple juice, currants, cranberries, and squash. Cover and cook for 15 minutes or until squash and cranberries are tender. Stir in salt, rice and barley and continue to cook until heated. Transfer to serving bowl, and mix in chopped celery and pecans.

FOOD FOR THOUGHT

"Integrated pest management" signs can be seen around cranberry bogs. This is good for the environment because it means farmers use fewer chemicals than conventional fruit farmers. Cranberry growers require bees for pollination of the plants, so no insecticides are used. However, the bogs are subject to invasive weeds and fungus. Like raspberries, cranberry crops can easily be wiped out by fungus. Many of the fungicides and herbicides sprayed on or around the plants are harsh and not as environmentally friendly as the term "integrated pest management" implies. On the other hand, organic cranberry crops are grown without chemical fertilizers, are not treated with fungicides and are hand-weeded. The quality and flavor of the organic berries is exceptional. Look for them in natural food stores during October and November.

Smoky Beans with Wild Rice, Leeks and Collards

(Serves 4)

Select collards with smaller leaves for more tender and flavorful greens. Save the stems for another dish. The stems can be sliced and add to a stir fry, soup or casserole. For a quick meal, prepare this dish in the pressure cooker.

2 tablespoons coconut oil
1 large leek, thinly sliced and rinsed well
3 or 4 cloves garlic, pressed or minced
1 chipotle chile in adobo sauce, chopped
1 bay leaf
3 cups water or 2 cups water and 1 cup stock
1 cup cranberry or red beans, soaked and drained
1 bunch collards, removed from stems, rolled into a chiffonade and cut in thin strips
1/2 teaspoon salt
1 cup cooked wild rice (p.291)
Juice of 1 lemon (about 1/3 cup)

Heat a heavy soup pot or a pressure cooker over medium heat. Add oil and leeks. Cook for a few minutes, then add garlic and chipotle chile. Stir. (If using a pressure cooker, remove from heat.) Add bay leaf, water and beans. Cook on stovetop for one hour or until beans are tender. (For pressure cooking, add bay leaf, 1 1/2 cups water or stock and cranberry beans, cover, return to heat, bring to pressure. Cook for 15 minutes.) When beans are done, add collards and salt. Cook on medium-low until collards are soft. Stir in cooked wild rice. Just before serving, remove bay leaf and blend in lemon juice.

Tip
In the South, collards are cooked with ham hocks for hours, sometimes all night long, until they are a soft mass. A healthier alternative is to leave out the ham and fat and simmer or braise collards with stock or wine for 15 to 20 minutes. They will be tender, have a good texture and will retain more vitamins than the traditional Southern version. Serve with lemon or lime blended with a little agave nectar and salt. Collards contain about the same amount of calcium as milk, and it is more easily absorbed. Eat them often in soups, stews and casseroles.

Black Bean Fiesta Pizza

(Serves 4)

A quick and easy dinner, this pizza is just right for those evenings when you don't feel like making a fuss cooking but want something special. Check around and you can find fairly good quality frozen pizza crusts, some are available in whole-wheat. I often use a frozen, thawed cornmeal pizza crust for this recipe.

1 tablespoon coconut oil or ghee
1 large yellow onion, peeled, cut in half and sliced
2 jalapeños, seeded and minced
2 to 3 cloves garlic, pressed
15-ounce can black beans, drained and rinsed
2 tablespoons lime juice
1/2 cup corn
1/4 teaspoon salt
1/2 to 1 cup grated sharp Samish Bay cheese (optional)
9-inch frozen pizza crust, thawed
1/4 cup chopped cilantro
Salsa

Preheat oven according to directions on crust. Heat a heavy skillet over medium heat. Add oil, onion, jalapeños and garlic. Stir for a minute, then cover, reduce heat and sweat onions until they are soft and beginning to brown. Blend in black beans, stir and cook for another minute. Stir in lime juice and corn and salt. Spread beans over crust, sprinkle with grated cheese over the top. Bake according to directions on crust. Sprinkle chopped cilantro on top before serving. Top with salsa before serving.

FOOD FOR THOUGHT

Commercially produced cheese sometimes uses rennet to coagulate the milk. Rennet is obtained from the stomach of cows or pigs. In the past, large-scale producers used rennet exclusively, but in 1988 chymosine, the first enzyme from genetically-altered microbes became available. Today, many large-scale cheese makers use chymosine. To be sure a cheese is actually vegetarian and doesn't contain rennet inquire about how the milk was coagulated. Samish Bay Cheese (p.232) uses natural microbial enzymes.

Stovetop Pasta

The essence of simplicity, pasta is something anyone can easily cook. Sauté, roast or grill different vegetables or mushrooms, add your favorite herbs and toss them with pasta. You can often find fresh pasta at the farmers market, but it's not usually organic or whole-grain. For nutritional content, whole-grain pasta is preferred. There are so many varieties of pasta, sauces and ingredients, you can practically eat pasta every day without ever getting bored.

Pasta requires plenty of water for room to move in the pot, so you'll need a large pot — one that holds 4 quarts of water. Boil the water and add a teaspoon of salt, unless you are serving your pasta with a sauce that contains salt. In that case, don't add any salt. Some cooks also add little olive oil so it won't stick together, but this isn't necessary. While the cooking time on the package is helpful, taste as you boil to see exactly when it's done, because various pots and stoves simmer at different rates. Pasta is done when it is al dente or slightly chewy. Drain and serve it with sauce or toss with your favorite vegetables. Garnish with parsley, toasted nuts or freshly grated cheese.

Ribbon Noodles with Sweet Onions, Summer Squash and Kale
(Serves 4)
With late summer selections from local farmers, this dish is one of my favorites.

> 2 tablespoon extra-virgin olive oil
> 2 sweet onions, medium dice
> 1 jalapeño, seeded and minced
> 3 or 4 cloves garlic, pressed
> 1 medium yellow or green summer squash, thinly sliced
> 1/3 cup marinated sundried tomatoes, chopped
> 1 tablespoon fresh chopped basil
> 1 tablespoon fresh marjoram
> 2 cups red Russian or black kale, removed from stems and sliced into ribbons
> Salt to taste
> 2 cups whole-wheat ribbons
> Freshly grated Romano or Parmesan cheese (optional)

Heat a heavy skillet over medium heat. Add oil, onions, jalapeño and garlic. Cover with a lid that fits directly over the onions, reduce heat and sweat the onions until soft. Add squash, sundried tomatoes, basil, marjoram and kale. Cover and cook until squash and kale are done — about 15 minutes. Stir in salt. While vegetables cook, bring a large pot water to a boil. Add pasta and salt. Stir and cook according to package directions, tasting to see when pasta is done, but not overcooked. Drain pasta, then combine with vegetables. Serve with Romano or Parmesan cheese, if desired.

Orzo with Pearl Onions, Spinach and Pine Nuts
(Serves 4)

One of the few varieties of pasta that is not available in whole-wheat, but the texture of orzo pasta makes it worth preparing this dish occasionally. Try 1 cup chopped shallots if you can't find pearl onions.

1 1/2 tablespoons extra-virgin olive oil
12 pearl onions, peeled and halved
Pinch of cayenne
1/2 cup dry Riesling wine
2 cups water
1/2 teaspoon salt
1 1/2 cups orzo pasta
2 cups packed, finely chopped fresh spinach, stems removed
1/2 cup lightly toasted pine nuts

Heat a heavy skillet over medium heat. Add oil, onions and cayenne. Stir and cook until onions are soft and slightly browned. Add Riesling and stir. Add water and salt and bring to a boil. Add orzo pasta. Reduce heat to medium, stir and cook 13 minutes or until liquid is absorbed by pasta. Blend in spinach and cook until wilted. Blend in pine nuts.

Angel Hair Pasta with Pesto
(Serves 4)

Roast the garlic with the red pepper ahead of time and you won't have long to wait for this meal. Grilled red pepper has a great smoky flavor.

1 large head garlic
1/2 tablespoon melted coconut oil
3 to 4 tablespoons extra-virgin olive oil
1 tablespoon lemon juice
1 1/2 cups fresh basil
1/4 cup lightly toasted pine nuts or walnuts, finely chopped
1/2 cup firm silken tofu
Salt and pepper to taste
1 pound angel hair pasta
1 roasted red pepper, peeled, seeded and cut into thin strips

Cut the top off a garlic head. Place garlic on a piece of tin foil. Drizzle coconut oil over garlic. Wrap the garlic in foil and bake in a 350° oven for 45 minutes or until very soft. Remove from oven, let cool slightly then squeeze the garlic out for the recipe. To make pesto, blend garlic, olive oil, lemon juice, basil, pine nuts and silken tofu in a food processor until smooth and creamy. Add salt and pepper to taste.

Cook pasta in a large pot of water. Drain and toss with pesto. Garnish each serving with roasted red pepper strips.

Fettuccine with Roasted Red Pepper Sauce
(Serves 4)

When peppers are in season, there is nothing more exquisite than roasted or grilled peppers pureed into this creamy-tasting sauce. Use a high quality goat yogurt like Port Madison. If you can't find Port Madison, use an organic nonfat yogurt.

1/2 tablespoon extra-virgin olive oil
1 large onion, chopped
2 red peppers
1/2 cup firm silken tofu (the type in the shelf-stable box)
2 cloves garlic, pressed
1/2 tablespoon chopped hot bottled peppers such as Mama Lil's
Salt to taste
1 pound fettuccine
Port Madison goat yogurt for garnish (optional)
1/2 cup lightly toasted chopped walnuts or pecans

Heat a heavy skillet over medium heat. Add oil and onion. Reduce heat, cover with a lid and sweat the onions until soft, stirring every once in awhile. This takes about 7 to 10 minutes. Set aside when done.

While onions cook, turn oven on to broil. Place peppers in a shallow pan under broiler. Turn peppers with tongs as the skin blackens. This takes about 10 minutes. When peppers are black, remove them and place in a paper bag or covered saucepan. *(Note: you can grill the peppers, if you like.)* While peppers cool, combine tofu, garlic and peppers in a blender. Peel and seed red peppers. Add to tofu mixture and puree until smooth and creamy. Add salt to taste. Cook pasta in a large pot of salted boiling water until al dente. Drain and serve topped with roasted pepper sauce and a swirl of goat yogurt. Top with toasted walnuts.

FOOD FOR THOUGHT
Peppers are divided into two categories — hot and sweet. Hot varieties are used as a spice, and sweet types are considered vegetables. A bright color indicates ripeness. Green peppers are less expensive than the yellow or red varieties because they are not mature and get to market sooner. Local peppers come into season late in the summer through early autumn.

Pasta Primavera with Cannellini Beans

(Serves 6)

Pureed beans are the base for this creamy sauce. Try different vegetables instead of asparagus as the seasons change. Mama Lil's Peppers make a good addition to this sauce.

1 cup cannellini beans, rinsed and soaked overnight
4 cups water
10 cloves garlic, peeled and sliced
1 large onion, chopped
1 carrot, sliced
1/2 teaspoon fennel seeds, toasted and ground (see p.165)
2 teaspoons dried basil, or 3 tablespoons fresh
1 teaspoon dried marjoram, or 1 tablespoon fresh
1 teaspoon salt
1 red pepper, chopped
1 bunch asparagus (about 1 pound), cut into 2-inch segments
4 crimini mushrooms, sliced
1 pound penne
1/3 cup finely chopped parsley
Freshly ground pepper to taste
Parmesan or Romano cheese (optional)

Drain beans and combine with water, garlic, onion, carrots, fennel, basil, and marjoram in a large soup pot. Simmer on low for one hour or until beans are tender. *(Hint: If you are using fresh herbs, do not add them until the final 15 minutes of cooking or the flavor fades away.)* Drain and reserve stock. Puree all but 1 cup of beans with 2 1/2 cups stock. Return soup to pot. Add salt, red pepper, asparagus and sliced mushrooms. Simmer, stirring occasionally, for 20 minutes or until vegetables are tender but still have some crispness to them. Add reserved beans and more salt to taste, if necessary.

Cook pasta in a large pot of salted boiling water until al dente. Drain. Serve with sauce. Garnish with parsley and freshly ground pepper. Sprinkle with Parmesan cheese, if desired.

Lemon-Tahini Channa Dal over Couscous

(Serves 4)

Channa dal are split baby garbanzos with an incredible nutty flavor. Look for them at natural and specialty food stores throughout the area. Cook the legumes ahead of time and this dish can be made quickly. If you can't find channa dal, use 1 1/2 cups cooked garbanzos. Kalamata olives are also good in this dish.

3 cups plus 1/4 cup water
3/4 cup channa dal, soaked overnight
2 cups boiling water
2 cups whole-wheat couscous
1/4 cup raw tahini
3 to 4 cloves garlic
Juice and zest of 1 lemon
2 tablespoons extra-virgin olive oil
Dash of cayenne
Hot water to thin
Salt to taste
1/4 cup chopped cilantro

Bring 3 cups water and channa dal to a boil. Reduce heat, cover and simmer until done — about one hour. Add a little more water, if necessary. Drain off excess water when done.

Pour 2 cups boiling water over couscous. Cover and let sit for 5 minutes. Fluff with a fork.

Combine channa dal, 1/4 cup water, tahini and garlic in a saucepan. Stir and heat gently for a few minutes or until heated through. Combine channa dal mixture in blender with lemon juice, zest, olive oil and cayenne. Add hot water and thin to desired consistency. Add salt to taste. Serve over couscous and garnish with cilantro.

Linguine with Fresh Tomatoes and Spinach
(Serves 4 to 6)

Jubilee Farm (www.jubileefarm.org) from Carnation usually comes to the University District Farmers market in August to sell great heirloom tomatoes that are perfect for this sauce. To peel tomatoes, see blanching tips on p. 161. For instructions on roasting an eggplant, see p.208.

> 2 tablespoons extra-virgin olive oil
> 1 red onion, finely chopped
> 2 to 3 cloves garlic, pressed
> 1 jalapeño, seeded and minced
> 2 cups sliced mushrooms
> 2 large tomatoes, peeled and seeded
> 1 small eggplant, roasted, peeled and cut into bite-size pieces
> 8-ounce can of tomato sauce
> 1/4 cup chopped fresh basil
> 1/2 cup shredded Parmesan cheese (optional)
> Salt and pepper to taste
> 2 cups fresh chopped spinach
> 1 pound linguini
> Additional Parmesan cheese for garnish

Heat a heavy skillet over medium heat. Add oil, onions, garlic and pepper, stir and cook until onions are soft. Stir in mushrooms, cover with a lid and cook until they release their juices. Remove lid, and simmer some of the liquid off. Add tomatoes, and cook for 10 to 15 minutes, stirring occasionally and breaking up tomatoes as you stir. Add eggplant, tomato sauce, basil and Parmesan cheese, if desired. Stir and cook for another 10 minutes or until tomatoes are very soft. Add salt and pepper to taste. Stir in spinach until wilted.

Cook linguini in a large pot of boiling, salted water according to package directions. Serve sauce over linguini. Garnish with additional cheese.

Hot Savory Sandwiches

Restaurants across the nation offer hot gourmet vegetarian sandwiches. You can find selections such as marinated, grilled portobello and goat cheese or smoked eggplant with grilled tofu and heirloom tomato sandwiches. There are also countless updated versions of the ubiquitous grilled cheese with additions like roasted onions and red peppers. Dining out as a vegetarian has never been easier, but the fat and sodium content of restaurant foods is usually quite high, the portions are huge and options are still limited.

In the 1960's, fast food was short-order cooking at home. Hot sandwiches and coleslaw or fries are easy and often fast meals. Variations are as endless as soup and salad recipes. The best tip for quick fix meals is to keep a variety of ingredients in the pantry like roasted peppers, sauerkraut, marinated artichokes, sliced olives, tapenade and pesto. Condiments and additions to hot sandwiches are as individual as our tastes. With a couple slices of whole-grain bread, some filling options, recipe suggestions and your imagination, you can quickly put together a warm, inviting meal.

Roasted Onion and Elephant Garlic Sandwiches with Spinach
(Makes 2 sandwiches)

Create variations by adding sliced zucchini, fresh or roasted red peppers, sundried tomatoes or whatever else strikes your fancy. Grilled vegetables are another savory option for sandwiches.

> 4 medium sweet onions, peeled
> 1/2 tablespoon melted coconut oil
> 1 head elephant garlic, cloves separated, peeled and sliced in half length-wise
> 2 ounces soft goat cheese like Port Madison
> 1 tablespoon chopped Mama Lil's Peppers
> Spinach leaves, rinsed and dried
> Mayonnaise, aïoli spread, or mustard
> 4 slices whole-grain bread

Preheat oven to 350°. Brush peeled onions with half of the ghee. Place onions in a baking dish. Toss elephant garlic with the rest of the ghee and add to the baking dish. Bake for 45 minutes or until onions are fork-tender. Remove from oven and slice onions in half. Spread one side of the bread with goat cheese. Flatten the onions and place them on the goat cheese, then top with garlic, hot peppers and spinach leaves. On the other slice of bread, spread a thin layer of mayonnaise or mustard before putting the sandwich together.

Coconut-Infused Asparagus with Hummus Sauce and Spinach

(Makes 4 sandwiches)

*Virgin coconut oil infuses the asparagus with a subtle coconut taste. For ordering information, see www.tropicaltraditions.com or www.eatraw.com. This sandwich goes well with **Balsamic Marinated Beets** (p.66).*

Roasted Asparagus:

1 1/2 pounds fresh asparagus, cut into 3-inch lengths, tough base discarded,
1 to 2 tablespoons melted coconut oil
2 tablespoons lemon juice
1 teaspoon honey or agave nectar
2 to 3 cloves garlic, pressed
Dash of cayenne
1/2 teaspoon salt

Hummus Sauce:

1/2 cup canned or precooked garbanzos (chickpeas)
4 to 5 cloves garlic, pressed
1/2 cup water
1/4 cup raw tahini
1 tablespoon chopped Mama Lil's Peppers
2 tablespoons lemon juice
2 tablespoons chopped cilantro
Salt to taste

Sandwich:

4 pieces of whole-wheat pita bread
2 cups washed, dried and torn spinach leaves
1 large, finely chopped tomato

Preheat oven to 350°. Combine oil, lemon juice, honey, garlic and cayenne in a small bowl. Toss with asparagus, then place asparagus in a shallow baking dish and roast for approximately 25 minutes.

While asparagus cooks, combine garbanzos, garlic, water, tahini and peppers in a small saucepan. Simmer for a few minutes. Puree with a hand blender, then add lemon juice, cilantro and salt to taste. Layer asparagus spears in pita bread. Top with hummus sauce then add spinach and tomatoes.

Grilled Eggplant, Caramelized Onion and Tomato Sandwiches

(Makes 4 sandwiches)

The eggplant I like best for sandwiches is a round purple eggplant called Rosa Bianca. White round eggplant, called Purple Blush, is also good. Conventional eggplant in grocery stores is tasteless and tough compared to locally grown varieties. Try grilled zucchini and pepper sandwiches with spinach for variation.

2 tablespoons melted coconut oil or ghee
1 tablespoon balsamic vinegar
1 clove garlic, pressed
1 onion, peeled and sliced into 1/2-inch slices
4 1/2-inch slices of a medium eggplant
1 ounce cheese, Port Madison goat cheese or Samish Bay Herbed Gouda (optional)
Tomato slices
Salsa, garlic aïoli spread or mayonnaise
Arugula leaves
4 French whole-grain rolls

Prepare grill. Combine oil, vinegar and garlic in a small bowl. Brush oil mixture over vegetables, then grill until vegetables are fairly soft. Lay the vegetables on bottom half of a roll. Spread or lay slices of cheese on top. Lay tomato slices and arugula leaves over the vegetables. Spread with salsa, garlic aïoli spread or mayonnaise on top roll.

Variation:

Fried Eggplant Sandwiches

1 onion, sliced
2 tablespoons melted coconut oil or ghee
2 to 3 cloves garlic, minced
1/2 cup cornmeal
1/4 teaspoon chipotle chile powder
4 1/2-inch slices eggplant
1 egg, beaten (or egg replacer p.283)
4 thin slices of cheese (optional)
Salsa or mayonnaise (or use a combination of the two)
Tomato slices
Arugula leaves
4 whole-grain rolls

Follow directions above for onion and garlic. Combine cornmeal and chipotle chile powder. Dip eggplant into egg then into cornmeal. Fry in a hot skillet with remaining oil until fork-tender. Melt cheese on top of eggplant, if desired. Prepare sandwiches according to directions above.

Smoked Tofu in Country Gravy over Biscuits

(Serves 4)

Corn Biscuits (p.23) make a good biscuit base in this recipe. Smoked tofu can be found in the refrigerated soy section of the grocery store, or grill your own sliced, firm tofu for an authentic smoky flavor. If red or yellow peppers are not in season, use 1 large green pepper. Serve this with a colorful salad like **Spicy Spinach and Red Cabbage Salad** *(p.63).*

1 ounce dry porcini mushrooms
1 cup boiling water
2 tablespoons coconut oil or ghee
1 onion, chopped
1 jalapeño, seeded and chopped (optional)
5 peeled, sliced garlic cloves (optional)
3 stalks celery, finely chopped
1/2 each: red, yellow and green pepper, sliced in thin strips
3 tablespoons whole-wheat flour
1 cup soymilk
1 tablespoon Bragg Liquid Aminos
1/2 teaspoon freshly ground pepper
8 ounces smoked tofu, cut into bite-size pieces
4 medium to large biscuits, cut in half

Pour boiling water over the porcini mushrooms. Let them rehydrate for about 1/2 hour. Heat a heavy skillet over medium heat. Add coconut oil and onion. Stir, cover and cook until onions are transparent and soft. Add jalapeño, garlic, celery and peppers. Cook until vegetables soften. Sprinkle flour over vegetables and stir to coat. Slowly add soymilk, about 1/4 cup at a time, mixing well after each addition for a smooth gravy. When all the liquid has been added and mixture is creamy, stir in mushrooms and liquid. Add 1 tablespoon Bragg Liquid Aminos, pepper and smoked tofu. Cook for 5 to 7 minutes. Serve over biscuit halves.

Chipotle Joes
(Makes 2 sandwiches)
With a meaty texture and high protein content, tempeh is perfect for sandwiches. It's also essential for the best sloppy joes.

1 tablespoon coconut oil or ghee
1 large onion, chopped
1/2 each: red and green pepper, coarsely chopped
4 cloves garlic, pressed
1/2 tablespoon chili powder
1/4 to 1/2 teaspoon chipotle chile powder
4 ounces tempeh, crumbled
8-ounce can tomato sauce
1 tablespoon apple cider vinegar
1 tablespoon molasses
Pinch of salt
2 whole-grain burger type buns

Heat a heavy skillet over medium heat. Add oil, onion and peppers. Stir, reduce heat, cover and cook until onions are transparent. Remove cover, add garlic, chili powder, chipotle powder and tempeh. Stir and cook for 5 minutes. Add tomato sauce, vinegar, molasses and salt. Stir, cover and cook for about 15 to 20 minutes or until tempeh is thoroughly heated. Taste and add more salt if necessary. Serve on buns.

FOOD FOR THOUGHT
Tempeh contains approximately 19.5 percent easily assimilated protein. A fermented soy product, tempeh was originally a staple in Indonesia. It has been popular with vegetarians in the United States since the 1970's. Tempeh is a powerhouse of nutrients, providing many valuable B vitamins. It is also rich in unsaturated fatty acids with Omega-3 oils and is low in saturated fat. Unlike tofu, tempeh should not be eaten raw. It needs to be cooked thoroughly.

Barbecue Tempeh Sandwiches

(Makes 2 good size sandwiches)

You can use 1 1/2 cups prepared barbecue sauce instead of making your own.

3 tablespoons coconut oil
8 ounces tempeh, cut in half horizontally, and sliced into 1/2-inch slices
1 cup water
1/2 cup catsup
2 1/2 tablespoons vegetarian Worcestershire sauce
1/2 tablespoon chili powder
Salt to taste
A few dashes hot sauce
1 onion, peeled and thinly sliced
1 lemon, sliced
2 whole-grain rolls or hamburger buns

Heat oil in a skillet over medium heat. When oil is hot, add tempeh. Cook for about 5 minutes on each side or until lightly browned. Remove from heat and transfer tempeh to a clean towel to drain.

In a small saucepan, combine water, catsup, Worcestershire sauce and chili powder. Simmer for 5 minutes, adding salt and hot sauce to taste. Place tempeh in a shallow baking dish. Pour sauce over tempeh. Lay onion slices and lemon on top. Cover and bake at 350° for 30 minutes. Remove from oven. Place under the broiler briefly to blacken onions slightly. Spoon tempeh pieces over buns and serve.

Tempeh Reuben Sandwiches

(Makes 2 sandwiches)

To make your own Russian dressing, blend mayonnaise with a little tomato paste, fruit sweetener and horseradish until the taste is right for you. Look for Fakin' Bacon in the refrigerated section of a natural foods store.

1 1/2 tablespoons coconut oil or ghee
4 slices smoky tempeh strips (Fakin' Bacon)
4 slices dark rye bread
Dijon mustard or Russian dressing
1 cup sauerkraut, heated
Thin slices of sharp cheese such as Samish Bay aged Gouda

Heat a skillet over medium heat. Add coconut oil and smoky tempeh strips. Toast the bread in the same skillet as the tempeh strips. Spread two of the toasted pieces of bread with mustard or Russian dressing. Layer sauerkraut, cheese and tempeh strips and cover with remaining slice of bread.

Black Bean and Avocado Tostadas
(Makes 12 tostadas)
Host a tostada party and everyone can create their own favorite version.

2 heads garlic
2 or 3 tablespoons melted coconut oil or ghee
1 large red pepper
12 corn tortillas
4 cups cooked black beans
1 1/2 cups cooked sweet brown rice
About 1/4 cup water
1 teaspoon coriander
1/4 teaspoon cayenne
1/2 teaspoon salt
1 cup sliced green onions
1 cup finely chopped tomato
1 large avocado, cut into thin slices

Preheat oven to 350º. Brush garlic heads with a little coconut oil, wrap in foil and bake for 45 minutes or until garlic is very tender. Broil or grill red pepper, turning with long tongs as the skin blackens. When the skin is charred all around, place pepper and in a bowl or pan and place a plate or lid on top. Let cool. Slip off the skin, remove the seeds, and slice into thin strips. Remove garlic from the oven. Let cool. Squeeze softened garlic into a small bowl.

Lay tortillas flat on a baking sheet and brush with remaining oil. Bake at 350º for 8 to 10 minutes, or until crisp. Place black beans, rice, water, coriander, cayenne and salt in a saucepan. Mash together and heat on low for 10 minutes, adding more water to keep mixture from sticking. Mixture should be very thick. Blend in roasted garlic and sliced green onions. Spread on crisp tortillas. Top with chopped tomato, strips of roasted red pepper and avocado.

Create Your Own Tostadas or Tacos
Use refried beans, sautéed tempeh or roasted vegetables as a base, then create your own tostadas and tacos by adding any of the following options.

Grilled or sautéed summer squash
Shredded lettuce or cabbage
Marinated artichoke hearts
Chopped fresh tomatoes
Marinated sundried tomatoes
Sliced cucumbers
Tomatillo salsa
Goat cheese or grated hard cheese

Pineapple chunks
Hot peppers
Sliced black or green olives
Sautéed mushrooms
Marinated beets
Roasted peppers
Toasted nuts
Sour cream

Curried Tempeh Tacos
(Makes 8 tacos)

Like tostadas, you can cut the fat in the tacos by lightly brushing oil or ghee on the tortillas and baking instead of frying them.

3 tablespoons coconut oil (see below) or ghee
1 large onion, chopped
1 jalapeño, seeded and minced
1 medium red pepper, seeded and chopped
2 cloves garlic, minced or pressed
2 teaspoons curry powder
1 medium carrot, cut into matchsticks
8-ounce package tempeh
1/2 teaspoon salt
1/3 cup cilantro (optional)
8 corn tortillas
1 1/2 cups finely shredded cabbage

Heat a heavy skillet over medium heat and add 1 1/2 tablespoons oil, onion, jalapeño, red pepper and garlic. Stir, reduce heat to low, cover with a lid that fits directly over the vegetables. Sweat them until the onions are limp and tender. Remove lid, stir in curry and carrot sticks. Crumble tempeh over all, stir, cover and cook on low for 10 minutes. Remove lid and continue to cook until mixture is quite thick — another 8 to 10 minutes. Blend in salt and cilantro, if desired.

Preheat oven to 350º. Lightly brush one side of the tortillas with remaining coconut oil. Lay flat, oil-side-up on a large baking sheet. Bake for 8 minutes or until tortillas are warm and soft.

Remove tortillas from oven, spread about 3 tablespoons of tempeh mixture down the middle of the tortillas and top with shredded cabbage. Fold over and enjoy!

Coconut oil tip
When using more than a very low heat, use unrefined coconut oil for cooking. Olive, sesame and other expeller-pressed oils degrade and are altered when higher heat is used. Though coconut oil is a saturated fat, it doesn't contain any of the trans-fatty acids found in beef, butterfat, milk, partially hydrogenated shortening and margarine. True expeller-pressed and virgin coconut oil are easily digested, and contain lauric acid (a medium-chain fatty acid) that enhances the immune system and brain functions.

A Taste of Excellence at Samish Bay Cheese

Nothing quite makes a region so unique and endearing as local artisan foods like Samish Bay Cheese. One of the best treats around, just a taste can perk up even the dreariest spirits in the winter when the rain pours down day after day. It was one of those days when we loaded the rain gear and hounds and set out for Samish Bay Cheese at Rootabaga Country Farm. From Seattle, it's a 45-minute drive northeast, past Mount Vernon, just beyond the tiny town of Bow.

The farm and small farmstead cheese company are owned and run by Suzanne and Roger Wechsler. For more than 30 years, they've been promoting, teaching about, selling and growing organic foods in the Pacific Northwest. In 1998, they bought a 150-acre farm and 11 cows and started making certified organic, small-batch handcrafted cheese. Today, at farmers markets and in natural food stores from Bellingham to Seattle, you can buy Samish Bay Cheese.

To make the cheese, Roger and Suzanne use only the milk from their own pastured cows. In fact, all the milk on their farm goes into cheese production. They use natural microbial enzymes to coagulate the milk. When the curd is firm, it is separated from the whey. The curds are then packed into molds and pressed. Each variety requires different processing and pressing times. The unique artisan cheese is turned each day until it dries. And it's all done in one of the most spotless rooms I've ever seen. When dry, the cheese is wrapped to prevent mold and over-drying. Then the cheese is aged in the temperature and humidity controlled room until it is ready for sale.

Three kinds of cheese are available from Samish Bay. Gouda is a creamy, rich melt-in-your-mouth cheese. At Whole Foods Market you can buy the mild Gouda cheese. Shop farmers markets or stop at the farm shop and you'll find all varieties. Try Gouda with cumin, herbs or nettles added. Mont Blanchard (named after a local mountain) is Samish Bay's own cheddar, which pairs well with crisp apples. The third kind is an Italian type of cheese called Montasio with a deep, complex flavor. Samish Bay Cheeses range from mild two-month varieties to those that are aged up to 15 months. The latter are delightfully sharp and tangy.

By the time we pulled up to the farm, the rain had let up and a rainbow magically illuminated the winter sky. Cows in the pasture gazed at us contentedly. Outside the tiny retail cheese shop was a cooler with a sign perched on top that said "Fresh Eggs." Before I had a chance to open the door, two customers came out with packages of cheese. A variety of cheese and a dozen eggs later, we were on our way back home. To learn more, check out www.samishbaycheese.com.

In August 2004, Samish Bay Cheese opened a guest house for those who want to stay overnight, relax in scenic surroundings and meet the cows. Contact Suzanne Weschler at cheese@rootabaga.com or 360-708-8998.

What's Organic and Who Says So

Ask any farmer who has been around for a long time, and you'll find farming without toxic pesticides and fertilizers was the way most of our food was once grown. Small farms with diverse crops marketed locally were the norm. People knew the farmers who grew their food and implicitly trusted what they ate. After World War II, farming changed dramatically. Industrial agriculture took over with large-scale conventional farms that relied on chemical pesticides and petroleum-based fertilizers. Increasingly, people began to demand food grown without using carcinogenic chemicals.

In the 1960's, small family farms struggled to survive. Many farmers were squeezed out by the low competitive prices of huge agribusiness farms. Organic agriculture was on the fringe. For years, there were many certifying agencies for organic farms across the country. Consumers had trouble sorting out various standards and claims about the way food was grown. Integrated pest management, unsprayed, transitional, no-spray or pesticide-free were some of the terms people were faced with. As organic food became more popular, consumers demanded nationally accepted organic standards that they could trust.

In 2002, the United States Department of Agriculture (USDA) began to certify farms that met criteria established as organic. A product can't be labeled "organic" unless a farm has been inspected and certified that it meets the national organic standards. These standards address everything from soil history and management to the seeds a farmer chooses. Even the containers and boxes filled with organic products fall under the guidelines. Today, consumers are reassured food is really organic when it's labeled so. It doesn't matter whether products come from Mexico, Japan or New York; they must all conform to the United States National Organic Standards.

According to the USDA, the basic aspects of the organic certification standards are:

- Food can only be classified as organic if it has been produced without hormones, antibiotics, herbicides, insecticides, chemical fertilizers, genetic modification or bacteria-killing ionizing radiation.
- If a label says 100 percent organic, it means that, by weight or volume, it must contain 95 to 100 percent organic ingredients. The USDA seal is voluntary.
- A label that says simply "organic" means that at least 70 percent of the ingredients are organic.
- Products with less than 70 percent organic ingredients can't make any claim other than listing organic ingredients on the ingredient list. No claims can be made on the front of the package.

Fabulous Fruit Desserts

A Fresh Fruit for Every Dessert

Profile: Jeff Miller, Willie Greens Organic Farm

Desserts With Raw Fruit
    Lemon-Tofu "Cream" with Fresh Fruit
    Melon With Sweetened Lime Juice
    Ambrosia
    Marinated Strawberries
    Melon with Fresh Apricot-Ginger Sauce
    Nectarines with Strawberry-Rose Sauce
    Fresh Berries with Lavender-Peach Sauce
    Autumn Fruit Delight
    Apples and Pears with Apricot Sauce
    Enhance Fruit Desserts with Herbs, Spices, Summer Flowers

Frozen Fruit Desserts
    Tips for Using an Ice Cream Maker
    Frozen Vanilla Treat with Fresh Fruit
    Frozen Strawberry Pops
    Cherry Red Bean Delight
    Brandied Strawberry Granita
    Creamy Frozen Maple Apricot Dessert

Easy Cooked Fruit Desserts
    Ginger Pears with Pineapple
    Stuffed Baked Apples
    Apricot-Almond Stuffed Pears
    Balsamic Poached Pears
    Baked Nectarines
    Maple-Glazed Grilled Peaches
    Ginger-Simmered Rhubarb and Nectarines
    Summer Fruit Compote
    Winter Compote with Ginger
    Honey Plums with Mint
    Cranberry Applesauce

Cranberry-Apple Whip
Sauteed Balsamic Cherries
Vanilla Baked Plums and Pears

Cobblers, Slumps, Crisps and More
Sour Cherry Bread Pudding
Sweet Baked Rice Pudding with Peaches
Cashew Cream
Strawberry-Rhubarb Cobbler (and variations)
Peach Crisp (and variations)
Cranberry-Raspberry Slump (and variations)
Apple Kuchen (and variations)
Nectarine Upside-Down Cake
Lemon-Cherry Upside-Down Cake
White Chocolate Raspberry Silk Pie
Blueberry White Chocolate Silk Pie
Fresh Cherry Cheesecake

"Life in Harmony with Nature" at Mair Farm-Taki

CSA Subscriptions: Connecting Farms and Cities

THINK ABOUT IT

Seattle Youth Garden Works is a nonprofit program where low-income and homeless teenagers learn employment skills by participating in a garden-marketing program. Vibrant vegetables and colorful flowers fill two gardens that are planted and cared for by work crewmembers between the ages of 14 and 22. These young urban gardeners sell produce and flowers at the University District and Columbia City farmers markets. In the spring, they market plant starts. Flowers and dried wreaths are available at holiday bazaars in the fall. Stopping by their booth for well-tended produce is another good reason to shop at and support local farmers markets.

Farm greenhouse in Monroe, Washington

Fabulous Fruit Desserts

Savor a juicy, sweet, flavorful peach, picked from the tree at the peak of ripeness and you've got the best dessert nature has to offer.

When I was young, we often visited my grandmother in Colorado. I couldn't resist lounging on her back porch in the late lingering sun, indulging in the best picks of her garden – juicy strawberries and perfect sweet-tart raspberries. In the autumn, the aroma of freshly baked apple pie filled her house. On a family vacation to the Northwest, we picked wild berries and stopped at roadside stands for succulent blueberries and plums. The crisp crunch of luscious Washington apples fresh off the tree created a lasting memory of the best fruit I'd ever had. Fruit-filled dreams led me to plant roots in the Northwest, where I could satisfy blueberry and apple cravings year after year.

Fresh fruit at the peak of harvest, with its incredibly seductive flavor, is food for the soul. Grown by farmer friends, these sweet, delectable treats are a celebration of life. Just a few bites of fruit can revitalize us when our energy is low. At markets in the spring, strawberries bursting with flavor are hard to resist and often don't make it home. By mid-summer, nectarines, peaches and melons packed with natural sugars are so ripe, the juice drips down your chin. Mouth-watering autumn apples range from sweet to tart. Special finds at markets like sour pie cherries, loganberries, huckleberries and elephant heart plums are cherished treats, worth the extra cost per pound for taste alone.

During harvest season, each week brings something new to market, but before you know it, the best of the season is over. There's no need to be wistful or resort to tasteless melons or cherries in January, because most fruit can be preserved. When you take the time to freeze extra berries and peaches or dehydrate cherries and apples, you can have a little bit of harvest season all year long. If you need help with techniques, check out *The Big Book of Preserving the Harvest* by Carol W. Costenbader *or Preserving Summer's Bounty: A Quick and Easy Guide to Freezing, Canning, Preserving and Drying What You Grow,* edited by Susan McClure and the staff of the Rodale Food Center.

For easy desserts, fruit can be sliced or served whole with cheese slices or simple biscotti on the side. Drizzle fruit with liquor or citrus juice, add a swirl of goat yogurt and a garnish of summer flowers for a sublime, simple presentation. Grilled peaches, apricot sorbet or raspberry poached pears are the perfect solution when you're in the mood for something different. Most fruits can be combined together or interchanged with other fruits in recipes. For example, if there aren't enough cranberries and apples for a cobbler, add raspberries from the freezer. The combination of flavors is enchanting!

A Fresh Fruit for Every Dessert

Different regions of the country begin and end seasons at slightly different times, and the type of produce grown varies from place to place. To check the approximate season for local fruit, see pages 301-303. Although I've included a few tropical fruits and standbys such as bananas, the focus is on locally grown fruit.

Apples: Members of the rose family, apples originated in Central Asia. Today, Washington produces more than half of the apples grown in this country. America's most popular fruit, apples come in many sizes and flavors from super-tart to very sweet. Thanks to farmers markets, we have access to many kinds of old-fashioned varieties of apples. Apples are convenient, pack easily into lunches and are excellent in baked desserts and breads. Apples can be grated and added raw to salads and desserts or cooked to enhance their sweetness. Combine raw grated apples with lemon or lime juice so they don't turn brown before using. Apples ripen too quickly at room temperature. Keep them in the refrigerator, and store them up to four weeks. When apples begin to get soft, they're better cooked.

Apricots: Though they originated in China thousands of years ago, the majority of our commercial apricot crop is grown in California today. Apricots are also cultivated in other states, and apricot trees are sold at nurseries for the home gardener. Access to farm fresh apricots is essential because they don't travel well. They're very soft when allowed to ripen naturally. Sometimes apricots are the first stone fruit of summer, but usually cherries are at the market weeks before them. You can bake, stew or grill apricots, or blend them with tofu for a creamy apricot pudding. Apricots can be stored at room temperature for only a day or so. In the refrigerator, they can be stored up to a week.

Bananas: A year-round tropical crop, most of which is imported from Central and South America, bananas are our third most popular fruit and one of the most frequently purchased items at the grocery store. Bananas have a higher sugar content as they ripen. They are rich in potassium and minerals and high in vitamin C. Slice and eat them raw, add them to smoothies or bake them in their skins for a special sweet treat. Store bananas at room temperature until very ripe. When they have lots of brown spots, eat or freeze them. A ripe banana is best for using in smoothies or baking.

Blackberries: Members of the rose family, blackberries originated in Asia, but now grow wild in temperate climates all over the world. Their season is late summer and early autumn. Pick them before a rain because after they get wet, many of the soft berries quickly mold. Some varieties are flavorful and sweet. Others simply taste like water with lots of seeds. They don't keep well, so use them within a day or two. Once one berry is moldy, it's a signal that mold is throughout the box even if you don't find it on other berries. Use blackberries in combination with any other berries. Orange and lemon are popular flavor complements for blackberries.

Blueberries: America and Canada produce 95 percent of the world's blueberry crops. Though they once only grew wild in the United States, domestic cultivation began in the early 1900's. The domesticated varieties are more popular now. After strawberries, blueberries are the nation's most popular berry. They are fairly firm and easy to ship as opposed to the delicate nature of other berries. They also freeze and defrost well and are excellent in berry cobbler during the winter months. Blueberry season is mid-summer through early fall. Before storing, sort through the berries and discard any crushed or moldy ones. Store in the refrigerator in a glass or plastic container and use within a few days. For longer storage, freeze them on a baking sheet in a single layer, then transfer to a freezer bag for later use.

Cherries: Cultivated in China over 3,000 years ago, cherries are one of the greatest pleasures of summer. Most of our nation's commercial crop comes from the Western states — Washington, Utah, Colorado, Idaho, and Oregon. These stone fruits are fragile and are better when purchased from the farmer who grew them. Vans and Lamberts have the best sweet cherry flavor. Sour pie cherries are softer and very perishable. If you are lucky enough to find a farmer who has these amazing tart delights, splurge and make a **Lemon-**

Cherry Upside Down Cake (p.275). Cherries need a cold temperature for storage, so keep them in the refrigerator either in plastic bags or in a container. They will keep for about four days. Sour cherries should be used or pitted and frozen the day you get them. The delectable tart fruit is also excellent when dehydrated.

Cranberries: A native fruit, cranberries were cultivated in natural bogs in Massachusetts by Native Americans in the early history of our country. Today crops are also cultivated in Washington, Wisconsin, Oregon and British Columbia. The tartness of cranberries requires the addition of sugar, fruit spread, frozen fruit concentrate or honey. You can combine them with other fruit like raspberries or apples and cut back on the amount of sweetener called for in a recipe by one-third or more. Look for plump, firm berries with no bruises or brown spots. Buy organic because conventionally grown cranberries are routinely sprayed with strong fungicides. Store cranberries for three weeks in a plastic bag in the refrigerator or freeze for up to a year.

Dates: Cultivated over 4,500 years ago in the Middle East, over 98 percent of the world's date crop today comes from Choachella Valley, California (near Palm Springs). There is no "date season" because dates dry on the palm trees and grow year-round. As the fruit dries, the sugar content increases up to 60 or 70 percent, making it one of the sweetest fruits. Along with fiber, they have a high enzyme content and contain a good amount of magnesium. Buy organic because conventionally grown dates are sometimes dusted with sulfur. Hard and soft dates should be stored in closed bags or containers in the refrigerator. Hard dates will keep for one year, while soft varieties should be eaten within a few weeks.

Figs: Native to southwestern Asia, figs were one of the first cultivated fruits. They have a significant amount of calcium and magnesium, and contain more fiber than prunes. Most our domestic fig crop comes from California. Figs are an autumn fruit. There are three different varieties — black, green and red. You can also find dried figs, which are perfect for snacking or making fig bars. Store fresh figs in a plastic bag or covered container in the refrigerator and use within a few days. Dried figs will keep for six months to one year in a plastic bag or covered container in the refrigerator.

Grapefruit: Considered a subtropical fruit, grapefruit is grown in Florida, Texas, California and Arizona. It is an excellent source of vitamin C and has a good amount of fiber. Choose fruit that is firm and heavy for its size. The best and sweetest tasting are the red varieties known as ruby grapefruit. Enjoy them raw or top them with whole organic sugar and run them under the broiler for a few minutes. Grapefruit can be kept at room temperature for about a week or stored in the refrigerator for up to two weeks. Store cut grapefruit on a plate, cut side down in the refrigerator for a few days.

240

Grapes: Cultivated since Biblical times, grapes originated in the Southern Caucus mountains. Two-thirds of the grapes cultivated in this country are processed into wine. Wine-making is the largest fruit industry. There are a number of varieties of grapes, and their season is June through December. Along with apples and strawberries, grapes are one of the most chemically treated fruits, so always search out local, organic varieties first. Pick up a stem of grapes and shake it. If many fall off, the grapes are not fresh. Store grapes in the coldest part of the refrigerator either in a bag or container. They will keep for about five days.

Huckleberries: The plants that bear these tiny berries have been around since prehistoric times and are said to be one of the oldest living plants on earth. Available at farmers markets and along hiking trails in the Pacific Northwest, huckleberries are a seasonal treat. Tiny red or blue berries, they have a more pronounced, sharper flavor than the blueberries they resemble but are not related to. Blue huckleberries are sometimes mistaken for wild blueberries, but wild blueberries are rarely found in this region. Huckleberries are transformed into a heavenly delight when cooked. Try combining them with nectarines. Red huckleberries are very tart and need more sugar than the blue variety for a sweet dessert. Stored in the refrigerator in an uncovered bowl, the berries will keep for a few days.

Kiwifruit: A China native, kiwifruit is now widely cultivated in New Zealand, Australia, Italy, France and the United States. Most of the commercial kiwis in the United States are grown in California, but they grow well in the Northwest and other mild-climate states. They contain a large amount of vitamin C and also have a significant amount of fiber, some of which is in the skin. Select plump, fairly firm unblemished fruit. There is no need to peel the skin when eating raw, but it can be too distracting in a salad or dessert. The best Northwest kiwis are available in October and November. At local markets, look for tiny kiwis with smooth skin called hardy kiwi. Grouse Mountain Farm at the University District Farmers Market usually offers some for sale in late September or early October. Eaten whole, these tiny green kiwis are delectable. Leave kiwi out at room temperature to ripen, then store in the refrigerator for up to one week.

Lemons: The most useful of all fruits, lemons should be on everyone's weekly shopping list. The skin or zest is great for flavoring a variety of dishes. Get organic so there is no need to worry about waxes or pesticide residues when using the zest. Lemon season is all year, but they are more expensive during summer months. Most of our lemon supply comes from Arizona and California. Select lemons that are firm and heavy for their size. Meyer lemons have thin skins and an intense lemon flavor. Stored loose in the refrigerator, they should last for up to three weeks. Cut lemons can be stored on a small plate, cut side down, and used within a few days.

Limes: The smallest members of the citrus family, limes are a little sweeter with a more assertive flavor than lemons. You can substitute limes for lemons in many recipes. They're grown in the same areas as lemons and have a year-round season. The best prices for limes are in the summer, just the opposite of lemons. Store in the refrigerator like lemons. Use them within a week or they will dry out and develop brown spots.

Loganberries: Considered a natural hybrid between raspberries and dewberries, loganberries are mostly cultivated for wine-making. They are soft, very tart and have a flavor similar to raspberries. Cooked, they need more sweetener added than other berries. There isn't a big commercial market for them, but look for them at farmers markets during July and August. Store them unwashed in the refrigerator in an uncovered container for one or two days at the most.

Mangoes: The leading fruit crop worldwide, mangoes have a peach-like flavor and texture. Most of the domestic crop comes from Hawaii, Florida and California. The season is spring and summer. Look for firm and unblemished organic mangoes. Leave them out at room temperature until there is some give when you press a finger into the skin. Peel with a paring knife and enjoy their juicy sweet flavor. Mangoes are good cooked or raw with lime squeezed over them. You can also puree them into fruit sauces. Once ripe, store mangos in a plastic bag in the refrigerator for one to three days.

Melons: Related to cucumbers and squash, melons most likely originated in Africa or Asia. Wild melons still grow in Africa, but they are not as sweet as the melons we find in grocery stores or farmers markets. Melons should be picked ripe in late summer or early autumn for the best flavor. The melons available in January are often shipped in from Mexico and lack flavor and sweetness. Some of the varieties you can find from Washington farmers are cantaloupe, Butterscotch, Casaba, Charentais, Crenshaw, honeydew and watermelon. Some farms, like River Farm in Ellensburg, grow for maximum flavor, checking the sugar content of their melons before they harvest. Local varieties may be more expensive, but the juicy, sweet taste is worth it. Store melon for a day or so at room temperature. Keep cut melon in the refrigerator in a covered container for a few days. River Farm sells their super-sweet melons at Columbia City and University District Farmers Markets.

Nectarines: Sometimes referred to as a fuzzless peach, nectarines are actually a separate species that has been around for at least 2,000 years. Nectarines from the past bear little resemblance to the sweet fruit we cherish today. You can find them with a white or pinkish-orange flesh and, unlike peaches, nectarines don't require peeling. Enjoy nectarines in July and August. Since the season is always much too short, freeze some for a winter treat. Select nectarines with a sweet fragrant aroma. They should be firm with a slight give when you touch them. Store at room temperature for a few days. Refrigerate in a perforated plastic bag and they will last up to five days.

Oranges: Originating in Malaysia, oranges have been cultivated for about 3,000 years. Spaniards first planted them at California missions in the mid-1700's. Not a local crop, most of our oranges come from California, Arizona and Florida. Navel and Valencia are the most common varieties, but there are many others. Blood oranges are red inside. Satsumas are very sweet and juicy with no seeds. Orange season is all year, though the selection tends to be better in the winter. Select fruit that is heavy for its size and has a sweet orange aroma. Avoid specimens with soft spots or ones that feel light and dry. Store them for several days at room temperature. Refrigerated, they keep for a couple of weeks.

Peaches: A stone fruit like cherries and plums, peaches originated in China. Classified as freestone or clingstone, the pit of peaches either breaks free of the flesh easily or clings to it. Like other stone fruits, if peaches are picked early they get softer but never sweeter. Peach season comes slightly before nectarines, late spring through August. Carefully carry the peaches you select at the market because they are ripe and will bruise with the slightest impact. Before using for a cobbler or pie, remove the skin first. You can do this by blanching the fruit for 30 seconds, then plunging each peach into cold water and slipping the skin off. Rama Farm and Cliffside Orchard sell perfectly ripe, sweet, juicy organic Red Haven peaches that can be held under running water and peeled. Red Haven is classified as a semi-cling peach but the pits come out easily. The aroma and flavor are heavenly. Refrigerate and store peaches for three to five days.

Pears: Pears have been grown in Europe and Asia since prehistoric times. There are nearly as many varieties of pears as apples today. Pears become ripe from the core outward. Unlike most soft fruits, pears are harvested early and ripen off the tree. When ripe, the sugar content has increased. One way to tell if a pear is ripe is a gentle give to pressure near the stem and a sweet pear aroma. Most of our commercial crop comes from Washington, then Oregon and California. Asian pears taste similar to pears, but are crisp like apples. Pears are available from July through October. Left out at room temperature, pears will ripen in five days. Store ripe pears in the refrigerator for three to five days.

Pineapples: A tropical fruit, pineapples originated in Brazil and have been cultivated for centuries. Most of our domestic crop comes from Hawaii. The best organic varieties appear in late spring though June. Even if pineapple isn't a local crop, it's a fun special occasion treat. Pineapple should smell fragrant when ripe. Store a ripe pineapple whole in a perforated plastic bag and keep it in the refrigerator for a few days. Cut-up chunks of pineapple keep well in a covered container in the refrigerator for up to a week.

Plums: Originating in Asia over 2,000 years ago, plums can still be found growing wild. There are many of varieties of domesticated plums to choose from. Unlike other stone fruits such as nectarines or apricots, select unripe plums. They will get sweeter and ripen at room temperature. Cooking enhances their sweet-tart flavor. Plums combine well with strawberries, peaches, nectarines and apricots. Their season is late summer to mid-fall. If the plums are very firm, leave them out at room temperature for a few days, otherwise, store them in a perforated bag in the refrigerator up to five days.

Raspberries: A delicate, fragile berry, the raspberry is a member of the rose family and has been around since prehistoric times. In addition to the familiar red raspberries, there are light yellow, deep amber and black raspberries (black caps). They don't travel or freeze as well as other berries, and the season is always too short. Raspberries have a coating of sugar on the outside of the berry. This sweet coating is easily rinsed off. If you know where your organic berries came from, resist washing them. Use them within a day or so because they spoil quickly. To freeze, place unblemished berries in a single layer on a baking sheet and freeze. Store them in a container or plastic bag in the freezer until you are ready to use them.

Rhubarb: Originating in Northern Asia, rhubarb is not a fruit, but a vegetable related to buckwheat. A hardy plant, it grows well in many areas of the country. Rhubarb is usually treated like a fruit and makes an excellent addition to baked goods. It can be made into tarts, jams, pies and compotes. Peak season is May and June. The leaves are very high in oxalic acid and are poisonous. The stalks also contain some and because oxalic acid blocks calcium absorption, eat rhubarb in moderation. Combining with other fruits such as apples or strawberries can be helpful if you want to cut down on the amount of sugar added to a rhubarb recipe. Use it with apples or pears in the fall. Fresh rhubarb stalks can be stored in a plastic bag in the refrigerator for about five days. Slice and freeze for longer storage.

Strawberries: As early as Roman times, people were cultivating strawberries. The perfect flavor and size of the strawberries we enjoy today was attained in the 19th century. Strawberries, along with grapes, apples and peaches are among the fruits most contaminated with pesticide residues. These should always be purchased from organic growers. The berries are deep red and firm with a sweet scent. Don't buy strawberries in large containers where you can't see most of the berries. Some of them underneath may be crushed or moldy. Local strawberries can be obtained from spring until fall in Western Washington and other areas of the country. Store unwashed berries in a covered container in the refrigerator for a few days.

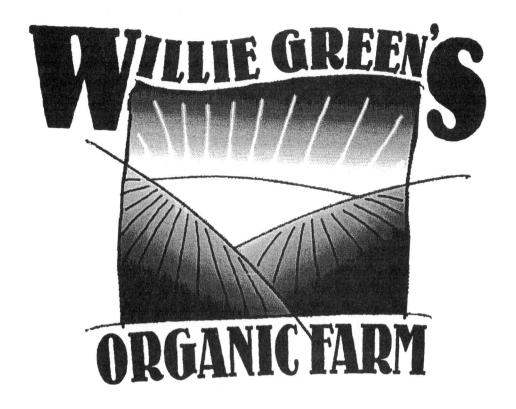

Jeff Miller

About thirty-five miles northeast of Seattle, just beyond Monroe and the north bank of the Skykomish River, you'll find Willie Green's Organic Farm, owned and run by Jeff Miller. Farms have been in this area since the early 1900's. Driving towards the farm, it seems as if you are passing one farm after another. The scenery generates a hopeful feeling that more family farms such as Willie Green's can return vitality to rural areas like this around the country.

I pulled up to Willie Green's Organic Farm on a warm spring day before the market season opened. The farm is named for Jeff's grandfather, Willie, and the greens that Jeff specializes in growing. His dog, Mokum (named for a variety of carrot Jeff grows) trotted up, sniffing as if to check me in. Then he headed off toward workers in a nearby field as if he was called to supervise the activity. Noah, Jeff's son, rode past on a small bike as Jeff came out of the house to greet me. Many crops had not been planted yet. It was a cool, wet spring. Some crops would be later than expected, but it was shaping up to be a good harvest. Four production houses were filled with broccoli and sugar snap peas. We walked farther down the driveway to the propagation house where there were rows upon rows of tiny starts. The earthy aroma of damp, fertile soil was intoxicating. The sweet smell of life made me want to linger just a little longer.

Farming seems to come naturally to Jeff, but he hasn't always been a farmer. A formally trained chef at the Culinary Institute of America (CIA), Jeff worked in restaurants in Pittsburgh and later at Stars in San Francisco. Working with all the good organic produce that came through his restaurant, he decided to try his hand at farming. He moved north and farmed outside of Woodinville in 1987. Later he moved to Monroe and got his own farm in 1996. Jeff grows produce on 17 acres of his own land and leases another 10 acres. He is easily one of the most organized farmers I've ever met, and he's excellent at marketing his picture perfect, flavorful produce. He says he does okay as a farmer. "You've got to love the lifestyle," he added.

At the University District Farmers Market, Willie Green's brilliant, perfectly prepped broccoli, cauliflower, carrots, greens and berries lure you over to his booth. The salad mix is one of my favorites, and the variety of broccoli he grows is sweet with no hint of bitter aftertaste. The sweet-tart Tulameen raspberries bring back fond memories of my grandmother's garden. You can also find Willie Green's at Columbia City, Bellevue, Lake City and West Seattle farmers markets. Jeff also wholesales through a local broker/farmer, Andrew Stout, from Full Circle Farm in Carnation. And he sells roughly two hundred pounds of lettuce and greens through Charlie's, another local produce broker, for many Seattle restaurants. In addition, Willie Green's offers seasonal CSA shares (p.279) and Winter Veggie boxes that extend harvest season a number of weeks in the fall.

However, farming isn't all beautiful produce. We only see the end result of a lot of hard work. It's an uncertain occupation, dependant on many things — weather, the price of organic seed, and market conditions among other things. When asked about certification and the national organic standards, Jeff explained that organic certification is based on what you sell. In 2002, he paid around $1,500 for his certification. "It's hard on small farmers," Jeff told me. "I had ten times more paperwork in 2002 than I did the year before the [national organic] standards went into effect. You have to keep track of all the yields."

"Organic farming is changing," Jeff said. One of the issues facing small farmers is that corporately owned organic farms like Cal-Organic plant so many acres that large-scale organic agriculture is becoming more like its conventional counterpart. Mass-produced produce from huge farms often tastes inferior, and as it descends on the marketplace, a surplus is created. Wholesale prices drop closer to conventional prices. The small organic farmer is challenged to generate more direct market sales rather than compete in grocery and natural food stores for produce space.

Marketing is the key for many smaller local farmers. In the 2004 harvest season, Jeff published a biweekly newsletter highlighting different produce items with news updates from his farm. This is available at his farm booth at the market. Jeff's website www.williegreensorganicfarm.com has details about his CSA program, produce information and recipes from past newsletters. Kristen, his outgoing better half, works with Jeff at the University District Farmers Market. Tracie, Kristen's sister and others work at various markets around town. Asked about his biggest challenge, Jeff replied: "Not being able to grow enough for market. [As a local farm] I'd like to get bigger, but not too much bigger," he added, smiling.

246

Desserts with Raw Fruit

Well-cultivated fruit grown by hardworking farmers has an enticing aroma and tastes as good as it smells. Good fruit needs little enhancement and requires no cooking. Fragrant vine-ripened, super-sweet Charentais melon, grown by River Farm in Ellensburg or Homestead Organic Produce in Quincy, can quicky satisfy a sweet craving. A perfect melon is more flavorful than any gourmet dessert and much healthier for you. Small, wild berries may be a hiker's delight but the large, luscious, cultivated blueberries sold by Rent's Due Ranch from Stanwood, quickly disappear by the pint, often before they make it home. Astonishingly juicy peaches, mouth-watering nectarines and plums, as well as crisp apples and pears ripened to perfection are transported from Chelan by Grouse Mountain Farm during the summer and fall. You can find all of these certified organic farmers at the University District Farmers Market. When considering desserts with raw fruit, it only takes a little imagination and, of course, ripe Washington-grown fruit.

Lemon-Tofu "Cream" with Fresh Fruit
(Serves 4 to 6)

Apricots, nectarines or strawberries are good choices for the fruit in this desssert. The silken tofu in shelf-stable boxes is the best choice for tofu.

> 2 cups organic, silken firm tofu
> 2 ripe bananas
> Juice and finely chopped zest of 1 lemon
> 3 to 4 tablespoons honey or agave nectar
> 1 1/2 cups fresh seasonal fruit, cut into bite-size pieces
> 2 tablespoons shredded coconut

Blend tofu, bananas, lemon juice, zest and honey in a blender. Gently blend in seasonal fruit. Top with coconut.

Melon with Sweetened Lime Juice
(Serves 4 to 6)

A desert-grown Washington-grown melon can be appreciated any time of day. Use another raw honey if you can't find lavender honey.

> 3 cups melon, cut into bite-size pieces
> 1/4 cup lime juice (approximately 2 limes)
> 1 to 2 teaspoons raw lavender honey
> Mint sprigs

Place melon in a bowl. Combine lime juice and honey and pour over melon. Garnish with mint sprigs.

Ambrosia

(Serves 4)

This is another heavenly dessert made with organic silken tofu. You can substitute nonfat plain yogurt for tofu. Use half the amount of lime juice if you make this with yogurt. Mangoes or nectarines can easily replace peaches here.

1 package shelf-stable silken tofu
1 cup cut-up pineapple chunks
1 ripe banana
1/4 cup lime juice
Honey to taste
1 cup sliced fresh strawberries or other fresh berries
2 ripe peaches, peeled and sliced
1 1/2 cups pitted cherries
2 tablespoons grated coconut

Combine tofu, pineapple chunks, banana and lime juice in a blender and puree until smooth. Gently mix in strawberries, peaches and cherries. Top with coconut.

Marinated Strawberries

(Serves 4)

A small amount of sugar pulls the juice from the berries. You can use raspberries, blackberries, sliced peaches or nectarines instead of strawberries.

2 cups sliced fresh strawberries
1 tablespoon Rapadura or organic sugar
2 tablespoons orange juice, Chambord, Grand Marnier, key lime liquor, Malibu rum or balsamic vinegar
Edible summer flowers for garnish (see note below)

Combine all ingredients and gently mix together. Refrigerate for at least one hour before serving. Garnish with flowers.

Note: Edible flowers can be found at markets or natural foods stores in the summer or in your own backyard. Some of the varieties are violet, Johnny-jump-up, Nasturtium, Anise Hyssop, Calendula, squash blossom, miniature rose and lavender.

Melon with Fresh Apricot-Ginger Sauce

(Serves 6)

Try a crenshaw melon from Homestead Organic Produce (p.5) or an orange honeydew from River Farm. For an easy fruit sauce, simply puree seasonal fruit. The best choices are the soft fruits like nectarines, apricots, strawberries, blueberries, etc. Add herbs, spices or flavorings of your choice and pour over seasonal fruit.

4 cups melon balls or chunks
8 ripe medium-size apricots
2 tablespoons apricot preserves (optional)
1 tablespoon grated ginger
1 tablespoon freshly grated coconut
Fresh seasonal flowers (see p.251 for ideas)

Place the melon balls in a serving bowl. Puree apricots and preserves together with a blender or hand blender and blend until smooth. Squeeze the juice from the grated ginger into the mixture, stir in and discard the pulp. Pour the sauce over the melon balls and gently mix. Garnish with grated coconut and fresh seasonal flowers.

Variations:

Nectarines with Strawberry-Rose Sauce

6 to 8 nectarines
1 cup ripe strawberries
1 tablespoon lemon juice
A few dashes rose water

Follow the directions above.

Fresh Berries with Lavender-Peach Sauce

4 cups mixed fresh berries
2 peaches, peeled with pit removed
1 teaspoon fresh lavender buds
2 tablespoons yogurt

Place berries in a serving bowl. Puree peaches, lavender and yogurt. Gently mix sauce with berries.

249

Autumn Fruit Delight
(Serves 4)

Nothing says autumn like succulent pears and crisp sweet-tart apples. Fuji apples are one of the best-tasting varieties. They have won many apple taste tests.

2 tablespoons lemon juice
1 tablespoon honey
Generous dash of cinnamon and nutmeg
2 Fuji apples, seeded and chopped
2 Bosc pears, chopped
1/4 cup chopped fresh dates
4 ripe figs, cut in half (optional)
1/4 cup chopped pecans

Blend lemon juice, honey, cinnamon and nutmeg together. Toss with apples and pears, making sure sauce coats all fruit. Blend in chopped dates. Place in separate serving bowls with fig halves. Garnish with pecans.

Variation:
Apples and Pears with Apricot Sauce

In the spring and summer, some farmers bring dried apricots to market. If you have an abundance of apricots, you can dehydrate your own.

8 to 10 dried apricots
Apricot nectar or apple cider to make 1 cup
1 tablespoon raw almond butter
2 sweet-tart apples, such as Fuji or Jonagold, seeded and chopped
2 Anjou or Bartlett pears, chopped
1/4 cup chopped fresh dates
1/4 cup slivered almonds

Soak apricots in apricot nectar or apple cider for about 2 hours in the refrigerator. Soak them overnight if you want. When apricots are very soft, puree with a hand blender or in a blender until smooth and creamy. Add almond butter and blend again. Pour the mixture over the apples, pears and dates and mix together. Sprinkle with slivered almonds.

Enhance Fruit Desserts with Herbs, Spices and Summer Flowers

Add generous pinches of your favorite spices to a fruit crisp, a few tablespoons of flavored liquor to raw, sliced fruit for a marinade or to a cobbler for a rich flavor. Garnish with flowers, citrus zest, coconut or mint sprigs. Below are ideas for specific fruits.

- **Apricots** — almond or vanilla extract, cardamom, ginger, nutmeg, lavender, apricot brandy, Grand Marnier (orange liquor), or hazelnut liquor
- **Apples** — lemon or orange zest, cardamom, cinnamon, nutmeg, cloves, ginger, Amaretto (almond-flavored liquor), Applejack brandy, Merlot, lilacs or lemon blossoms
- **Berries** — coconut extract, lemon or orange zest, rose water, mint, lemon verbena, Kirsch (cherry brandy), Triple Sec (orange liquor), Crème de Casiss (black currant liquor), Chambord (black raspberry liquor), key lime cream liquor, Zinfandel, lavender or pansies
- **Cherries** — lemon or orange zest, almond extract, Cherry Herring (cherry brandy) Kirsch, hazelnut liquor, banana liquor, Grand Marnier, cognac, rose geranium, violets, lavender or balsamic vinegar
- **Figs** — cardamom, nutmeg, cinnamon, cloves, anise, star anise, lavender, almond extract, vanilla, coconut flavoring, orange or lemon zest, balsamic vinegar, rose or orange flower water, or Malibu rum
- **Mangos** — lemon, lime or orange zest, lemon verbena, ginger, cardamom, nutmeg, Malibu rum, coconut schnapps, banana liquor, Alize (passion fruit liquor), violets, lavender sprigs, rose or orange water
- **Melons** — lime or orange zest, mint, ginger, star anise, Alize, Midori melon liquor, key lime liquor, Malibu rum, Japanese plum wine, sparkling white wine, nasturtiums, lavender or violets
- **Nectarines and peaches** — vanilla, maple syrup, cardamom, cloves, cinnamon, ginger, bourbon, Kahlua, peach schnapps, hazelnut liquor, key lime liquor, Marsala wine, or pansies
- **Pears** — lemon verbena, mint, cardamom, cinnamon, cloves, ginger, balsamic vinegar, Clavados (applejack brandy), bourbon, Reisling, or Ruby Port
- **Plums** — vanilla, orange or lemon zest, anise, cloves, ginger, Cointreau (orange liquor), gin, or Japanese plum wine
- **Strawberries** — lemon, orange or lime zest, rose water, mint, tequila, coconut schnapps, strawberry liquor, banana liquor, key lime liquor, Grand Marnier, white chocolate liquor, hazelnut liquor, Malibu rum, port wine, balsamic vinegar, pansies, violets or lavender

Frozen Fruit Desserts

Sizzling summer days and cooling, creamy frozen treats naturally go together. But if your choice is lower fat with a creamy texture and no dairy, a short trip down the frozen dessert aisle in any grocery store reveals a limited selection. However, your options don't have to end there. With a few basic recipes, your own creativity, and flavor enhancing suggestions, you can make your own fabulous frozen desserts.

Though an ice cream maker isn't absolutely necessary, you'll get better results if you have one for most of these desserts. Without one, it takes a more work but you can do the freeze and stir method for these recipes. For this method, take your dessert out every half hour for about three hours and stir to incorporate air into it. Use a hand blender or mixer until the mixture gets very thick. The texture with this method isn't equal to the creamy texture you get with an ice cream mixer.

Versions of the recipes in this section first appeared in an article in Vegetarian Journal in July 2001. Check out the Vegetarian Resource Group website at www.vrg.org.

Tips for using an ice cream maker

♦ Read through the recipe before beginning.

♦ Blend all your ingredients, except the agar and liquid, the day before you make the frozen dessert. This gives flavors a chance to marry. Refrigerate until you're ready to make the dessert.

♦ Place the ice cream maker base in the freezer at least eight hours before making the dessert. You can store it in your freezer if you have room.

♦ When mixing your dessert, turn on the ice cream maker first before adding the mixture, otherwise the dessert will stick to the sides of the base and freeze up and it will freeze unevenly.

♦ Most ice cream makers direct you to churn for 20 to 25 minutes but let it churn for 35 minutes and you'll have a thicker texture. Sample liberally, of course, to make sure it has the right consistency before turning off the machine.

♦ Enjoy your sweet rewards immediately, if possible. These desserts have a lower fat content and the water molecules begin linking up, changing the texture from creamy to hard and grainy as the dessert sits in the freezer.

♦ Experiment with flavorings and fruits, but keep the same proportion of tofu or beans, sweeteners, liquid ingredients and agar. Once you have the recipes down, take a stroll down an ice cream aisle for flavoring ideas.

Frozen Vanilla Treat with Fresh Fruit

(Serves 4 to 5)

This is the basic recipe. Amazake is a naturally sweet rice beverage found in the refrigerated section of natural food stores. Agar can be found in flake, granule or powder form. Top this frozen dessert with seasonal fruit selections or mix in your favorite dried fruit.

2 vanilla beans, slit down the middle
1 cup vanilla-pecan or almond shake amazake
1 package shelf-stable, firm silken tofu
1/4 cup organic sugar
1/8 teaspoon salt
Pinch of freshly grated nutmeg
2 tablespoons melted coconut oil
2 1/2 teaspoons agar
3/4 cup water
Fresh seasonal fruit

Scrape seeds out of vanilla beans into amazake and blend with tofu, sugar, salt, nutmeg and oil in a blender. Puree until creamy. Chill for at least 2 hours. Sprinkle agar over the water in a small saucepan. Bring to a boil, then reduce heat and simmer for 5 minutes or until dissolved. Let cool for about 10 minutes before adding to cold mixture. Have ice cream maker ready to go (chilled overnight in the freezer). Turn on and pour mixture in. Churn for 35 minutes or until very thick. Serve within a few hours. Top with fresh fruit.

Frozen Strawberry Pops

(Makes 12 pops)

This easy dessert doesn't even need churning! Fruit sweetener can be found in natural food stores near the sugar or in the refrigerated section.

1 cup fresh strawberries, stems removed
1 shelf-stable package firm silken tofu
2 tablespoons lemon juice
3 tablespoons strawberry preserves or orange marmalade
1 tablespoon finely chopped orange zest (optional)
1 teaspoon agar
1/2 cup mixed berry frozen concentrate
1/2 cup water

Combine strawberries, tofu, lemon juice, preserves and orange zest, if desired, in a blender. Blend until smooth and creamy. In a small saucepan, sprinkle agar over berry concentrate and water. Bring to a boil, reduce heat and simmer for 5 minutes or until agar dissolves. Add to strawberry-tofu mixture and puree until smooth. Pour into Popsicle molds and freeze until solid, or pour into small paper cups and freeze until slushy. Insert a stick, then freeze until solid.

For easy removal from plastic molds, run water over mold, twist the handle and pull gently.

Tip

Don't soak berries in water or they become waterlogged. Wash strawberries briefly, or wipe large berries off with a damp cloth. Scoop the stem out with a spoon and use the berries as soon as possible. Very ripe berries are pink all the way through. They usually need nothing more than a splash of balsamic vinegar or a squeeze of citrus to enhance the flavor.

Cherry Red Bean Delight

(Serves 6)

In one of my cooking classes, an assistant mentioned a frozen red bean (adzuki) dessert she had as a child. The idea of a bean dessert was intriguing, so I went home, experimented, and came up with this irresistible recipe.

1/3 cup adzuki beans, soaked overnight
1 cup vanilla soymilk
1/4 cup cherry preserves
2 tablespoons lemon juice
1 teaspoon almond extract
1/8 teaspoon salt
2 1/2 tablespoons agar
3/4 cup cherry juice or coconut milk
Pitted sweet cherries or flowers for topping

Add approximately 2 cups of water to adzuki beans in a saucepan and bring to a boil. Reduce heat, partially cover and slow-simmer until done — 1 to 1 1/2 hours or until beans are soft. Remove from heat, drain and let cool. In a blender, combine adzuki beans and 1/2 cup soymilk. Blend until smooth and creamy. Add remaining soymilk, preserves, lemon juice, almond extract and salt. Continue to process until creamy. Refrigerate for at least two hours or overnight. Sprinkle agar over cherry juice in a small saucepan. Bring to a boil, reduce heat and simmer 5 minutes or until agar dissolves. Let cool 10 minutes, then add to adzuki bean mixture and blend until smooth. Turn on ice cream maker and add mixture. Churn for 35 minutes or until done. Top frozen dessert with fresh, pitted cherries or flowers.

Brandied Strawberry Granita
(Serves 4)

Bursts of tantalizing summer berry flavor come from the combination of fresh berries, frozen raspberry concentrate and Kirsch (a cherry brandy) in this rich-tasting, Italian-style frozen ice. You only need a blender and some time for this delicious treat.

1/2 tablespoon agar
1 cup frozen raspberry concentrate
3 tablespoons sugar
2 cups fresh strawberries
3 tablespoons fresh lemon juice
1/4 cup Kirsch (cherry brandy)
1 cup water
Pansies, lavender or other edible summer flowers

Sprinkle agar over raspberry concentrate. Let it soak for a few minutes while it softens. Bring the liquid to a boil, then reduce heat and cook over medium-heat, stirring constantly for 5 minutes. Remove from heat and stir in sugar. Let mixture sit while you blend the remaining ingredients in a blender or food processor.

Add the raspberry concentrate mixture to the strawberry mixture and blend on low until they are well mixed. Pour into ice cube trays and freeze solid. At least two hours before serving, remove from freezer and let the cubes thaw for 5 minutes. Then place about 1/3 of the cubes into a food processor or blender and pulse the machine on and off until the cubes are the consistency of coarse snow. Then, run the machine until the mixture is creamy looking but not runny. Process the remaining cubes in the same way. Cover and freeze a few hours. There is no need to let this dessert sit out before serving. Garnish with edible summer flowers.

Creamy Frozen Maple Apricot Dessert
(Serves 6)

This can easily be made with other fruits and flavorings. Nectarines, peaches or mangoes are all good options in this recipe.

3 cups sliced apricots
1 shelf-stable package firm silken tofu
1/4 cup maple syrup
1 tablespoon lemon juice
Generous pinch of nutmeg or cardamom
1/8 teaspoon salt
2 teaspoon agar
1 cup peach or apricot juice
Maple syrup for topping

Combine apricots, tofu, maple syrup, lemon juice, nutmeg or cardamom and salt in a blender and blend until smooth and creamy. Pour into a container and refrigerate for at least a few hours before churning.

In a small saucepan, sprinkle agar over juice, bring to a boil, then reduce heat and simmer for 5 minutes or until agar is dissolved. Let cool 10 minutes before blending with the cold mixture. Turn on ice cream maker and add mixture. Churn for 35 minutes or until very thick. Serve with a swirl of maple syrup on top.

R & R Farms

Every summer at the University District Farmers Market, I watch for my favorite apricot farmers to make an appearance. Some of the best apricots around come from R & R Farms, a homestead orchard on 6 1/2 acres near Wenatchee, owned and run by Ron and Roslyn Lawrence. The old orchard was abandoned around 1948, and when Ron and Roslyn took over, they didn't have to use chemical sprays or fertilizers because there weren't any pest problems. The apricot trees were thriving and coexisting with many native plants. The orchard was in balance with nature, and that's the way they kept it. Their method of agriculture is called "wildcrafting." They don't add compost to the soil or rely on irrigation to force size growth. They depend on the rainfall received, and encourage plants and animals that enhance their crops. The orchard is also a haven for many wild animals. They share their harvest with local bears and coyotes. Buy more than you think you need because you can't eat just one, and those small Royal and Tilton apricots disappear quickly.

Easy Cooked Fruit Desserts

When you want something sweet and warm, there are many easy cooked or baked fruit desserts that can be put together at the last minute. Grilled peaches or nectarines are heavenly. Pears sautéed in virgin coconut oil topped with a simple apricot or raspberry sauce (p. 20-21) are absolutely decadent. When fruit is perfect, let the natural flavors shine through. These sweet indulgences create a perfect ending for simple as well as elegant meals. Check out the bounty of local selections. You won't be disappointed with taste.

Baked Ginger Pears with Pineapple
(Serves 4)

Goldie Caughlan, Nutrition Education Manager for PCC Natural Markets, once shared a great baked pear recipe similar to this.

> 4 to 6 Bosc pears
> 2 cups apple cider
> 1 cup canned pineapple chunks, drained
> 1 to 2 tablespoons freshly grated ginger
> Sprinkling of grated coconut

Cut pears in quarters. (There is no need to seed the pears because the seeds are soft enough to eat.) Place pears in a shallow baking dish with pineapple chunks. Pour apple cider over the pears and sprinkle with ginger. Cover and bake at 325° for one hour or more until pears soak up most of the cider. When pears are soft and done, sprinkle with coconut. Place them under the broiler for a few minutes so they will brown lightly on top.

FOOD FOR THOUGHT

Pears originated in the Middle East. They used to be called "butter fruit" because of their smooth texture. A member of the rose family, they are related to apples. Both fruits contain boron, an essential mineral for healthy bones. Pears are also a good source of fiber, folate, potassium and iron.

Stuffed Baked Apples
(Serves 4)

Apples and raw almond butter go together naturally. Add some dates for a sensual sweet dessert.

3/4 cup apple juice
1/4 cup Applejack brandy, or more apple juice
1 tablespoon arrowroot
2 large baking apples (Newton Pippin, Granny Smith, Fuji or Winesap)
1 1/2 tablespoons maple syrup
3 tablespoons almond butter
3 Medjool dates, pitted and cut into small pieces

Preheat oven to 350º. In a baking dish, combine apple juice, Applejack brandy and arrowroot. Stir until arrowroot is dissolved. Peel, halve and core apples, hollowing a space in the center for the filling. Mix maple syrup, almond butter and dates. Fill apples, place in baking dish, cover and bake for 45 minutes or until apples are done.

Variation:

Apricot-Almond Stuffed Pears
8 dried apricots
Apple juice to cover to 1/2 cup
1 tablespoon almond butter
1 teaspoon maple syrup
1 tablespoon raisins
4 large Bosc pears
1 cup apple juice
1 tablespoon arrowroot
Freshly grated nutmeg

Soak apricots in apple juice for at least one hour. In a blender, puree soaked apricots and juice, almond butter and maple syrup. When blended, mix in raisins by hand. Preheat oven to 350º.

Wash and core pears, scooping out a hole in the middle of the pear. Combine apple juice and arrowroot and stir until arrowroot is dissolved. Place pears in a shallow baking dish. Spoon apricot mixture into the pears. Pour apple juice with arrowroot over the stuffed pears. Top with a sprinkling of freshly grated nutmeg. Cover and bake for 45 minutes or until pears are tender.

Balsamic Poached Pears

(Serves 4)

Poaching is a technique where fruit is simmered in a sugar-based liquid until tender. Pears, peaches, apricots, nectarines, and apples can also be poached, You could use a light dry red, ruby port or white wine with a sweetener in this recipe instead of balsamic vinegar.

2 tablespoons orange marmalade
2 tablespoons Rapadura or organic sugar
1/4 cup balsamic vinegar
1 1/2 cups water
2 large Bosc pears, cut in half with cores removed
Sprinkling of grated coconut (optional)

Combine marmalade, Rapadura and balsamic vinegar. Mix well and stir into water in a shallow saucepan. Bring mixture to a boil. Add pears, reduce heat and gently simmer for about 10 minutes. Let pears cool in liquid, then remove pears to a serving dish. Spoon sauce over the pears. Garnish with coconut before serving.

Baked Nectarines

(Serves 4)

Nectarines are good any way you slice them. These baked delights are great over vanilla ice cream or frozen soy dessert. Grilling is another option. Add a tablespoon of melted coconut oil to a small amount of apricot nectar or balsamic vinegar and baste the fruit as it grills. When done, sprinkle with freshly grated nutmeg.

4 nectarines, sliced in half and pitted
1 tablespoon lemon juice
1 cup peach or apricot nectar
1 tablespoon Rapadura or date sugar
Freshly grated nutmeg

Preheat oven to 350°. Place nectarine halves, cut side down, in a shallow baking dish. Sprinkle with lemon juice. Pour peach nectar over peaches. Sprinkle with Rapadura and freshly grated nutmeg. Bake uncovered for 30 minutes or until very tender.

Maple-Glazed Grilled Peaches

(Serves 6)

Peaches are the best when eaten fresh off the tree on a warm afternoon or grilled. Apricots, nectarines or mangoes are also good grilled.

6 peaches, blanched and peeled
3 tablespoons maple syrup
2 1/2 tablespoons orange juice
1/2 tablespoon Grand Marnier liqueur
Generous pinch of nutmeg or cardamom
Vanilla or lemon yogurt or organic vanilla ice cream (optional)
Mint sprigs

Lightly spray the grill grid with oil to prevent sticking. Preheat grill. Slice the peaches in half and remove pits. Combine maple syrup, orange juice, Grand Marnier, and nutmeg or cardamom. Brush the cut side of the peaches with the mixture. When grill is ready, place peaches cut side down on the grill. Brush the tops with maple glaze. After 5 minutes turn the peaches. Cook for 5 minutes. Peaches should be lightly browned. Pour any remaining glaze over peaches and serve with a dollop of yogurt. Garnish with mint sprigs.

Ginger-Simmered Rhubarb and Nectarines

(Serves 4)

*Serve this dessert with **Lemon–Pecan Biscotti** (p.30) or top each serving with a spoonful of lemon yogurt.*

2 cups rhubarb, cut into 1/2-inch lengths
4 nectarines, pitted and sliced
1 cup peach nectar
1/4 cup Rapadura or organic sugar
1 tablespoon grated ginger

Place rhubarb, nectarines, peach nectar and Rapadura in a medium-size saucepan. Squeeze juice from ginger over the fruit mixture. Discard ginger pulp. Bring to a boil, then reduce heat and simmer until fruit is very tender.

Summer Fruit Compote
(Serves 4)

*This compote is delicious over vanilla ice cream, pound cake or **Ginger-Peach Scones** (p.25). You can also chill the simmered fruit for a few hours, then serve it with oatmeal cookies (p.31).*

3 peeled, pitted peaches, sliced
4 pitted, quartered apricots
4 pitted, quartered plums
3/4 cup apricot nectar or apple juice
1/4 cup coconut milk
1 tablespoon fruit sweetener
1 or 2 tablespoons Malibu rum
1/2 tablespoon kudzu or arrowroot

Preheat oven to 350º. Combine all ingredients in an 8X8-inch baking dish. Mix until arrowroot is dissolved. Cover and bake for about 45 minutes or until fruit is very soft.

Winter Ginger Fruit Compote
(Serves 4 to 6)

During the autumn and winter, some of my favorite fruits aren't in season. I often use dried fruit instead of resorting to fruit that was transported from hundreds of miles away. You can use 4 cups of fruit juice instead of fruit concentrate. Juice your own apples for the juice, if you want.

3 cup assorted dried fruit (use peaches, nectarines, apples,
apricots, apples, pears, figs, mangoes or cherries)
3/4 to 1 cup frozen apple or peach concentrate
3 cups water
1 1/2 to 2 tablespoons grated ginger

Place dried fruit in an oven-proof ceramic or glass bowl. Combine apple or peach concentrate and water. Blend well, then stir the concentrate and dried fruit together. Squeeze juice from the grated ginger over the dried fruit and discard ginger pulp. Let the fruit sit overnight in the refrigerator. Bake uncovered in a 350º oven for about 75 minutes, basting occasionally. Fruit should be plump and soft.

Honey Plums with Mint

(Serves 4)

Cooking enhances the sweet-tart flavor of plums. This dessert is good by itself or served over plain cake.

2/3 cup water
1 tablespoon lemon juice
1 tablespoon finely chopped lemon zest
2 tablespoons honey
Fresh mint sprigs
14 to 16 small plums, pitted and cut in half
Pinch of salt
6 ounces lemon yogurt (optional)

Place water in a small saucepan. Add lemon juice, zest and honey. Bring to a boil. Add mint sprigs, plums and pinch of salt. Reduce heat and cook on low for 10 minutes or until plums are soft. Remove from heat, cool and serve with a dollop of yogurt and fresh mint sprigs.

Cranberry Applesauce

(Makes 2 cups)

You can use this recipe as an alternative to cranberry sauce and enjoy it as an accompaniment to a holiday meal. Or, serve it with shortbread for a humble dessert.

2 cups sliced apples
2 cups fresh cranberries
1/2 cup apple juice
1/4 cup Rapadura
1 teaspoon almond extract

Place all ingredients in a saucepan and cook on medium-low until fruit is tender, about 5 to 10 minutes. Puree 2 cups at a time in the blender, then return to saucepan and cook until mixture thickens to desired consistency.

Variation:

Cranberry-Apple Whip

1 cup cranberry-applesauce
1 cup firm silken tofu
2 to 4 tablespoons finely chopped, toasted walnuts or pecans

Blend cranberry-applesauce and silken tofu in a blender or with a hand blender until smooth and creamy. Stir in toasted nuts and serve.

Sautéed Balsamic Cherries

(Makes about 2 cups)

Serve these deep-flavored cherries over your favorite frozen nondairy dessert or vanilla ice cream. Use only the best balsamic vinegar. It enhances the flavor of the cherries.

1/2 tablespoon coconut oil
2 1/2 cups pitted sweet cherries
2 tablespoons balsamic vinegar
1 to 2 tablespoons Rapadura or organic sugar
Grated coconut

Heat a heavy skillet over medium heat. Add coconut oil. When the skillet is hot, stir in cherries. Sauté until cherries are soft. Sprinkle sugar over the cherries. Stir until all cherries are coated. Add balsamic vinegar, stir and cook for another 30 seconds. Remove from heat, garnish with coconut and serve.

Vanilla Baked Plums and Pears

(Serves 4)

Plums and pears usually overlap seasons and the taste of both enhance each other.

12 Italian plums (or 8 to 10 larger plums), cut in half and pitted
2 Bosc pears, cut in half and sliced
1/2 cup water
1 tablespoon lemon juice
1/4 cup Rapadura or organic sugar
1 tablespoon arrowroot
1 vanilla bean, sliced in half lengthwise, or 1/2 teaspoon vanilla
Topping:
1/2 cup whole-wheat flour
1/4 cup oatmeal
3 tablespoons organic brown sugar
3 tablespoons coconut oil or butter
1/4 cup chopped, toasted walnuts

Preheat oven to 350º. Combine fruit, water, lemon juice, sugar and arrowroot in a small bowl and mix well. Pour into a 9X9-inch baking dish. Scrape the inside of a vanilla bean into the mixture and stir. Discard vanilla shell. Combine topping ingredients, mixing until oil is well blended. Sprinkle over the fruit mixture. Bake covered for 40 minutes. Uncover the dish and continue to bake for another 10 minutes. You can run this dish under the broiler to brown the topping, if desired.

Cobblers, Slumps, Crisps and more

Cooked fruit desserts bring back memories of my grandmother's pies – sour cherry and sweet-tart apple were favorites. Grandma showed me how to roll out a perfect piecrust and taught me the art of making cookies with the leftover pastry dough. Everyone raved about her flaky, tender piecrusts. But to get those delectable crusts light and flaky, she used a lot of butter or lard. It was rich comfort food, but all that saturated animal fat in one bite would make me cringe now. These days I'm challenged to create the same dynamic flavors with more healthful options.

Bread and rice puddings, cobblers and crisps are long-time traditional favorites. Because the egg whites are whipped, bread pudding is better with the addition of farm fresh eggs for perfect texture. Rice pudding holds together well when you use kudzu (kuzu) or arrowroot. It is downright decadent when made with cashew cream. Cobblers are healthy options for dessert because there is only one rich-tasting biscuit crust. A New England slump is fruit simmered in a large, deep skillet with sweet biscuit dough dropped onto it like dumplings. A crisp is fruit baked with a crumb topping. Using maple syrup instead of sugar makes the topping become crisp.

The following recipes are dedicated to inspired memories of my grandmother's kitchen.

Sour Cherry Bread Pudding

(Serves 6)

Try using bread from The Essential Baking Company (p. 40) for this recipe.

> 5 cups of artisan bread cubes, crusts removed
> 1 1/2 cups pitted sour cherries
> 1/2 cup Rapadura or organic sugar
> 1 1/2 cups vanilla soymilk
> 3 eggs, separated
> 2 tablespoons rum or 1/2 tablespoon vanilla
> 1/2 teaspoon salt

Combine bread cubes, sour cherries and sugar. Mix well. Preheat oven to 325°. Lightly oil the sides and bottom of a 9X9-inch pan. Heat vanilla soymilk in a small saucepan over medium heat. When warm, stir in egg yolks, blending well. Add rum or vanilla and salt. Stir and cook for a few minutes. Remove from heat and mix in with the bread cubes.

Whip egg whites until soft peaks form. Fold egg whites into the bread mixture. Turn into the prepared baking dish and bake for 45 minutes or until pudding is set. Serve warm with a little vanilla soymilk poured over it. Or be decadent and use a dab of whipped cream or ice cream.

Sweet Baked Rice Pudding with Peaches

(Serves 6)

This dessert can also be made with other fruit such as apples, pears, blueberries or apricots. To blanch and peel the peaches, bring a large pot of water to a boil. Plunge ripe peaches in for 30 seconds, then remove and peel peach while holding under running cold water. Pour a little cashew cream over the top (see recipe below) and this pudding is like a taste of heaven.

Zest and juice of 1/2 lemon
2 cups cashew cream
1/3 cup kudzu or arrowroot
1/4 cup maple syrup
1/2 teaspoon freshly grated nutmeg
1/4 teaspoon salt
2 cups cooked brown Jasmine rice
2 peeled ripe medium-size peaches
2 tablespoons Rapadura
1/2 to 1 teaspoon cardamom

Preheat oven to 325°. Combine lemon zest, juice, cashew cream, arrowroot, maple syrup, nutmeg and salt in a blender and mix until foamy. Combine this with brown rice and pour into a lightly oiled 9X9-inch pan. Bake for 35 minutes or until thick.

Remove from oven and spread sliced peaches over the top. In a small bowl, combine Rapadura and cardamom. Sprinkle over the peaches, return to oven and bake for another 15 minutes or until peaches are tender. Remove from oven. Pudding thickens as it cools.

Cashew Cream

(Makes about 2 cups)

This topping makes cobbler, crisp, rice or bread pudding sublime. You can also use it to top fresh sliced peaches, nectarines or apples and dates.

1 cup water
1 cup cashews
1/2 teaspoon vanilla extract
1 tablespoon maple syrup
1 tablespoon lemon juice
Dash of salt
Pinch of cayenne

Soak cashews in water for an hour. Puree cashews and water in a blender with remaining ingredients. Sweeten to taste with additional maple syrup.

266

Strawberry-Rhubarb Cobbler
(Serves 6)

The first cobbler of the season begins with strawberries. You can make plain rhubarb cobbler, but you will have to double the sugar in the recipe.

Filling:
2 cups strawberries
2 cups rhubarb, cut into 1/2-inch slices
1/2 cup Rapadura or organic sugar
1/4 cup orange juice
2 tablespoons Triple Sec or finely chopped orange zest
2 tablespoons kudzu

Crust:
1 1/4 cups whole-wheat pastry flour
1/2 tablespoon baking powder
2 tablespoons plus 1 tablespoon Rapadura, or organic brown sugar
1/4 cup coconut oil or cold butter
1/3 cup vanilla soymilk
1 tablespoon melted coconut oil or butter (optional)

Preheat oven to 350º. Combine strawberries, rhubarb, sugar, orange juice Triple Sec and kudzu, in a 2-quart casserole dish.

In a separate bowl, blend flour, baking powder and 2 tablespoons organic sugar. Mix well. With a pastry blender or fork, mix in 1/4 cup coconut oil until mixture resembles coarse meal. Stir in soymilk until a dough forms. Knead about 3 turns, then on a lightly floured board, pat dough to an 8-inch round, or large enough to cover fruit in the casserole dish. Lift and place dough over fruit. Cut about 5 slits into the dough, radiating out from the center. Brush melted oil on top and sprinkle with Rapadura. Place cobbler on a baking sheet. Bake 35 to 45 minutes or until top is golden brown. Cool for 10 minutes before serving.

Variations:
Apple-Pear Cobbler
2 large Granny Smith apples, peeled, cored and thinly sliced
2 large Bosc pears, cored and thinly sliced
1/4 cup lemon juice
1/4 cup Rapadura, or agave nectar
2 tablespoons arrowroot
1/2 teaspoon cinnamon

Combine filling ingredients and prepare dough for crust as directed above. Follow baking instructions above.

Mixed Berry Cobbler

4 to 5 cups mixed summer berries
1/4 cup organic sugar or Rapadura
2 tablespoons lemon juice
2 Tablespoons Chambord or Crème de Casiss (optional)
3 tablespoons arrowroot or kudzu

Combine ingredients. Prepare dough for crust. Follow baking instructions above.

Cherry Cobbler

4 cups pitted sour cherries
1/2 cup organic sugar or Rapadura
3 tablespoons arrowroot or kudzu
2 tablespoons lemon juice
1 tablespoon finely chopped lemon zest

Combine ingredients. Prepare dough for crust. Follow baking instructions above.

Nectarine Cobbler

4 cups sliced ripe nectarines
1/4 cup maple syrup
1/4 teaspoon freshly grated nutmeg
2 tablespoons Malibu rum or coconut milk (optional)
3 tablespoons arrowroot or kudzu

Combine ingredients. Prepare dough for crust. Follow baking instructions above.

Plum-Strawberry Cobbler

3 cups sliced plums
2 cups sliced strawberries
1/2 cup strawberry preserves
2 tablespoons lime juice
3 tablespoons arrowroot or kudzu

Combine ingredients. Prepare dough for crust. Follow baking instructions above.

Cranberry-Raspberry Cobbler

3 cups raspberries
2 cups cranberries
1/4 cup frozen raspberry concentrate
1/2 cup organic sugar
3 tablespoons arrowroot or kudzu

Combine ingredients. Prepare dough for crust. Follow baking instructions above.

Peach Crisp
(Serves 6)

Almond or cashew butter takes the place of butter in this recipe, giving the topping a crisp texture and a wonderful flavor. Leave out the Rapadura, and the maple syrup imparts a subtle sweet flavor to the topping.

Filling:
5 to 6 cups peeled and sliced ripe peaches
2 tablespoons lemon juice
2 tablespoons arrowroot or kudzu
1/2 teaspoon freshly ground cardamom
Topping:
1 cup whole-wheat or spelt flour
1 cup rolled oats
1/2 cup Rapadura or organic brown sugar (optional)
1/2 teaspoon baking soda
1/2 teaspoon cinnamon
1/2 cup almond or cashew butter
1/2 cup maple syrup

Preheat oven to 350°. Combine the apple filling ingredients in a 2-quart casserole dish and stir gently. Set aside. In a medium mixing bowl, combine flour, oats, Rapadura, soda and cinnamon in a bowl and mix thoroughly, making sure there are no small lumps.

In another bowl, mix almond butter with maple syrup. Blend well. Pour wet ingredients into dry mixture and blend together until all particles are coated. Sprinkle the topping over the apples and pat down. Bake for 45 minutes or until the filling is bubbling. Let cool before serving.

Variations:
Pear-Cranberry Crisp
4 large pears, cored and sliced, use Bosc or Anjou
1 cup fresh cranberries
1/4 cup cranberry juice
1/4 cup Rapadura or agave nectar
1 tablespoon orange zest
1 tablespoon arrowroot or kudzu
Omit cinnamon from crust in recipe above

Combine pears, cranberries, cranberry juice, Rapadura, orange zest and arrowroot. Place fruit mixture in casserole dish; prepare topping in recipe above, spread over fruit and bake as directed at 350° for 45 minutes.

Cinnamon-Apple Crisp
Filling:
6 large sweet-tart baking apples such as Fuji or Granny Smith
1/4 cup apple juice
1 1/2 tablespoons lemon juice
1 tablespoon maple syrup
1 tablespoons arrowroot or kudzu
1 teaspoon cinnamon
Topping:
1 cup whole-wheat or spelt flour
1 cup rolled oats
1/2 to 3/4 cup organic brown sugar
1/2 teaspoon baking soda
1/2 cup coconut oil or butter

Combine apples, apple juice, lemon juice, maple syrup, arrowroot and cinnamon in a 2-quart casserole dish. Combine flour, oats, sugar and baking soda. Mix thoroughly. Cut coconut oil or butter into the dry ingredients. Sprinkle over fruit mixture, pat down and bake at 350° for 45 minutes. Serve with **Cashew Cream** (p.266), frozen vanilla soy dessert or organic vanilla ice cream, if desired.

Blueberry Crisp
5 cups blueberries
1 tablespoon lemon juice
2 tablespoons Crème de Casiss
1/4 cup Rapadura or organic sugar (optional)
2 tablespoons arrowroot or kudzu

Combine blueberries, lemon juice, Crème de Casiss and arrowroot. Place in 2-quart casserole dish. Prepare topping in the preceding recipe and bake at 350° for 45 minutes.

Cranberry-Raspberry Slump

(Serves 6)

A tantalizing blend of cranberries and raspberries create a sweet-tart flavor in this simmered old-fashioned New England fruit dessert with orange dumplings.

Base:
2 cups fresh cranberries
2 cups frozen raspberries
1/3 cup orange juice
1/2 cup Rapadura
1 tablespoon arrowroot
1 tablespoon Grand Marnier or 1 tablespoon orange zest
Dumplings:
1/3 cup vanilla soymilk
1 tablespoon lemon juice
1 cup whole-wheat pastry flour
2 tablespoons organic sugar or Rapadura
2 tablespoons baking powder
1/2 teaspoon baking soda
1/2 teaspoon salt
1 tablespoon finely chopped orange zest
2 tablespoons coconut oil or cold butter

Combine cranberries, raspberries, orange juice, sugar, arrowroot and Grand Marnier in a heavy skillet (not cast iron because acidic ingredients tend to pull more iron out creating metallic taste). Simmer for 5 minutes. While the fruit cooks, prepare dumplings.

Combine soymilk with lemon juice and set aside. In a medium mixing bowl, combine flour, sugar, baking powder, soda, salt and orange zest. Mix well, making sure there are no small lumps of baking soda. Cut in coconut oil or butter until mixture has a mealy consistency. Add soymilk and lemon juice and stir until a batter forms. Batter will be fairly thick but still sticky. Drop from a heaping teaspoon onto the simmering liquid, going around the outside of the pan until you reach the middle, covering almost all of the fruit mixture. Cover and simmer for 40 minutes or until dumplings are done. Serve in individual dishes with the hot simmering fruit ladled over the dumplings. Add a dollop of vanilla yogurt, vanilla ice cream or frozen soy dessert, if desired.

Variations:

Strawberry-Raspberry-Rhubarb Slump
2 cups strawberries
2 cups rhubarb, cut into 1/2-inch slices
1 cup raspberries
1/2 cup frozen strawberry-daiquiri mix
2 tablespoons lemon juice
2 tablespoons arrowroot

Combine ingredients in a skillet. Bring to a boil, then reduce heat and simmer for 5 minutes. Prepare dumplings (p. 271). Combine soymilk and lemon juice, then mix dry ingredients, blending well. Cut in coconut oil or butter until mixture has a coarse mealy consistency, then add soymilk, stirring until a batter forms. Drop from spoonful onto simmering fruit. Cover and simmer for 30 to 40 minutes or until rhubarb is fork-tender.

Peach-Blueberry Slump
3 cups peeled peaches, sliced
2 cups fresh blueberries
Juice and zest of 1 orange
1 teaspoon fresh lavender buds
1 tablespoon arrowroot

Combine ingredients in a skillet. Bring to a boil, then reduce heat and simmer for 5 minutes. Prepare dumplings (p. 271). Combine soymilk and lemon juice, then mix dry ingredients, blending well. Cut in coconut oil or butter until mixture has a coarse mealy consistency, then add soymilk, stirring until a batter forms. Drop from spoonful on simmering fruit. Cover and cook for 30 to 40 minutes.

Plum-Pear Slump with Lemon Dumplings
3 cups sliced pears (Bosc or Anjou)
2 cups pitted sliced plums
1/2 cup apple juice
2 tablespoons lemon juice
1 tablespoon arrowroot
1 tablespoon lemon zest to replace orange zest in dumplings

Combine pears, plums, apple juice, lemon juice and arrowroot in a skillet. Bring to a boil, then reduce heat and simmer for 5 minutes. Prepare dumplings (p.271). Combine soymilk and lemon juice, then mix dry ingredients, substituting lemon for orange zest. Cut in coconut oil or butter until mixture is mealy, then add soymilk, stirring until a batter forms. Drop from spoonful on simmering fruit and cover and simmer for 30 to 40 minutes.

Apple Kuchen
(Serves 6)

If you make this homey German coffeecake with eggs, the crust will be more cake-like. Made with tofu, the crust works but is smaller and the texture is more dense. Sweet-tart apples such as Fuji, Jonathan or Jonagold are good in this recipe.

Topping:
3 medium apples, peeled, cored and thinly sliced
2 tablespoons lemon juice
2 tablespoons maple syrup
1 tablespoon Grand Marnier or 1 teaspoon orange zest
1/2 tablespoon arrowroot
Crust:
1 1/4 cups whole-wheat pastry or barley flour
1/2 cup Rapadura
1 teaspoon baking powder
1 teaspoon baking soda
1 teaspoon cinnamon or cardamom
3 tablespoons plus 1 tablespoon butter or coconut oil
2 beaten eggs or 1/2 cup Mori Nu silken tofu
1/3 cup vanilla soymilk
2 tablespoons organic powdered sugar (optional)

Preheat oven to 350º. Lightly oil a 14-inch pizza pan. Place apples, lemon juice, maple syrup and Grand Marnier in a bowl. Mix well, then let fruit marinate while you prepare the crust.

Combine dry ingredients and mix well. Cut in butter with a pasty blender or fork until mixture resembles coarse crumbs. Whip beaten eggs or silken tofu and soymilk together in a blender or with a hand blender until smooth. Stir in with dry ingredients. Batter consistency will be between cake batter and a brownie mix — a little too stiff to pour and a little too sticky to pat out. Scrape the batter onto the pizza pan and spread with a knife or bowl scraper to about an inch from the edge. Crust will be thin.

Mix arrowroot in with the apples and lemon juice mixture until apples are coated. Place apples, one at a time, on the crust radiating out from the center. The crust should be covered with apples. Drizzle the juice left in the bowl over the apples. Bake for 25 minutes or until crust is browned around the edges. Remove from oven and let sit for 5 minutes. With a large wide spatula, carefully remove kuchen from pan and place on a cooling rack. Sprinkle with powdered sugar before serving, if desired.

Variation:

Blueberry Kuchen
3 cups fresh blueberries
1 tablespoon orange zest
1 tablespoon Grand Marnier
1 tablespoon arrowroot

Follow directions above, substituting the blueberry combination for the apples. Prepare crust on p. 273 and bake as directed.

Pear-Cherry Kuchen
1/3 cup dried sour cherries, chopped
2 medium-large Bosc or Anjou pears, cored and thinly sliced
2 tablespoons lemon juice
2 tablespoons Rapadura
Generous pinch of cardamom

Pour about 1/2 cup water over cherries and let soak for about 5 minutes. Pour off water, then combine cherries, pears, lemon juice, sugar and nutmeg. Mix well. Follow directions on p.273 for crust and baking.

FOOD FOR THOUGHT
Pears have alkaline elements and a strong diuretic action, which is good for digestion. They contain iodine, necessary for good thyroid function, and are also an excellent source of soluble fiber, which is helpful for constipation. Pears have a higher pectin content than apples. They can be used in any recipe that calls for apples. They are best when ripened after picking.

Nectarine Upside-Down Cake

(Makes one 9-inch cake)

Pineapple upside-down cake was the pattern for this recipe that uses nectarines from local farmers. Incorporating an egg makes the cake lighter with more cake-like texture than an egg replacer.

3 cups sliced nectarines
1/2 teaspoon cardamom
2 to 4 tablespoons Rapadura
1 tablespoon arrowroot
2 tablespoons plus 1 tablespoon lemon juice
1/3 cup vanilla soymilk
1 cup whole-wheat pastry flour
1/2 tablespoon baking powder
1/2 teaspoon baking soda
1/2 cup Rapadura
1/3 cup butter or coconut oil
1 egg, beaten or egg replacer for one egg
Edible flowers

Combine nectarines, cardamom, Rapadura, arrowroot and 2 tablespoons lemon juice in a saucepan. Heat on medium heat until liquid is clear and thick, about 10 minutes. Remove from heat. Set aside.

Preheat oven to 350°. Lightly oil a 9-inch cake pan on the bottom and sides. Mix soymilk and remaining tablespoon lemon juice together. Set aside. Combine flour, baking powder and baking soda. In another bowl, cream butter and 1/2 cup Rapadura until soft and creamy. Add beaten egg. Make a well in the dry ingredients. Stir in half of the soymilk, then add half of the egg-sugar mixture. Repeat. The consistency should be on the thick side. Place an even layer of cooked nectarines on the bottom of the cake pan. Spread the cake batter on top of nectarines. Bake for 40 minutes or until cake lightly springs back when touched. Cool, then cut the cake and flip it over to serve. Garnish with seasonal flowers.

Variation:

Lemon-Cherry Upside-Down Cake

3 cups pitted pie cherries
1/2 to 1 cup plus 1/2 cup organic sugar
2 tablespoons lemon juice
2 tablespoons arrowroot
1 tablespoon minced lemon zest

Follow directions for recipe above, substituting sour pie cherries for nectarines.

White Chocolate Raspberry Silk Pie

(Makes one 9-inch pie, serves 8)

If you want to make this pie without dairy, use dairy-free dark chocolate and add a little more honey or agave nectar. For the crust, choose cookies made without hydrogenated fat. Make the crust a day ahead for quick preparation.

Crust:
2 cups crushed plain chocolate cookies
3 1/2 tablespoons melted coconut oil or butter
1 tablespoon water
1 teaspoon vanilla extract

Filling:
1 package extra-firm silken tofu
2 tablespoons white chocolate liquor or 2 teaspoons vanilla extract
1 1/2 tablespoons honey
1 cup fresh raspberries, plus about 1/2 cup raspberries for garnish
2 1/2 cups grated white chocolate plus 2 tablespoons for garnish (about 6 ounces)
2 tablespoons chocolate syrup

Preheat oven to 350°. Lightly oil the bottom of a 9-inch pie pan or a springform pan. Crush cookies into crumbs in a food processor. Blend crumbs with butter, water and vanilla extract. When this is completely mixed, press crust into prepared pan. Bake for 10 minutes. The crust will be soft but will get firm as it cools. Let crust cool completely before filling.

Place raspberries, tofu, honey and vanilla extract in a blender and process until smooth and creamy. Grate white chocolate. Heat all but 1 tablespoon (reserving it for the top) in a cup in the microwave on high for one minute. Alternatively, you can melt the white chocolate in a double boiler. This takes 8 to10 minutes. Stir chocolate before combining with the tofu-raspberry mixture in the blender. Blend for one minute. Pour filling into cooled pie shell.

Refrigerate pie two hours before serving. Pie hardens as it cools. Garnish with 1/2-cup raspberries and reserved grated chocolate. Drizzle chocolate syrup in a decorative pattern over the pie.

Variation:

Blueberry White Chocolate Silk Pie
Replace raspberries with blueberries and omit honey from filling.

Fresh Cherry Cheesecake

(Makes one 9-inch pie)

My husband's friend, Hoby, makes this most delectable cheesecake. Here, I've I've used farm-fresh sour pie cherries from Mair Farm-Taki (p.278). A springform pan works best for this recipe.

Crust:
8-ounce package shortbread cookies
1/4 cup melted butter or coconut oil
Pie:
Two 8-ounce packages cream cheese, softened
2 eggs
2/3 cup organic sugar or Rapadura
2 tablespoons white chocolate liquor, or 1 1/2 teaspoons vanilla
1/2 cup sour cream
Topping:
1 1/2 cups pitted sour pie cherries
1/2 cup sugar or Rapadura
1 tablespoon arrowroot

In a blender or food processor, crush the cookies until they are crumbs. Mix with melted butter. Press crumbs firmly into the bottom of the springform pan, pressing 1 1/2 inches up the sides. You can use glass pie pan that has been lightly oiled, but it will be hard to remove a slice without leaving some of the crust in the pan.

Preheat oven to 350°. With an electric mixer, beat the softened cream cheese until fluffy. Beat in eggs, one at a time, gradually adding sugar. Add the white chocolate liquor, and finally the sour cream. Mix until well blended. Spread the mixture evenly over the crust. Bake for 60 minutes or until cake is firm.

Prepare the topping while cheesecake bakes. In a small saucepan, combine cherries, sugar and arrowroot. Cook on medium-low, stirring frequently, until the color changes from opaque to clear. Keep stirring until it thickens, then remove from heat and let cool. When cheesecake is done, turn off the oven, open the door and let cake sit for another hour. Remove from oven and gently release from the springform pan onto a serving platter. Spread the cooled topping over the top. Chill for a few hours before serving.

"Life in Harmony With Nature" at Mair Farm-Taki

Katsumi Taki, the son of a Buddhist minister, moved from Japan to Connecticut in 1989. Then through the influence of a professor, he moved to Eastern Washington in 1990. In 1993, the owner of Mair Farm, south of Yakima, passed away. Katsumi, with a background in fish biology and agriculture, took over the 36.5-acre farm and renamed it Mair Farm-Taki. You can find Katsumi's certified organic produce stand at four markets during the summer – Yakima, Pike Place, Magnolia and the University District.

Katsumi grows a wide variety of vegetables, fruits and herbs – all destined for market. His main crops are soft fruits such as apricots, nectarines, peaches and cherries. Some of the bing cherry trees on his farm are over 50 years old and still produce excellent cherries. At Katsumi's University District Farmers Market booth, apricots can be purchased by the case. And you can often find bins of slightly blemished fruits and vegetables labeled #2 or #3 for a lower price. Besides being a great place for soft fruit, apples and pears, there are always some unusual finds like Japanese cucumbers, bitter melon, burdock root, daikon, dried fruit and the delightfully tart and salty umeboshi (sun-dried, salt and red-shiso pickled immature apricots).

At 36.5-acres, Mair Farm-Taki is a small farm here, but would be considered large by Japanese standards. Katsumi told me that in Japan, space is precious. Many things are grown vertically on poles or with nets. Even watermelons are grown with nets there. Though Japanese farms are considered among the most productive in the world, the average farm size is a mere 3.3 acres.

Katsumi finds his greatest farming challenges are the ubiquitous weeds and ever-present insects. His orchards and fields are mostly hand-weeded. The most looming insect problem is the coddling moth. The proverbial worm in the apple hatches in developing fruit, and the larvae burrows its way through the apple until it is full grown. The cycle is about 4 weeks. Then it starts all over again. The conventional approach may use pesticides like Diazinon or Malathion. Katsumi applies an odorous fish oil spray, which works by suffocating the eggs, but this must be reapplied frequently to be effective. It's a nontoxic solution and the smell eventually goes away. On the other hand, toxic residues of conventional sprays can remain on the apples.

An organic oasis, a part of the grounds at Mair Farm-Taki is available to rent for weddings, anniversaries or reunions. A manmade pond with a gazebo provides an elegant atmosphere for special occasions. You can also arrange field trips or picnics and enjoy the serene atmosphere near the Yakima River. Next time you're traveling through Yakima, you might want to make reservations and pack a lunch. For more information about Mair Farm-Taki stop by Katsumi's booth at the market and get a brochure, or call (509) 877-4051.

CSA Subscriptions: Connecting Farms and Cities

In Japan in the 1970's, a group of women farmers got together after becoming concerned about the increasing amount of fresh food imports and the decreasing number of family farms. These women started the concept of subscription farming – selling shares of the harvest to consumers in exchange for weekly produce deliveries. The idea spread to Europe and was later imported to the United States in the 1980's. Here, community supported agriculture (CSA) began as an attempt by small farmers to regain a foothold in a market dominated by large agribusiness farms.

CSA agriculture is a unique relationship between local farms and consumers. Joining a CSA usually requires a lump sum of cash before harvest season. In exchange, vegetable boxes are delivered each week for a specified amount of time. Depending on the farm, you may arrange to pay this in payments. Some farms allow you to work on the farm as a barter payment for a "share." I found the amount of weekly produce delivered in a CSA box is equal to or more than what you can purchase in a natural foods store. Also, farmers receive necessary capital to continue farming. Choosing to support small farmers this way, consumers become CSA members and form part of an economic loop that bypasses anonymous corporate farms, brokers and middlemen. Not subject to the whims of the marketplace, farmers have the option of growing heirloom varieties of produce. CSA members have the benefit of sampling vegetables they might not ordinarily buy. A CSA subscription also offers a personal touch in a world where purchases have grown increasingly impersonal with warehouse-size grocery stores selling produce that comes from anonymous corporate farms that are often hundreds of miles away.

Each CSA farm offers a different package. There are a variety of prices and drop-off places. Some have newsletters with weekly recipes, and others hold potlucks where members can mingle and get to know each other. There may be member U-pick days for flowers or berries on the farm. Some CSA farms unite with other farmers, buying additional produce to provide a greater variety for members. With some CSAs, home delivery is an option instead of a weekly drop-off point. Pickles or dried fruits, locally produced bread, jam or even herbal tinctures are sometimes included in a weekly box. Whatever your choice, a weekly veggie box challenges you to plan and cook your weekly meals according to seasonal offerings. The element of surprise means planning meals around sugar pumpkin, braising greens or tomatoes. I've grown so fond of fresh Brussels sprouts on the stalk, I get a winter CSA share just to get them each year. An overload of some item might mean finding a friend with whom to share the harvest.

Being a CSA member creates a sense of time, history, purpose and belonging. For more information about local CSA subscriptions visit a farmers market and talk to farmers and get recommendations from friends. Or, check out www.usda.gov and search for CSA farms in the area.

Hunter dreaming about Buckwheat Bunnies

Healthy Canine Treats

Share farm-fresh produce and homemade organic treats with your canine friends and they'll never stray.

We've had dogs ever since I can remember. They've always been part of the family and it seems only natural to feed them nutritious food and treats. My grandmother's sleepy old cocker spaniel never moved off the back porch on lazy summer days. However, when dinner was served, she was suddenly alert and sitting near the table. The beagles I grew up with loved any kind of treats handed out. I've always given biscuits to the dogs in my life, but it wasn't until a decade ago that I decided to try my hand at baking biscuits for my treat-motivated basset hounds. It's gratifying that the fruits of my labor, even my failures, are so wildly appreciated by canine companions.

To get started, you need a few basic recipes. If you want to create biscuits tailored to your dog's tastes, you'll need an understanding of ingredient options and how they function in recipes. Then, once you have that down, you can experiment with different flours, dry ingredients, liquids, fats, eggs and egg replacers. Biscuit experiments never go to waste with dogs. I've found over the years that even flops receive more than a passing bark.

Biscuit Basics

Biscuit recipes include two parts: dry and wet ingredients. These are mixed separately, then combined. When blended, the ingredient combinations should result in a dough that has a texture thicker than cookie dough. When the dough pulls away from the sides of the bowl, gather it up into a ball. If the dough is too tacky, add more flour for a very stiff dough. It's helpful to lightly oil your hands when forming the dough into a ball. Place the dough in covered container or plastic bag and refrigerate it for a few hours or overnight. For quicker biscuits, you can add more flour and roll it out right away, but the dough is often too sticky to roll out easily. You can also put the dough in the freezer for at least 1/2 hour before rolling it out. Cold, hard dough makes rolling and cutting easier. Biscotti dough should be firm enough to work with right away.

High-gluten flours such as wheat, spelt and kamut tend to make a heavier, stickier dough. High-gluten flour-based biscuits often take longer to bake and harden. Non-gluten flours like millet, buckwheat, amaranth and teff combined with tapioca or arrowroot are easier to roll and cut into shapes. Biscuits made with these flours get crisp more quickly when baked.

Flour alternatives

Whole grains are staples used in baking throughout the world. Refined grains have been stripped of vitamins, minerals and fiber. Whole-grain flour is the ideal choice for biscuits. Whole-wheat, spelt, kamut, triticale, rye and to a lesser extent, barley and oats contain gluten, which creates a springy, resilient texture. Gluten holds the biscuit dough together so you can shape it. Oats and barley contain so little gluten that they should be used in combination with other grains for best results.

Non-gluten flours include amaranth, buckwheat, millet, quinoa, rice, sorghum and teff. In case your dog is sensitive to one of these grains, use only one new whole-grain flour at a time. Wait a week, then try another new grain. With non-gluten flour, use 1/2 cup of tapioca flour or arrowroot for each 2 1/2 cups of flour. Tapioca and arrowroot flour bind the dough together, making it easy to roll out and lending a crispy texture to the baked biscuits.

Seeds, nuts and other dry ingredients

For better digestibility, grind seeds and nuts before adding to the dough. Sunflower, sesame and pumpkin seeds add minerals as well as flavor. Other nut options include ground walnuts, hazelnuts, pecans or pine nuts. Carob can partly take the place of flour in a recipe. It adds calcium and other minerals, plus a unique flavor that most dogs love. Use 1/4 to 1/2 cup carob powder. Other dry ingredients to add for recipe variations include Parmesan cheese, a tablespoon of nutritional yeast, a teaspoon of herbs such as rosemary, basil or sage. Add a teaspoon of dried kelp for flavor and additional minerals.

Eggs and egg replacers

In cookie recipes, eggs make up part of the liquid ingredients. They contribute to a softer texture, and egg whites add a slight rise for baked treats. They are not absolutely essential to gluten or non-gluten flour based biscuits. A good egg-replacer is flax seed-water mixture. To make this, grind 1/4 cup flax seeds in a coffee or seed grinder until they resemble a coarse powder. In a blender, combine ground flax seeds and 3/4 cup water or stock. Blend until frothy and thick. This mixture will replace 4 eggs. Each 1/4 cup flax seed-egg replacer equals one egg. It will keep refrigerated for one week. Use this mixture like you would use eggs in a recipe, combining it with liquid or semi-liquid ingredients.

Fat

Dog biscuits require little or no fat for a crisp biscuit. For 5 cups of flour, you may want to add 1/4 cup butter or coconut oil. You can also use nut or seed butter like peanut, almond, tahini or cashew butter. Dogs will come quickly for a warm-from-the-oven peanut butter-molasses biscuit.

Vegetables

I often use baked pureed pumpkin, squash, yams or sweet potatoes in dog treats. Steamed and pureed carrots, parsnips or rutabaga work well, too. These vegetables are added to the liquid ingredients. Grated carrots add some color and sweetness when mixed in with the dry ingredients.

Liquid ingredients

Use homemade or processed vegetarian soup stock. The commercial variety usually contains more sodium so use 1:1 ratio of packaged or canned stock to water. Another liquid option that dogs like is applesauce. Molasses, maple syrup and agave nectar can be added in moderation, but keep sweeteners to a minimum. Dogs don't need or care about a sweet taste.

Ingredients to avoid

Some ingredients are toxic to dogs and should be avoided. Never use chocolate, onions and raisins. Since garlic is related to onions, I don't ever use it. While dog biscuits are a good way to use up flour and other ingredients, don't add rancid, moldy or unacceptable items you wouldn't eat.

Buckwheat Bunnies
(Makes about 76 biscuits)
The only bunnies my hounds catch are these crispy peanut butter flavored treats. If you don't have bunny cookie cutters, use another shape or cut them into small squares – the size of squares is up to you.

3 cups buckwheat flour
1 cup millet flour
1 cup tapioca flour or arrowroot
1 teaspoon kelp
1 teaspoon cinnamon
1 large baked and mashed yam or one 14-ounce can yam puree
1/2 to 3/4 cup peanut butter
1/4 cup molasses
1 to 1 1/2 cups stock or water

Combine dry ingredients in a large mixing bowl. Place yam, peanut butter, molasses and 1 cup vegetarian stock in the blender and puree until smooth. Stir liquid ingredients into flour ingredients, adding more stock if necessary. Keep stirring until a stiff dough is formed. Oil your hands before attempting to shape the dough into a ball.

Work with the dough immediately or place it in a covered container or a plastic bag and refrigerate for up to a week if you want. When you are ready to roll the dough, preheat oven to 350º. Line a few baking sheets with parchment paper. Divide dough in half and put half back in the refrigerator. Roll out the dough to about 1/4-inch thick. Cut with cookie cutters and place as many as you can on a baking sheet. It doesn't matter if they are touching. They will break apart when done. Bake for 40 minutes. They should be fairly hard when baked. For a very crisp texture, turn off the oven and leave overnight.

Doggie Biscotti
(Makes approximately 70 biscotti)
My dogs are crazy about this savory biscotti. Toast the pumpkin seeds for 10 minutes at 325° and cool. Then, grind the seeds in a seed or coffee grinder or with a mortar and pestle.

3 cups spelt flour
1 cup barley flour
1 cup toasted, ground pumpkin seeds
1 teaspoon kelp
Generous pinch of sage (optional)
1/2 cup grated sharp cheddar cheese
3 tablespoons ground flax seeds
1/2 cup cold water
1/2 cup unsweetened applesauce
1/2 cup vegetable stock (p.97, without onions or commercial stock)

Combine spelt, barley flour, pumpkin seeds, kelp and sage, if desired. Mix well. Blend in grated cheese. Set aside. Place the flax seeds and water in a blender and blend on high until frothy and thick. Add applesauce and vegetable stock. Blend on medium speed.

Preheat oven to 350°. Line a baking sheet with parchment paper. Pour wet ingredients into dry ingredients and mix until a stiff dough is formed. Gather into a ball, then divide the dough into three equal sections. Roll each section into a 14-inch log and place on baking sheet. Flatten slightly with the palm of your hand. Bake for 30 minutes. Remove from oven and let cool before slicing.

Reduce oven temperature to 325°. Slice biscotti on the diagonal. Make 1/4 to 1/2-inch slices with a sharp serrated bread knife. Place biscotti on a pizza screen and bake for 30 minutes or until hard. Remove from oven and cool on a cooling rack; or after turning the oven off, leave the biscuits in the oven overnight and they will be very crisp in the morning.

Options:
♦ Use any high-gluten flour such as whole-wheat or kamut instead of spelt. Try any low-gluten flour like oat, amaranth, teff or millet to replace barley flour.
♦ Add lightly toasted, ground sesame or sunflower seeds instead of pumpkin seeds.
♦ Rosemary, basil or oregano can substitute for sage in this recipe.
♦ Parmesan or grated Romano cheese are good options.

Pumpkin-Parmesan Rosemary Squares
(Makes up to 200 squares, depending on the size cut)
This is a popular treat because of the Parmesan cheese. If you want a stronger cheese flavor, add an additional 1/2 cup cheese.

2 1/4 cups kamut flour
2 cups teff flour
1/2 cup arrowroot
1/2 cup Parmesan cheese
1 teaspoon chopped fresh rosemary
1 can pumpkin puree (about 14 ounces)
1/2 cup unsweetened applesauce
1 cup vegetable stock (p.97, without onions or commercial stock)

Combine kamut, teff flour, arrowroot, Parmesan cheese and rosemary. Mix well and set aside. Blend pumpkin puree, applesauce and vegetable stock with a hand blender. Pour wet ingredients into dry ingredients. Stir until a stiff dough is formed, adding more flour if necessary. Gather into a ball and place in a container or plastic bag. Refrigerate overnight or place in the freezer for at least 1/2 hour before rolling it out.

Preheat oven to 350°. Line a baking sheet with parchment paper. Roll dough to 1/4-inch thickness. Cut into 1-inch squares. Bake for 45 minutes or until biscuits are fairly firm. Turn the oven off and leave them overnight or for at least a few hours.

Dog biscuit tips and tidbits

♦ Always use the best quality organic ingredients. Purchase whole-grain flours in small amounts and store in the freezer to retain freshness.

♦ After blending wet and dry ingredients together, you may find you need a little more liquid. Add a little more vegetable stock or water and stir. Touch the dough to make sure it isn't too sticky before picking it up. Oil your hands before gathering the dough into a ball. If you use a non-gluten flour and tapioca, the dough may not need refrigeration before rolling out. Biscotti doesn't require refrigeration before baking.

♦ Wheat or high-gluten flour dough, is easier to work with when it's cold. If the dough is too tacky, add a little more flour.

♦ Fun cookie cutter shapes can be found at any cooking store. There are different sizes of bones or various animals and theme cutters such as barnyard animals, bats, pumpkins or hearts for holidays.

♦ Bake the biscuits on parchment paper (which can be reused) for easy removal. Leave them in the oven until they become hard. Depending on the flour used, you may have to leave them in longer, up to an hour longer with the oven at 200° may be helpful to crisp-up a batch of biscuits.

♦ If your dog is old, small or has few teeth and you need softer biscuits, bake the biscuits for a shorter period of time. Biscotti can be baked once to produce treats that are easier to chew.

Appendix

The World of Whole Grains

Cultivated for at least 8,700 years, grains are a staple in every cuisine around the world. Ancestors of barley and wheat were originally grown almost nine thousand years ago in the Tigris-Euphrates Valley in what is now Iraq. Teff, the tiny grain from Ethiopia, has been ground into flour to make fermented flatbread for centuries. Millet is native to the West Indies, and it has been cultivated in India and the Middle East before the Roman Empire. Millet was also a staple in China before rice displaced it. Quinoa sustained Andean civilizations for centuries before Spanish colonization.

No other food in history has been as vital as whole grains in nourishing traditional civilizations. In some parts of China, rice makes up 70 percent of the average Chinese daily diet. In Mexico, the Tarahumara Indians have a long history as endurance athletes. Over half of their daily calories come from corn. Studies have shown that muscles perform better on energy from complex carbohydrates. According to Ellen Coleman in *Eating for Endurance*, carbohydrate-rich diets help maintain muscle glycogen stores that allow the body to exercise longer and harder without fatigue.

Whole grains contain all the major nutrients needed by the body — carbohydrates, protein, essential fatty acids, vitamins and minerals. When grains are refined, the nutrient-rich germ, bran and fiber are removed. All that's left are the starch and protein components. Enriched means just a few vitamins and minerals are added back. Each grain has a slightly different nutritional profile. The greater variety of grains incorporated into your daily diet, the wider the range of nutrients taken in.

Buying and storing

Whole grains contain natural oils. The shelf life is much shorter than for refined grains. Purchase whole grains from bulk bins at stores where the turnover is rapid. Buy small quantities that can be used in a few months. Label and store grains in containers away from the light, which depletes some B vitamins. Use them within six months. Alternatively, store whole grains up to a year in the freezer.

Because of the natural oils, whole grains tend to attract more bugs than refined grains. When you bring whole grains home, place them in the freezer for about 20 minutes. Then, transfer to a jar and label them with name and purchase date before storing.

Preparation

Whole grains are minimally processed. They may contain small stones, sticks and dirt. Place all but very tiny whole grains in a double-mesh strainer, pick out any rocks and rinse them. Small grains like teff and amaranth have been air-cleaned. If you want to rinse these grains, place them in a mason jar with a piece of cheesecloth covering the opening. Rinse, then use them in recipes.

Soaking grains before cooking is often recommended. Both whole grains and legumes contain phytic acid, which binds with magnesium, calcum, zinc and other minerals, preventing them from being absorbed. For better digestibility, soak grains and legumes before cooking to neutralize the phytic acid. For more information about phytic acid in beans and whole grains, see *Healing with Whole Foods* by Paul Pitchford. After soaking you can discard the water and use fresh water to cook grains. If you want a fluffy dinner grain, dry-roast the grains in a cast-iron skillet. Dry-roasting also makes the grains more alkaline. Heat the skillet over medium heat, add the grains, stir and toast until grains are a few shades darker with a toasted nutty aroma. Dry-roasting usually takes from 5 to 7 minutes. You can also sauté the grains in a little ghee or coconut oil for a richer taste. Use 1/2 to 1 tablespoon ghee or oil and cook for 5 minutes. Remove from heat and cook as directed. If you dry-roast or sauté grains, cook them right away because the oil contained in the grain is more vulnerable to rancidity when heated.

Cooking

Cooking whole grains doesn't always go according to instructions because there are many variables. Use a grain cooking chart as a guide. The age of the grain, the weight of the pot, the fit of the lid and the stove's temperament – all these are variables when cooking whole grains. Find out what works on your stove with your pans. For best results, write down exactly how you cook the grain each time. Starting with less water than most cooking charts call for, I discovered it's easier to add hot water to undercooked grains than to simmer too much water off grains that are fully cooked. A rice cooker is another option to use for other grains.

For a sticky grain, start your grains in cold water. Bring the water to a boil, reduce heat, cover and simmer for specified time. To get a perfect, fluffy dinner grain, add dry grains when the water is already boiling. Toss in a pinch of sea salt for digestibility. Once the grains are cooking, resist the urge to stir. Air pockets are formed between the grains as they cook. When these air pockets are disturbed, the starch molecules on the outside of the grains move together, creating a sticky grain. The texture can become quite glue-like if you continue stirring. To check and see if there is still liquid in the pan before the grains are done, gently move the grains on one side with a fork. Add a little hot water or stock, if necessary. Check again in 5 to 10 minutes.

WHOLE GRAIN COOKING GUIDE

One cup	Liquid	Time	Yield
Amaranth✷	2 cups	30 minutes	2 cups
Whole or hull-less barley	2 cups	60 to 75 minutes	3 1/2 cups
Buckwheat	1 3/4 cups	15 to 20 minutes	3 cups
Kamut	1 3/4 cups	60 to 75 minutes	2 cups
Millet	2 cups	20 to 30 minutes	4 cups
Oats—groats✷	2 cups	60 minutes	2 to 2 1/2 cups
steel-cut	2 cups	10 minutes	2 to 2 1/2 cups
Quinoa	1 3/4 cups	15 to 20 minutes	3 cups
Rice	1 3/4 cups	50 minutes	2 1/2 cups
Rye	2 cups	60 to 75 minutes	2 cups
Spelt	1 1/4 cups	60 to 75 minutes	2 1/2 cups
Teff✷	2 cups	20 minutes	2 cups
Wheat berries	1 3/4 to 2 cups	60 to 75 minutes	2 1/2 cups
Wild rice	2 to 2 1/2 cups	60 minutes	2 1/2 to 4 cups

✷ Amaranth, oats and teff are naturally sticky. These grains will never be fluffy like rice or quinoa. Start them in cold water and stir them often when cooking.

The Grains

Amaranth – An ancient grain cultivated by the Aztecs in Mexico, amaranth was also known in ancient China and has been found growing wild on five continents. A drought-tolerant, hearty plant, much of the amaranth in this country is grown in Nebraska. Classified as a supergrain, it has a significant amount of protein and calcium. Amaranth also contains magnesium and silicon – important minerals for strong bones. With a glutinous texture, it imparts a sweet taste slightly reminiscent of corn.

Barley – With origins from either western Asia or the Ethiopian highlands, barley was a grain staple in Europe before being replaced by wheat and rye. Most of the barley found in stores is pearled barley, which means the outer hulls and an inner layer were mechanically removed, leaving it similar to refined rice in nutritional quality. In Chinese medicine, barley is cooling and thermal in nature. It stimulates the appetite and strengthens the intestines and soothing to the digestive tract. Barley has cholesterol-lowering capabilities, and it contains more magnesium than calcium.

Buckwheat – Not a true grain, buckwheat is a hearty plant that thrives in poor soil where other crops fail. It originated in Siberia and is used extensively in Eastern European cooking. Buckwheat has a strong, earthy flavor that is intensified when dry-roasted. Kasha is toasted buckwheat. The grain is porous and absorbs water easily, so rinse it quickly before roasting and cooking. Buckwheat is high in calcium, vitamin E and B vitamins and contains a significant amount of rutin, a bioflavonoid that helps strengthen capillaries.

Kamut – Originating about six thousand years ago in the fertile Tigris-Euphrates River basin (in what is Iraq today), kamut is an ancient relative of durham wheat, the variety used to make pasta. Unlike wheat, kamut is not a hybridized grain, but a true heirloom. It contains more protein and B vitamins than wheat. Because of the gluten content, you can bake bread or make pasta with kamut flour. Cooked, whole-grain kamut is large and chewy like wheat berries with a sweeter taste.

Millet – Native to the East Indies, millet was the staple grain in Northern China before rice was hybridized to grow in cooler climates. A small, round, golden grain, millet is easily digestible, gluten-free and rich in B vitamins and silicon. Millet is considered an anti-fungal grain and is good for people who have Candida. It contains about 11 percent protein and is considered by most nutritional authorities to be the most alkaline grain.

Oats – With a long history as a staple grain for people in Central Asia, oats were also the staple grain of the Celts. Oats have a higher fat content than most other grains and contain a natural antioxidant that resists rancidity. They

Oat groats refers to the whole grain. Oat straw or oat groat tea improves calcium metabolism and calms nerves. Steel-cut oats have been cut with steel blades so they cook quicker. Rolled oats and oatmeal are whole oats that have been steamed and rolled.

Quinoa – Pronounced *keen-wah*, this nutritional powerhouse was the principal grain of the Incas. Quinoa flourishes at high altitudes (above 10,000 feet), in extreme weather conditions and in poor soil. A beet and spinach relative, quinoa isn't a true grain, but it fits in the grain category because it cooks like a grain. Quinoa is considered strengthening and energizing for the whole body. It contains more calcium than milk and has about 16 percent protein. Quinoa is also a good source for many other nutrients such as iron, phosphorus, B-complex and vitamin E.

Rice – A staple for more than half the world's population, there are over 7,000 varieties of rice. Rice became cultivated from wild grasses found in Asia and Indochina centuries ago. It reached Japan in the second century, where the amount of rice a landlord grew determined his wealth. Rice contains a number of B vitamins and is considered useful for the nervous system and helps relieve irritability. It also contains iron, vitamin E and linoleic acid. Rice is lower in protein than many other grains.

Rye – Developed from a species of a northeastern European grain, rye can sustain itself in cold severe climates. Rye bread has long been a staple in Russia. Rye is nutritionally similar to wheat, but the flavor is stronger and slightly bitter. It contains all the B vitamins, protein and iron. Rye berries are quite chewy and are rarely cooked by themselves. Use them in place of spelt, kamut or wheat berries in recipes. The main use of rye in the United States is rye whiskey.

Spelt – An ancient wheat relative, sometimes referred to as *farro*, spelt was grown over 9,000 years ago in the Middle East. Like kamut, spelt is a true grain that contains more B vitamins and protein than wheat. Cooked spelt has a texture similar to wheat berries. As a flour, spelt makes excellent bread, but when made into pasta, it does not hold together well when boiled. Long used in Europe, spelt is becoming more familiar in American households.

Teff – Wild and drought-resistant, teff looks like prairie grass with seeds. Native to Ethiopia, this tiniest of grains was eventually cultivated. The word teff translates as "lost." In Ethiopia, the grain is ground into a bread grain and made into a naturally fermented flatbread called *injera.* A millet relative, teff is high in protein, calcium and iron and contains lesser amounts of zinc and copper. Gluten-free, teff can be used by many who have wheat or corn allergies. Cooked teff has glutinous texture and a sweet molasses-like taste.

Wheat – Wheat was cultivated in the Middle East about 10,000 years ago. American colonists from Europe brought wheat with them. Then grains of wheat were carried west with the pioneers. Eastern Washington still has many wheat farms today. Wheat is the most frequently eaten grain in the United States, and though wheat allergies are common, it is suspected that a large number of wheat allergies may be due in part to hybridization and over-consumption of refined wheat products. Whole wheat contains 12 B vitamins, vitamin E, protein and a number of important minerals such as zinc, iron and magnesium. Cooked wheat berries have a chewy texture.

Wild rice – The seed of an aquatic grass, wild rice is native to the Great Lakes region of the United States. It grows along streams in shallow water in Minnesota. Harvesting is still done by canoe and the rice is parched over open fires. On the other hand, cultivated "wild" rice seeds are shot from low flying planes into manmade paddies in California, the largest producer of "wild" rice. This paddy rice is left to cure and slightly ferment for weeks after machine harvesting. It is then heated, which alters the starch and the rice turns a dark shiny hue. It's worth it to search out true wild rice because it is much sweeter with no bitter aftertaste. It's also higher in protein, minerals and B vitamins than wheat, barley, oats or rye. For more information about obtaining traditionally harvested wild rice, contact the Leech Lake Wild Rice Company at 218-751-9750. This rice is organically grown and harvested by the Leech Lake Band of Ojibwe.

Legume Basics

The world of legumes includes peas, lentils and beans. First mentioned in the Bible, there are over 14,000 members in the legume family. Of those, about 700 are listed by the Seed Saver Exchange as edible varieties. Many are heirloom or old-fashioned varieties that have been handed down within families for generations.

Along with grains, legumes are the cornerstone of nutrition in various cuisines around the world. An inexpensive protein source, they can be grown in relatively poor soil and still give a high yield per acre. They are known for putting nitrogen back into the ground and building up the soil. Farmers often rotate legumes with other crops to enrich their soil. Alfalfa is an amazing legume whose root system can penetrate up to a hundred feet and bring up trace minerals that other root systems can't reach. Alfalfa is often alternated with wheat for a number of years to enrich farmland in Eastern Washington.

Some varieties of legumes are eaten fresh, in or out of the pod, but the beans more familiar to most of us are the dried varieties. Dried beans should be soaked and rehydrated before cooking. Traditional cooking simmers beans from the outside in. Pressure-cooking cooks beans from the inside out. A long, slow simmer assures beans' digestibility. A pressure cooker produces beans with speed, digestibility and exceptional texture. Beans have a melt-in-your-mouth quality when cooked in a pressure cooker.

Buying, storing and soaking

Beans are not very perishable. The optimal shelf life is about one year, but you can keep them for a few years. The longer they're stored, the more beans dry out and lose nutrients. Trying to tenderize and cook very old beans can be like attempting to tenderize gravel on a country road. Buy dry beans at natural food stores for a fresher product. If you select beans in a bag, choose a bag without moldy, broken, chipped or split beans. Uniformity of shape and color is not important. Purchase fresh-harvested dry beans from farmers markets in the fall.

Store beans in covered glass containers away from the light. Left out in the light, pyridoxal and pyridoxine, two natural forms of a B vitamin, deteriorate rapidly. This vitamin is essential for the metabolism of amino acids and starch. Cooked beans should be refrigerated as soon as they cool. They will keep for about one week in the refrigerator. You can also store cooked beans in the freezer for about six months.

Before cooking legumes, spread them out on a tray and pick out any stones or small sticks. Discard any shriveled or otherwise unsightly beans. Rinse all legumes except red lentils, which can stick together like cement after rinsing. To soak, place the beans in a pot and cover with three times the amount of water. Soak overnight. Long soaking is ideal, but use the quick soak method if pressed for time.

Quick soak for beans

Use three times the amount of water over beans in a pot and bring to a boil. Boil for about 10 minutes. Remove from heat and let the beans sit for another 10 to 20 minutes. To check and see if your beans have finished soaking, cut a bean in half. If there is a dark spot in the middle, continue soaking. If it is uniform all the way through, the beans are finished soaking. Discard the soaking water and cook according to directions.

Cooking

Pour off the soaking water, cover beans with three times the amount of water and bring to a boil. Add a 1-inch strip of kombu, a sea vegetable, to make beans more digestible. Cook until beans are done – about 1 to 1 1/2 hours. To determine if beans are done, gently mash the bean against the roof of your mouth. It should crush easily. Some beans such as garbanzo or scarlet runners have a firm grainy texture when done. Beans are delicious when slow simmered all day in a crockpot. A pressure cooker is another option when you want beans without waiting.

Nutrition

Legumes range from 17 to 25 percent protein, significantly higher than whole grains and vegetables. Soybeans contain about 35 percent protein. Beans have a wide range of B vitamins as well as minerals – calcium, potassium, magnesium, iron and zinc. They also contain complex carbohydrates and soluble fiber, which has a stabilizing effect on blood sugar imbalances. Beans help reduce blood cholesterol levels and regulate colon functions. According to Paul Pitchford in *Healing With Whole Foods,* Chinese medicine embraces beans and promotes their consumption for good kidney function.

BEAN COOKING GUIDE

1 cup	Soaking	Stove-top Bean/water 1:3	Pressure Bean/water 1:1 1/4	Yield
Adzuki (aduki)	Yes	1 hour	9 minutes	2 1/2 cups
Black	Yes	1 1/2 hours	6 to 9 minutes	2 1/2 cups
Cannellini	Yes	1 1/2 hours	10 to12 minutes	2 cups
Cranberry	Yes	1 1/4 hours	9 to 12 minutes	2 1/4 cups
Fava	Yes	2 to 3 hours	18 minutes	2 cups
Flagelot	Yes	1 hour	12 minutes	2 cups
Garbanzo	Yes	2 1/2 hours	18 minutes	2 1/2 cups
Great Northern	Yes	1 hour	12 minutes	2 cups
Lentils Brown French	No	40 minutes	6 to 10 minutes	2 cups
Split Peas	No	40 minutes	6 to 10 minutes	2 cups
Pinto	Yes	1 1/2 hours	8 to 10 minutes	2 1/4 cups
Red	Yes	1 hour	12 minutes	2 cups
Scarlet Runner	Yes	2 hours	14 minutes	1 1/2 cups

For pressure-cooked quick-release, run water over the pressure cooker until the pressure drops. Natural release means waiting until the pressure drops naturally. You can cook the beans for a few minutes less if you let the pressure come down naturally.

Digestion

All around the world, you can find tips to make beans more digestible. In India, *asafetida*, a resin from a giant fennel, is said to lower gas-producing tendencies. In Mexico, *epazote*, a tropic native, is added to bean dishes to enhance digestion. In Japan, *kombu*, a sea vegetable, helps speed up cooking time, enhances flavor and helps de-gas beans. The digestive problems with beans stem from their complex sugars (stachyose and raffinose). The human digestive system can't break these sugars down, and they end up in our large intestines. To enhance digestibility and decrease the possibility of having gas, try any of the following tips.

♦ Soaking beans overnight leaches out indigestible sugars responsible for causing gas. When you soak beans, pour the soaking water off and use fresh water to cook your beans. If gas is a problem, change the soaking water frequently.

♦ Cut a strip of kombu into small pieces and cook it with the beans. Kombu also adds vitamins and minerals to the cooking water.

♦ Do not add salt until the beans are thoroughly cooked. Salt retards the cooking process and toughens the beans.

♦ Eat small portions of beans on a regular basis to build up your body's tolerance level and develop the digestive enzymes needed to break down and absorb beans.

♦ Sprouting beans reduces gas, increases protein content, lowers the starch and reduces the cooking time.

A Few Varieties of Beans

Adzuki (aduki, azuki)
Known as the "king of beans" in China and Japan, adzuki beans have been cultivated there for centuries. They can be enjoyed fresh, dried or sprouted, and they are sometimes ground into flour. In Asian countries, adzuki beans are often made into sweet desserts. Earthy with a slight sweet taste, adzuki beans easily substitute for beans such as pinto, red, and white beans.

Anasazi
An heirloom variety of bean that has been discovered in the ruins in Mesa Verde, Colorado. This bean was eventually displaced by pinto beans in the Southwest. Anasazi beans have a more buttery texture and better flavor than pinto beans. Cook them like you would pinto beans.

Black
A native of Mexico, black beans are earthy and sweet. They can be substituted for other beans, but the liquid tends to turn things black. They are often made into soup in Cuba and are traditional in *feijoada* in Brazil. They are widely available in grocery stores. Growing Things (p.197) at farmers markets often has fresh black beans available in the autumn.

Cannellini
A white bean with a creamy texture, cannellini beans were originally cultivated in Argentina. They are favorites in Italian recipes like *pasta e fagioli*. Longer and bigger than navy beans, cannellini beans are good in salads or soups.

Cranberry
About the size of a pinto bean with the same creamy texture, cranberry beans are grown by a number of farmers in the Northwest. The Meyer's of Stoney Plains (p.84) often have a good crop that they sell in the autumn. When you purchase cranberry beans fresh from the farmers market and cook them, they have a wonderful buttery texture.

Fava
More ancient than most other legumes, fava beans are widely used in cuisines throughout the world. The fresh version is often used in the Northwest. Fresh favas demand more preparation than other legumes – shelling, blanching and then peeling the outside skin – but they offer a distinct flavor and personality, best savored on their own and not hidden in soups or stews. Bob Meyer of Stoney Plains once said that when fava beans are fresh, they don't require a second peeling. The skin will be transparent and the flavor is more like a green vegetable than a legume. Serve them simply with lemon and butter.

Flageolet

Immature kidney beans, flageolet beans are often mentioned in French cooking. Pale green, delicate and tender, these small buttery beans can make any dish shine. Look for fresh flageolet beans during late summer at the farmers market. Cook them with a little ghee, salt and pepper.

French lentil

Idaho, Eastern Washington and parts of Oregon are considered the best region in the world for growing lentils, peas and chickpeas. More are cultivated and harvested here than anywhere else, and they are exported worldwide. Per ounce, compared to beef, they contain more protein and also have vitamins, minerals and iron. A "Persian" variety, French lentils hold their shape well when cooked and have a sweet, subtle earthy flavor. They are the most savory of the lentils and add richness to soups and stews. Lentils don't contain sulfur and are more easily digested than beans.

Garbanzo (chickpea, ceci)

Though they have Old World origins, garbanzos and other legume crops are extensively grown and alternated with wheat in Eastern Washington. Garbanzos are round beans with wrinkly skins and a distinctly nutty taste. The texture is firm. You can also find black or split baby garbanzos, but the beige variety is more common. Garbanzos are also ground into flour, which adds a nutty flavor to baked goods. The beans need to be soaked, then simmered for a long time. When pressure-cooked, they are creamy and delicious.

Red

These beans are similar in color to kidney beans, but closer in texture to white or Great Northern beans. Along with black beans, they are popular in Cuban cooking. Red beans are also the peas in Jamaican peas and rice. A good all-occasion bean, this should be a staple in the pantry.

Scarlet runner

First cultivated in South and Central America, scarlet runners grow easily in the Pacific Northwest. Many grow the plants for the flowers, which are big and scarlet. With a compact, fine-grained texture, scarlet runners are more like lima beans. They hold their shape well and are excellent, colorful additions to salads. Subtly sweet, they are also tasty additions to soups or casseroles.

Local Seasonal Picks

In the Pacific Northwest, the season for vegetables and fruits varies slightly from region to region and from year to year. On the Penninsula, things are slightly behind our season around Seattle. Traveling east, crops such as peaches in central Washington come into season earlier than those crops closer to Idaho. In addition, farmers often plant the same crops at different times. The quality you can find is dependant on many things – soil, sun and even the minerals in the water. Thanks to Michaele Blakeley for helping me with the following seasonal dates.

Apples	late July – October
Apricots	June – August
Artichokes	April – July
Asparagus	May – June
Basil	June – September
Beans, green	July – October
Beans, shell (dried)	August – October
Beets	May – November
Blackberries	August – September
Blueberries	June – September
Bok choy	can be year-round
Boysenberries	July – August
Broccoli	can be year-round
Brussels sprouts	November – December
Cabbage	can be year-round
Carrots	can be year-round
Cauliflower	can be year-round
Celeriac	September – October
Cherries	June – July
Corn	August – October
Cranberries	October – November

Cucumbers	July – September
Currants	August
Eggplant	July – August
Fava beans	throughout harvest season
Garlic	June – October
Grapes	August – September
Greens, specialty	can be year-round
Greens, wild	March – June
Herbs	June – September
Jerusalem artichokes	fall through winter
Kale	year-round
Kiwi, hardy	September – October
Kohlrabi	year-round
Lavender	July – August
Leeks	year-round
Lettuce	year-round
Melons	August – November
Mushrooms, wild	June – November
Nectarines	July – August
Nuts	June – October
Okra	July – September
Onions	June – November (winter storage)
Parsley	May – September
Parsley root	October
Parsnips	October – early spring
Peaches	July – August

Pears	August – October
Peas	June – fall
Peppers	June – fall
Plums	August – September
Potatoes	July – November (winter storage)
Pumpkins	October – November
Purslane	June – September
Radishes	can be year-round
Raspberries	June – October
Rhubarb	May – September
Rutabaga	October – throughout winter
Shallots	August – September
Soybeans, green	July – October
Spinach	can be year-round
Squash, summer	June – till frost
Squash, winter	September – November (storage)
Strawberries	June – October
Swiss Chard	can be year-round
Tomatoes	July – September
Turnips	can be year-round

Market finds and highlights

Year-round

During the off-season, you can often find farmers selling their harvest and preserved items such as jam or pickles, tucked in various locations around Seattle. There are a few farmers markets that remain open such as Pike Place and the Ballard Market. Other markets in the state have extended seasons as well such as the Olympia Farmers Market, which is open from April through December and the Port Angeles Farmers Market is open year-round. For information about farmers market locations, look for the current edition of the *Washington Tilth Producers Directory* or call (206) 442-7620.

Some of the items you can find all year include a variety of cheese, goat milk products, dried fruit and tomatoes, eggs, nuts, hazelnut oil, seasonal greens, root vegetables, broccoli, cauliflower, cabbage, jam, locally produced organic bread, pickled peppers and vegetables, fruit or herb vinegar.

May – June

The beginning of market season you can find some exceptional items such as:
♦ Flower and vegetable starts
♦ Wild foraged greens, pea vines and mushrooms (dried)
♦ Asparagus, young greens, beets, peas, new potatoes, cherries, rhubarb
♦ Pickles, jam, dried herbs
♦ Roasted peanuts, nuts

July – September

The height of harvest season, be sure to include some of the following in your weekly shopping trips.
♦ Soft fruits such as berries, apricots, nectarines, peaches, plums
♦ Melons
♦ Peppers, eggplant, heirloom tomatoes, peas, green beans, fava beans, summer squash, corn, turnips
♦ Sweet onions, garlic
♦ Wild mushrooms, foraged greens and berries
♦ Roasted peppers, salsa, fruit vinegar

October – December

♦ Apples, pears
♦ Shell beans — cranberry, cannellini, black
♦ Brussels sprouts
♦ Root vegetables – beets, parsley root, parsnips, celeriac, carrots
♦ Winter squash, pumpkins, gourds
♦ Nuts – walnuts, hazelnuts
♦ Flower bulbs
♦ Pickles, jam, dried summer fruit, dried herbs

Recommended Reading

Atkinson, Greg, *The Northwest Essentials Cookbook: Cooking with the Ingredients that Define a Regional Cuisine,* Sasquatch Books, Seattle, 1999.

Ballister, Barry, *The Fruit and Vegetable Stand: The Complete Guide to the Selection, Preparation and Nutrition of Fresh Produce,* The Overlook Press, Woodstock and New York, 1987.

Cooper, Ann with Lisa M. Holmes, *Bitter Harvest: A Chef's Perspective on the Hidden Dangers in the Foods We Eat and What You Can Do About It,* Rutledge, New York, 2000.

Costenbader, Carol W., *The Big Book of Preserving the Harvest: 150 Recipes for Freezing, Canning, Drying and Pickling Fruits and Vegetables,* Storey Books, North Adams MA, 2002

Erasmus, Udo, *Fats that Heal, Fats that Kill,* Alive Books, Burnaby BC, Canada, 1993.

Hawkes, Alex D., *A World of Vegetable Cookery,* Simon and Schuster, Inc. New York, 1968.

Henderson, Elizabeth with Robyn Van En, *Sharing the Harvest: A Guide to Community Supported Agriculture,* Chelsea Green Publishing Company, 1999.

Jackson, Wes, *Becoming Native to this Place,* Lexington University Press of Kentucky, 1994.

Jones, Doug, *My Brother's Farm: Reflections of Life, Farming and the Pleasures of Food,* GP Putman's Son's, New York, 1999.

Kimbrell, Andrew (editor), *Fatal Harvest: The Tragedy of Industrial Agriculture,* California, The Foundation for Deep Ecology, Island Press, 2002

Lambrecht, Bill, *Dinner at the New Gene Café: How Genetic Engineering is Changing What We Eat, How We Live and the Global Politics of Food,* Thomas Dunne Books/St.Martin's Press, New York, 2001.

Lappé, Francis Moore and Anna Lappé, *Hope's Edge,* Penguin Putman, Inc, New York, 2002.

Masumoto, David Mas, *Epitaph for a Peach: Four Seasons on My Family Farm,* Harper Collins, New York, 1995.
------, *Harvest Son: Planting Roots in American Soil,* W.W. Norton & Company, New York, 1998

McClure, Susan (editor) and the staff of the Rodale Food Center, *Preserving Summer's Bounty: A Quick and Easy Guide to Freezing, Canning, Preserving and Drying What Your Grow,* Rodale Books, Allentown PA, 1998.

Morash, Marian, *The Victory Garden Cookbook,* New York, Alfred A. Knopf, Inc., 1982.

Morgan, Lane, *Winter Harvest Cookbook: How to Select and Prepare Fresh Seasonal Produce all Winter Long,* Seattle, Sasquatch Books, 1990.

Nabhan, Gary Paul, *Coming Home to Eat: The Pleasures and Politics of Local Foods,* W.W. Norton & Company, New York, 2002.

Onstad, Dianne, *Whole Foods Companion: A Guide for Adventurous Cooks, Curious Shoppers & Lovers of Natural Foods,* Chelsea Green Publishing Company, Vermont, 1996

Pitchford, Paul, *Healing With Whole Foods; Oriental Traditions and Modern Nutrition,* North Atlantic Books, Berkeley, CA, 1993.

Rex-Johnson, Braiden. *Pike Place Market Cookbook: Recipes, Anecdotes and Personalities from Seattle's Renowned Public Market,* Sasquatch Books, Seattle, 1992.

Rothenberg, Daniel, *With These Hands: The Hidden World of Migrant Farmworkers Today,* Harcourt, New York, 1998.

Schneider, Elizabeth, *The Essential Reference: Vegetables from Amaranth to Zucchini,* William Morrow, New York, 2001.

Soloman, Jay, *Lean Bean Cuisine,* Prima Publishing, Rocklin, CA, 1995.

Williams, Jacqueline, *Wagon Wheel Kitchens: Food on the Oregon Trail,* University Press of Kansas, Kansas, 1993.

Wilson, Duff, *Fateful Harvest: The True Story of a Small Town, A Global Industry, and a Toxic Secret,* New York, Harper Collins, 2001.

Wood, Rebecca, *The New Whole Foods Encyclopedia,* Penguin Books, New York, 1989.

Index

312

T

317

ORDER FORM

Special Discount Rate

_____ copies *Local Vegetarian Cooking* at $17.00 each   _____

Shipping (see chart)   _____

Washington residents add 8.9% tax   _____

Total amount   _____
Check or money order only

Shipping & Handling Rates

U.S.: $4.00 first book
Additional books add $1.00 per book
International: $9.50 first book
Additional books add $5.00 per book

Name(print)_____

Street_____

City/State/Zip_____

Pay by check or cashiers check
Please allow ten days for delivery
Mail this form to:

LOC Press
Debra Daniels-Zeller
P.O. Box 412
Lynnwood, WA 98026